Quentin Tarantino's
Django Unchained

Dani Laufman

Quentin Tarantino's *Django Unchained*

The Continuation of Metacinema

EDITED BY OLIVER C. SPECK

B L O O M S B U R Y

NEW YORK · LONDON · NEW DELHI · SYDNEY

Bloomsbury Academic

An imprint of Bloomsbury Publishing Plc

1385 Broadway	50 Bedford Square
New York	London
NY 10018	WC1B 3DP
USA	UK

www.bloomsbury.com

Bloomsbury is a registered trade mark of Bloomsbury Publishing Plc

First published 2014

Library of Congress Cataloging-in-Publication Data
Quentin Tarantino's Django unchained : the continuation of
metacinema / edited by Oliver C. Speck.
pages cm
Includes bibliographical references and index.
ISBN 978-1-62892-660-6 (paperback) – ISBN 978-1-62892-839-6 (hardback)
1. Django unchained (Motion picture) I. Speck, Oliver C., editor of compilation.
PN1997.D533Q46 2014
791.43'72 – dc23
2014006389

ISBN: HB: 978-1-6289-2839-6
PB: 978-1-6289-2660-6
ePub: 978-1-6235-6780-4
ePDF: 978-1-6289-2655-2

Typeset by Integra Software Services Pvt. Ltd.
Printed and bound in the United States of America

Contents

Introduction: A Southern State of Exception

Oliver C. Speck

Django Unchained has been widely seen as a companion to Tarantino's 2009 film Inglourious Basterds. Again, references to Germany and German culture abound and the role of the "übercultured German" is played by Christoph Waltz, with similar panache. While both films share stylistic and thematic similarities with other films by Tarantino, they belong to a unique genre that this American auteur himself has invented, the historical revenge fantasy. Indeed, most assessments critical of Tarantino's two most recent films take offense with the basic plot idea of pairing a tired Hollywood cliché, the vigilante taking revenge, with a historical crime.

There are, of course, countless films that are set in the past and that take liberties with historical accuracy. Gone with the Wind (1939), for example, famously shows an idyllic American South before the Civil War, and many World War II films feature a wish fulfillment in the form of ultimate justice dealt to heel-clicking Nazis. However, only Django Unchained and Inglourious Basterds allow to imagine the revenge of the tortured—the Jews, the slaves—on the leader of the oppressive regime—Hitler, the slaveholder.

It is my contention that Tarantino's provocative shift from films that deal with race and violence (e.g. Pulp Fiction [1994], or Jackie Brown [1997]), but are set in a never–never land of an unspecified presence, to films that deal with slavery and the Holocaust is a move to be taken seriously as a real auteur. Further, this seriousness stems from a political/critical impetus. Indeed, some of the most shocking attributes of *Django Unchained* are the implicit political assumptions about slavery and race that carry this film and that have not been explored by critics: slavery in *Django Unchained* is linked to capitalism and, in turn, the absolute ownership of slaves is on a par with fascism and the Holocaust. In other words, *Django Unchained* seals the political turn the work of Quentin Tarantino has taken.

In Tarantino's film, the slave appears as a shadowy companion to the *homo sacer*. The *homo sacer*,[1] the figure at the heart of the philosophical project of the Italian political philosopher Giorgio Agamben, appears to exist in a paradoxical state. Banned from the community, he lives in a permanent State of Exception. Having lost all intrinsic value, he can thus not be sacrificed. Indeed, literally an outlaw, he does not enjoy any legal protection and can therefore be killed without impunity. According to Agamben, a concentration camp inmate—stripped of all political rights—has nothing more than his life as sheer biological existence. As personal property, the slave appears to have value. However, this value is purely an exchange value and is not reflected in the monetary gain that could be derived from exploiting his labor, a point that the film stresses on several occasions. Here, *Django Unchained* shows an astute awareness of the mechanisms of biopolitics.[2] In one memorable scene, a fugitive slave is torn apart by dogs. While his owner watches his investment being torn to pieces, the titular hero uses the bloody spectacle to gain symbolic value in the eyes of the slave owner. The only loss appears to be the miserable and valueless life of the slave.

This introductory chapter will frame the South in *Django Unchained* as a State of Exception. As I argue, Tarantino represents slavery and racism as a proto-fascist function of capitalism. In this "Southern State of Exception," Stephen, the house slave who seems to be the manipulative mastermind behind the workings of the Candie plantation, is the key figure. As portrayed by Samuel L. Jackson in "Uncle Ben" attire, Stephen is paradoxically the *homo sacer* who embraces his position to the point where he becomes the leader.

The *homo sacer*

That Giorgio Agamben's project is based on the decisive insight of a Nazi philosopher is not as surprising as it might at first appear. Carl Schmitt's definition is formidable in its simplicity: "Sovereign is he who decides on the exception."[3] Declaring a state of emergency puts the persons in power as well as their subjects in a paradoxical space, a legal gray zone, where any act against the sovereign can be met with lethal power. In other words, a slave owner is at once inside the law, as well as outside of it—on his land, he can do whatever he wants, to whomever, because he *is* the law. As Agamben explains, such a suspension of the law should not be confused with anomie, on the contrary: the partial or complete abrogation of the law in a state of emergency, such as the right to protect your own property, serves exactly to stave off a lawless state of nature. In times of crisis—be it natural disasters or wars—the authorities can temporarily commandeer housing and transportation in order to help those in need and prevent civil unrest. Here, Agamben points to the often forgotten historical fact that during the fascist rule the Weimar constitution was never really abolished, but rather suspended.[4]

While the German philosopher of law directs his attention to the person or institution in power, the political philosopher Agamben is interested in what happens to the other people when such a State of Exception is declared, that is when all laws are suspended. The figure that comes into existence when the leader declares a state of exception, as mentioned earlier, is the *homo sacer*. Once martial law is declared, a group of people can be stripped of all their political rights. For the sake of simplicity, we can say here that the slave or the concentration camp inmate is the material expression of the *homo sacer* as Agamben describes him. The use of force is crucial to an understanding of this mechanism: if there is no law to protect life and limb of a person, by definition, no use of force can ever be unlawful. The German soldier who methodically kills completely innocent civilians in Roman Polanski's *The Pianist* (2002), to refer to another harrowing filmic example, does not break any law because the life of a person in the Jewish ghetto is, as Agamben calls it, a "bare life," a life that enjoys absolutely no protection.[5]

What does enjoy protection—and *Django Unchained* leaves no doubt about that—are the rights of an owner who can dispose of or sell his own property, count on help from the authorities when this property is stolen, and sell or even destroy it. Dr. Schultz has clearly understood the importance of this mechanism. When he encounters Django at the beginning of the film, he takes pains to ensure that all the paperwork is in order, even if that means signing the bill of sale himself and paying the former owner who is pinned under a horse and who will certainly be dead in the near future. This farcical insistence to follow the letter of the law provides an important insight. When all human rights are stripped away, the law that now remains is an empty shell, a hollowed-out form without content.

To paint Quentin Tarantino now only as an avid reader of Agamben would not do the political analysis of the film, or the filmmaker, justice. Indeed, as the film stresses, in regard to private property, the hollowing-out of the law leaves the question of value intact; it even allows the complete uncoupling of exchange value from use value. As many scholars—also in this book—have pointed out, so-called "Mandingo fights"[6] to the death probably did not happen. However, Tarantino's point is that the betting on such fights is akin to enticing pit bulls to fight each other—the chance of a monetary gain and the added entertainment value justify the potential loss of a fighter. Morality is not an issue, only value counts.

Keeping in mind Candie's perverted sexuality (including the incestuous relationship with his Southern Belle sister), the actual role of Sheba, the attractive and well-dressed slave girl at his side, is not quite clear. As sexual commodity, however, she makes perfect sense, since she provides her master with the necessary value, being a high-class prostitute from his own establishment. Further, *Django Unchained* contains an entire sequence that is dedicated to the careful planning of the charade concerning the purchase of Broomhilda—of course, any interest in her as an object of value would immediately raise the price. This potential surplus value is only bound to the body, dead or alive. In the words of Dr. Schultz, "the way the slave trade deals in human lives for cash, a bounty hunter deals in corpses."

Django Unchained features many scenes that allude to the relative monetary value of a *homo sacer*. The mauling of a dispensable fugitive slave, as mentioned earlier, serves to terrorize the other slaves and invests Django with a symbolic value. Here, the film offers another insight into the precarious bare life of the *homo sacer*: without the proper papers, Django can lose the status of a freeman immediately. After he is caught by the white posse, Django can be sold to be worked to death in the mines without any legal issues resulting. Again, the thousands of concentration camp inmates who were worked to death in Nazi-Germany in so-called "labor camps," such as the underground factory of the infamous V2 rockets, come to mind. The recent adaptation of the eponymous slave narrative, *12 Years a Slave*, makes a similar point. Once the free African American is transported over the state line, his rights are lost and he becomes a commodifiable object that can be traded or sold. In other words, in a State of Exception, anyone can potentially become a *homo sacer*.

Genre as palimpsest

The generic roots of *Django Unchained*, which have been mentioned in nearly every review of the film, but never analyzed in depth, are worth considering. The lack of critical interest is due to these genres' status as not being serious. Here, the commonly used monikers for these popular genres, "Spaghetti Western" and "Blaxploitation," already hint at cheap entertainment without any artistic value. Certainly, Tarantino's overabundant use of reference to generic tropes, for example, in *Kill Bill, Vols. 1 & 2* (2003 and 2004), has resulted in considering all allusions to prior films as mere postmodern in-jokes. However, if we treat the many references in *Django Unchained* not as a simple nod to fan expectations but as real intertexts, a political dimension is opened.

The European Spaghetti Western understands that the American Western was never about the creation myth of a new nation or even the dialectics of nature versus culture. As in many American *Sur-Westerns*[7] of the 1950s, such as *Rancho Notorious* (Fritz Lang, 1952),

Shane (George Stevens, 1953), *Johnny Guitar* (Nicholas Ray, 1954), and *The Searchers* (John Ford, 1956), most Spaghetti Westerns feature a barren landscape, a veritable existentialist hell, in which the dust-covered characters engage in their life or death struggles. Men and women are reduced to the base motives that drive them— lust, greed, revenge. Often, the hero, or, rather, antihero, is a bounty hunter as in Sergio Leone's famous "Man with No Name—Trilogy," *Per un pugno di dollari/A Fistful of Dollars* (1964), *Per qualche dollaro in più/For a Few Dollars More* (1965), and *Il buono, il brutto, il cattivo/ The Good, the Bad and the Ugly* (1966). The setting and the archetypal characters of these tales reflect the allegorical element of a State of Exception in which everybody is potentially an executioner or a *homo sacer*.

Such a State of Exception should not be confused with the Hobbesian State of Nature that can be found in lesser Westerns. In the latter, the Marshall, the Sheriff, or whoever represents the Law is also the incarnation of order that tames the uncivilized nature of the frontier town. In a Sur-or a Spaghetti Western, there is no threat of anomie because the law is always already suspended. A look at the last entry in Sergio Leone's above-mentioned trilogy can quickly explain this decisive difference. The film—greatly admired by Tarantino, as is well known[8]—is nominally set during the American Civil War, but is clearly allegorizing this conflict as prototype of the mass-slaughters of the twentieth century. Two of the most memorable scenes in *The Good, the Bad and the Ugly* refer directly to the martial law that suspends all humanitarian norms. First, a brutal torture scene in a POW camp for Confederate soldiers is clearly designed to remind the viewer of a concentration camp—the prisoners can be killed or tortured without any interference. Then, later in the film, a bridge located in the no-man's-land between the Confederate and Union armies symbolizes the brutal nature of the static warfare of World War I, as well as the meaningless death modern warfare causes. The crucial difference between a State of Nature, where only the fittest survive, and a State of Exception is that a split second can decide who lives and who dies, or, in other words, who may become a *homo sacer* and who has the power to exterminate others.

Another memorable example for an intertextual dialogue would be *Il Grande Silenzio/The Great Silence* (1968) by Sergio Corbucci, a film set in a snow-covered no-man's-land where the sadistic bounty hunter is able to kill the hero, a hired killer who still has a quantum of feelings left.[9] Notably, the first bounty for Django and Schultz is the Sheriff of a small town. Only the German's sangfroid and a hidden Derringer can win the duel with this elected lawman who has a price on his head. To repeat what was said above, in this zone of indistinction, anybody can become a leader or a *homo sacer*.

The most obvious cinematic intertext to Tarantino's film is *Django* (1966), also by the above-mentioned Sergio Corbucci. The Italian film's music is even played over the credits of *Django Unchained*. *Django* is an inspired remake of *Yojimbo* by Akira Kurosawa (1961), as is Leone's first installment of the "Man with No Name—Trilogy," *Per un pugno di dollari/A Fistful of Dollars*. In all these films, and, of course, in the literary source, the short pulp novel "Red Harvest" from 1929 by Dashiell Hammett, the ruthless (and nameless) antihero arrives in a dusty town and plays two equally matched gangs against each other. The bounty hunter's almost mystical mastery over his weapon, be it sword, six-shooter, or machine gun, breaks the equilibrium and results in a bloody spectacle of annihilation: the sovereign can be judge, jury, and executioner at once. Remarkably, *Django Unchained* transfers three decisive characteristic of the nameless killer onto Dr. Schultz. Not only is this jovial German bounty hunter an ethical person who always keeps his word, he is certainly a crack shot and also has a soft spot for true love.

There is an interesting precedent to the genre mash up of *Django Unchained* that has barely been mentioned in any review and that serves clearly as model:[10] the 1975 Blaxploitation Western *Boss Nigger* written by Fred Williamson, who also plays the lead. This last installment of a trilogy (with *The Legend of Nigger Charley* [1972] and *The Soul of Nigger Charley* [1973]) features a couple of black bounty hunters who end up as sheriffs of a white town. As the effective sovereigns of this isolated community, they can make up any laws they want.

The Fred Williamson trilogy and the story of "Red Harvest" provide a link to Blaxploitation cinema, the other genre to which *Django Unchained* pays homage. Here, a look at Tarantino's 1997 *Jackie Brown*, an ode to Pam Grier and the character she portrays in the films where she is featured, can help to understand the complexities that are involved. Quentin Tarantino does not just simply fashion *Jackie Brown* after *Foxy Brown*, a lurid tale of revenge from 1974 by the white director Jack Hill, or other films of the genre, such as the famous *Shaft* (1971) by the African American Gordon Parks, which inspired the name of Broomhilda von Shaft. Tarantino understands that the basic premise for these films is that the law does not provide justice for black people. It is instead up to the ethical hero to provide justice, often by playing one faction against another. In order to prevent a race-war, Shaft drives the Italian mob out of Harlem with the help of black militants. But he is still making sure that the black crime lord pays the bills, and he certainly does not feel much solidarity for the black gangsters or even the militants just because of the color of their skin. Indeed, the best Blaxploitation films are always neo-noir films, where the ethical hero disregards prevalent morality and, in the absence of a functioning legal framework, only follows his professional duty. In this context, it is telling that Django does not free the other slaves, or become the leader of a slave revolt, even after he frees Broomhilda and kills his actual adversary, Stephen, revealed as the slave-turned-secret-master, and blows up the oppressor's mansion.

Schultz arguably sacrifices himself for Django and Broomhilda. However, what costs him his life is actually his steadfast refusal to shake hands with Candie after he has been forced to pay an extraordinary amount of money for Broomhilda's freedom. Choosing death before dishonoring his own beliefs is a perfect example of what Slavoj Žižek calls the *beau geste*: "One sacrifices oneself [...] to maintain the appearance of the Other's honor."[11] For this ethical hero, a simple handshake is a gesture of commitment that appears to be almost sacred. From this perspective, finally, Tarantino appears as a hopeless romantic. Just as the film noir detective obeys only his professional code of conduct, Schultz is the sovereign who sacrifices himself to end the State of Exception.

The politics of provocation

At the time of this writing, *Django Unchained* has made more than 425 million dollars worldwide, according to boxofficemojo.com, a website that tracks the domestic and international gross income of movies. This is significantly more than Tarantino's second to last film, *Inglourious Basterds*, but certainly pales against, for example, *Skyfall* (2013), which was released around the same time and made over 1 billion dollars. Still, a year after its initial release, the film continues to cause controversy. For example, at the 2013 conference of the National Communication Association, no less than three panels were dedicated to the film, with often heated arguments concerning the merits or flaws of the film following the presentations.[12]

12 Years a Slave and *Lincoln*, two films that were widely seen as a timely comment on the first African American president, might be historically more accurate, and they might have a strong cathartic effect on the viewer, but *Django Unchained* does not aim at a representation of race, as these films do, but rather provides a meta-commentary on the politics of racial representation. The complexity of this subject is clearly expressed by the chapters in this book. Indeed, many contributions are themselves the result of a discussion between two or even three scholars. All contributors bring their own scholarly expertise to their respective close readings of *Django Unchained*, but, without doubt, they also bring a definite passion to unraveling elements of this fascinating film.

The first part of this book explores the intertextual dialogues with Europe and the United States. Robert von Dassanowsky examines the character of Dr. "King" Schultz, who fled his native Germany after the failed 1848 revolution. As von Dassanowsky argues, Tarantino does not repeat the allohistorical mode of *Inglourious Basterds*, but suggests how (fictional) personal history is lost in the fiction of a dominant "official history." While not as polyglot as *Inglourious Basterds*, *Django Unchained* features many references to language. Here, Margaret Ozierski analyzes the notable instances where the French language and phenomena of French culture make a programmatic appearance in the film. Her chapter understands the ideal of liberation as it is developed in the film by locating it within the speaker, the user of language in a minor register who accedes to the status of (liberated) subjecthood. These chapters help to understand Django's breaking through the chains of linguistic enslavement to become a new speaking subject.

Dana Weber explores the German cultural subtext: the medieval *Nibelungenlied* and its retellings in Richard Wagner's *Ring* cycle and Fritz Lang's *Nibelungen* (1924). As it becomes apparent, it is not coincidental that the film brings forth a powerful political statement when it (controversially) associates American slavery with the Holocaust by drawing precisely from these German cultural models.

Gregory L. Kaster's contribution compares Quentin Tarantino's *Django Unchained* and Steven Spielberg's *Lincoln*. Especially when viewed historically from the standpoint of American slavery and abolition in Abraham Lincoln's day, the two films offer complementary perspectives and lessons on these and related topics. Both movies tackle questions of means and ends, as well as agency, in the context of struggle against antebellum slavery.

The second part of this book, "Philosophy Unchained: Ethics, Body Space, and Evil," is dedicated to another meta-cinematic perspective: Alexander D. Ornella underlines in his chapter that skin and skin colors are markers of difference as well as surfaces that are subject to identity politics. Skin color grants a body access to or prohibits this body from inhabiting certain spaces. If bodies violate these ascribed spaces, social actors have measures in place to express this dislocation and restore the boundaries.

Django Unchained and *Inglourious Basterds* depict two notorious events in history, the American slave trade and the Holocaust of World War II, respectively, and are certainly presenting a revised version of history. Still, according to Kate E. Temoney, Tarantino's stylistic choices lend themselves to human rights discourse in an unexpected, inventive, and albeit most likely unintended manner, by providing an artistic and bearable space for confronting and grappling with the complex, incongruous, and seemingly inscrutable phenomena of human atrocities depicted in these two films. Manufacturing the intensity of these conditions for the viewer tempered by a jocularity and historical redemption permits the viewer to directly attend to the real horrors of human rights abuses.

Dara Waldron asserts that Tarantino's film, by taking issue with the problem of radical evil, is a purposeful attempt to explore the relationship between evil and slavery. He then explores the relevance of the character of King Schultz to this debate, addressing his character as exemplar of the moral concerns in the film. In Waldron's view, Schultz's purpose is to make the revenge narrative—in which revenge is normally considered an expression of premodern archaism—a more complex, more modern moral activity.

William Brown states that complications in *Django Unchained* are a result of a distinctly capitalist logic whereby if one does not make maximum profit based upon the perceived value of the product being bought (in this case, a human being), then somehow one has failed. *Django Unchained* offers a critique of the way in which the relative concept of value (this is valuable to me, but not necessarily to you) breeds greed, which in turn breeds violence and destruction.

After these detailed analyses, Part III, "Questions of Race and Representation," asks the pertinent question: What is a "Black Film"? The first chapter in this section is by Heather Ashley Hayes and Gilbert B. Rodman and takes up some of the major historical, cultural, and political issues with which the film presents us. This discussion of the complex problems of representation and authenticity provides a framework for the following chapters, each of which critique aspects of the film. The archetypal figure of the Frontier Hero is at the center of Samuel P. Perry's contribution. Tarantino's whitewashing of violence and the history of slavery in *Django Unchained*, as Perry argues, results in a loss of historical contextualization.

Reynaldo Anderson, D. L. Stephenson, and Chante Anderson discuss problematic aspects of the aesthetic choices in the film. For them, the film ultimately fails because it falls back on stereotypical representations of race, gender, and class. Ryan J. Weaver and Nichole K. Kathol argue that Tarantino's *Django Unchained* offers mainstream, that is, white audiences, redemption from the sins of the past. Like Samuel Perry, the co-authors criticize the use of cinematic stereotypes. In their reading, the clichés of the "cowboy" and the "Magical Negro" still wield rhetorical power even though the attributes are reversed in the film.

This book ends with a provocative critique of this controversial film. David J. Leonard focuses particularly on the themes of white redemption and its white-centered narrative. He argues that *Django Unchained* is a story of whiteness (and white masculinity) and a movie that lifts Tarantino himself to the status of great white savior.

Notes

1   According to Giorgio Agamben, the *homo sacer* is "an obscure figure of archaic Roman law," *Homo Sacer: Sovereign Power and Bare Life* (Stanford, Calif: Stanford University Press, 1998), 8.

2   Michel Foucault defines "biopolitics" as a form of government control, whose emergence is linked to modernity here: "biological existence was reflected in political existence; the fact of living was no longer an inaccessible substrate that only emerged from time to time, amid the randomness of death and its fatality; part of it passed into knowledge's field of control and power's sphere of intervention"—Michel Foucault, *The History of Sexuality—Vol. 1: An Introduction* (New York: Vintage, 1990), 142. See also my chapter in *Quentin Tarantino's* Inglourious Basterds*: A Manipulation of Metacinema*, ed. Robert von Dassanowsky (New York/London: Continuum, 2012), 193–213.

3   *Homo Sacer*, 11.

4   See here, esp., *Homo Sacer*, 168–170. Agamben describes the declaration of a state of emergency that suspended the constitution and the construction of concentration camps.

5   A plantation and a concentration camp do not hold prisoners who are still protected by the penal code, but rather objects who have nothing but their "bare life" (*Homo Sacer*, 20).

6   The term "Mandingo fighting" refers to the 1975 film *Mandingo* by Richard Fleischer, where slave owners organize bare knuckle fights.

7   A concept coined by André Bazin. Hillier translates this as "Super Western" in his introduction—Jim Hillier, ed. *Cahiers Du Cinéma, The 1950s: Neo-realism, Hollywood, New Wave* (Cambridge, Mass: Harvard University Press, 1985), 82.

8   2012 Greatest Film Poll Sight & Sound, http://explore.bfi.org.uk/sightandsoundpolls/2012/voter/1134 n.d. (accessed November 20, 2013). See also Geoffrey Macnab, "Quentin Tarantino—The Good, the Bad and the Movie Geek," where Quentin Tarantino is quoted, commenting on the film: "I think a case can even be made that with Leone and [Ennio] Morricone that they are the best director-composer team in the history of film." http://www.independent.co.uk/arts-entertainment/films/features/quentin-tarantino–the-good-the-bad-and-the-movie-geek-2283148.html, Friday May 13, 2011 (accessed November 20, 2013).

9   We can safely assume that Quentin Tarantino is familiar with the film. The winter scenes in *Django Unchained* could be seen as homage to this famous Spaghetti Western.

10 Aisha Harris, "When Blaxploitation Went West: Django Unchained Seems Tame by Comparison," *Slate*, December 25, 2012, http://www.slate.com/articles/arts/culturebox/2012/12/django_unchained_tarantino_s_movie_seems_tame_compared_with_the_blaxploitation.html (accessed November 20, 2013).

11 "Death's Merciless Love," http://www.lacan.com/zizek-love.htm (accessed November 30, 2013). *True Romance* (1993), directed by Tony Scott and written by Quentin Tarantino, and *Inglourious Basterds* contain similarly noble and futile gestures.

12 Early versions of the chapters by Heather Ashley Hayes and Gilbert B. Rodman, Samuel P. Perry, Reynaldo Anderson, D. L. Stephenson, and Chante Anderson, and Ryan J. Weaver and Nichole K. Kathol were introduced here.

PART ONE

Cultural Roots and Intertexts: Germany, France, and the United States

1

Dr. "King" Schultz as Ideologue and Emblem: The German Enlightenment and the Legacy of the 1848 Revolutions in *Django Unchained*

Robert von Dassanowsky

Austrian actor Christoph Waltz embodied a negative take on Austria's troubled postimperial identity and relationship with Nazism as the identity shifting SS officer Hans Landa in Tarantino's *Inglourious Basterds* (2009). The director creates an intertextuality with that film through Waltz's character in his *Django Unchained* (2012) in order to create a Tarantinian dialectic that moves between the German-speaking world and the United States in the nineteenth and twentieth centuries. Waltz's Dr. "King" Schultz, a German immigrant dentist and thus a member of the emerging *Biedermeier*,[1] bourgeois intelligentsia, recreates himself as an American bounty hunter. It is the removal of "bad teeth" on a social level, but also represents the ease of identity re-creation in the antebellum. While it is known that Tarantino creates extended backstories for his characters which are only suggested in their actions on screen, *Django Unchained*, while less populated and intricate than the narrative of *Inglourious Basterds*, represents a much more theoretically complex characterization by actor Christoph Waltz. This chapter will examine the possible ideology of Tarantino's Dr. "King" Schultz and how the character's actions reveal his past and represent the first part of the director's allohistorical filmic exploration of the collisions of humanism and social Darwinism as they reverberate from post-Napoleonic Europe to pre–Civil War America, and eventually (back) to fascist Europe.

It has been speculated that Tarantino wanted to help "redeem the Germans a little after his last picture, *Inglourious Basterds*, depicted the brutal nature of the Holocaust."[2] Far more than just echoing Roberto Rossellini's creation of *Germania Anno Zero* (1948) to show the plight of postwar Germany and balance out the negative images of the German occupation of Italy in *Roma citta aperta* (1945) and *Paisan* (1946), and because the central character of *Inglourious Basterds* is an Austrian not a German (and a focal part of the national identity clichés that rise and fall throughout the film), there is a more complex structure that binds Tarantino's *Bastards* with *Django* beyond making up for the image of the "bad Germans." The simplistic binary of good and evil Tarantino borrows from B-movies, exploitation films, and Hollywood propaganda film is, after all, his unique style.

Unlike the reaction to *Inglourious Basterds* which, beyond opinion and basic review, gave rise to informed and critical analysis of the film on blog sites, *Django Unchained* inspired little critical blogging beyond the opinion piece. U.S.-based blogs particularly suggested some anxiety, even irritation at Tarantino's treatment of American history in the iconoclastic way he had looked at Europe. One of the more informed blogs that set up the intertext between the films through the development of racist ideology and the director's questioning of the relationship between culture, control, and dehumanization was from Michael J. Anderson:

The incontrovertibly major *Inglourious Basterds* indeed provides a point of departure in almost every sense, beginning with its ontological status as an object of psychic historical revision: where *Inglourious Basterds* provides a fantastic, contingent counter-reality in which Jews and members of the cinematic colony bring about the destruction of the Third Reich, in an orgiastic final act explosion of extreme cartoon violence, *Django Unchained* gives agency to the victims of the Trans-Atlantic slave trade, whether it is the unshackled slaves in the opening set-piece, Django in his role as homicidal bounty-hunter, or the latter in his final, ruthless, John Woo-coded devastation of Candieland (which will include slavers and complicit whites and blacks alike). *Django Unchained* also responds to and revises *Inglourious Basterds'* negative Germanic archetype, with former film Nazi Waltz recast as the "good guy." At the same time, the World War II film's heroic Americans are now cast as their villainous, slave-owning ancestors in what will prove the first of *Django Unchained's* many provocations.[3]

Waltz's King Schultz, the film's enlightened and moral center, bears more than a passing resemblance in name and visage to Carl Schurtz (1829–1906), the young history student whose doctoral studies were interrupted by the 1848 Revolution in the German Confederation. Joining one of the many student movements that called for a democratic system, Schurtz fought in clashes with the Prussian army. After the failure of the 1848 revolts, he fled to Switzerland and then returned to the Confederation at the risk of death, to rescue a compatriot. He lived in France and England before coming to the United States, where he joined the Republican Party and was subsequently appointed Ambassador to Spain by President Lincoln. Having influenced Spain not to side with the Confederacy and returning to the United States at onset of the Civil War, he was made Union Brigadier General. After the war, he became the first German-born American to be elected to Senator. Schurtz was reform-minded and staunchly anti-imperialistic. He opposed President Grant's attempt to annex the Dominican Republic in 1869, and enabled arms sales to the French during the Franco-Prussian War. He also rejected President McKinley's desire to annex land following victory in the Spanish American War. Despite these anti-imperialistic beliefs, he was supportive of Anglo-American superiority. He had not only been strongly involved with Lincoln's anti-slavery campaign, but he also supported state's rights and therefore dismissed national laws protecting African American civil rights under Reconstruction. In his later role as Secretary of the Interior under President Hayes, he attempted to mediate the racist attitudes toward Native Americans and clean up corruption as head of the Indian Affairs Office, but repression continued in the maintenance of the reservation system and Schurtz later aimed for assimilation. He is commemorated widely as perhaps the most important German American in U.S. political history and as a positive force in Native American Affairs, for undertaking civil service reforms and in his later years as a New York newspaper editor and independent political gadfly.[4]

Schurtz was by far the most prominent German "Forty-Eighter" in the United States. The term refers to Europeans (Germans, Austrians, Irish, French, Hungarians, Poles) who united against the post-Napoleonic era of reaction (the Metternich System) to demand democratic governments and protection of civil rights in the mass movements that resulted in the pan-European revolutions of 1848. For Germans, there was an additional, most important demand—the unification of Germany. The emergent middle class and new political movements (constitutional monarchists, republicans, nationalists, and Marxists) all supported the revolutions and mourned the strengthening of reactionary forces in its failure. The European revolts began as the February Revolution in France, which toppled King Louis Philippe, and then spread throughout Europe, but the movements were crushed within the year, with massive loss, casualties, and exile.

One of the most remarkable events in the German Confederation was the establishment of the Frankfurt National Assembly or Parliament, with its over 400 delegates composed of intellectuals, professors, teachers, middle-class merchants, physicians, and even members of the nobility. The future of what would be a unified Germany (with or without Austria) and what its political form should be (various versions of monarchy or republic) was central to the Assembly's work, but so were the concepts of a document of basic rights. The Assembly ultimately offered the Prussian King the crown as reigning dynasty over a constitutionally united German Empire. It was rejected, and the Assembly was disbanded by military intervention. Reforms that had been passed earlier in several German states in the Confederation were rescinded in a wave of reaction and repression. Fearing long imprisonment or even execution, many "Forty-Eighters"—like Carl Schurtz or Tarantino's fictional emblem of this past, Dr. "King" Schultz—fled to the United States.

Schultz, or the education and the revolution

While we never learn the true first name of Dr. Schultz, his nickname "King" is part of the complex and reflective dualism that runs through Tarantino's *Basterds* and *Django* films. Tarantino's American history suggests a whimsical genealogical link with the future Dr. [Martin Luther] King, just as Django's bride, the slave who has taken on her German mistress' surname as "von S[c]haft," also suggests she is a possible ancestor of the 1970s Blaxploitation film hero John Shaft. A more political reflection might be that "King" may have been a nickname won as an ironic moniker of his leadership in a revolt, or as a staunch anti-monarchist. Along with the fantasy of a Brunhilde von Schaft (misspelled and demythologized as "Broomhilda von Shaft"), a slave "inheriting" a name of (fictional) German nobility, Tarantino's "name game" reflects the growing rejection of royalty and the nobility as "racially" (later biologically) superior in Europe, from the French Revolution to the revolutions of 1848. Tarantino avoids giving Schultz articulated Marxist leanings despite the strong influence of Marxism among the "Forty-Eighters" like Carl Schurtz, for the obvious reason that both the concept of nationalism in the nineteenth century as a popular anti-dynastic unification movement and Marxism, which was not tied to the evolution of "communisms" in the twentieth century, would have been confusing to a general audience.[5] But it is clear that Dr. Schultz is well aware of the privileged superiority of the aristocratic landowners of his homeland in his reaction to its American translation in plantation owners such as Candie, as well as with German/Austrian intellectual humanism, here most tangibly represented by his staunch adherence to the law, his disgust with and desire to battle corruption, and his love of Beethoven. As a dentist "from Düsseldorf" who appears in the American South in ten years after the European revolutions as a bounty hunter with excellent English skills, soft-spoken but in a highly intelligent manner, little fear of confrontation, an abhorrence for inhumane society, self-appointed despots, and expertise with firearms, Schultz's identity as a "Forty-Eighter" is hardly a stretch of the imagination.

It is important to understand the roots of Schultz's ideology, his abilities as a "Forty-Eighter," and why he is so intent on educating his assistant, the ex-slave Django (Jamie Foxx), even before he decides to help him reclaim his enslaved wife Brunhilde/Broomhilda (Kerry Washington). The eighteenth-century German Enlightenment, particularly the concepts of philosopher Immanuel Kant (1724–1804) and playwright Gotthold Ephraim Lessing (1729–1781), have a strong bearing on Tarantino's exiled dentist, who may also possibly have served as a delegate at the Frankfurt National Assembly, given his logical discourses and persuasive legal debates with other figures in the film. Like *Inglourious Basterds*, this is indeed also a film about language. Unlike the previous film, it is not a question of Hans Landa's fluency in Italian because he is an Austrian not a German, the monolingual failure of the American "Basterds," or the lack of English that dooms the hiding French Jewish family, but it is also one of miscommunication and misunderstanding—in one's own language. The running joke of the film is that Americans cannot understand Schultz's elegant and erudite English, and not because of a German accent. The slave traders that Schultz encounters and from whom he liberates Django exhort him to "speak English" because they do not recognize his advance vocabulary and refined phrasing in what is, of course, a second language to him. This actually displays a deepening of Tarantino's concerns about the "language problem" in *Basterds* and the subversion of the Americans as heroic, because they cannot speak any other language beyond English and do not have the ability to comprehend cultures (French, German, Italian) to which they believe they are superior. In *Django*, Tarantino attacks such ignorance by portraying Americans who hold sway of the lives of other enslaved "Americans." His pre-KKK lynch mob can barely communicate their simple thoughts or commands, and most important to the narrative, the plantation owner named Candie (Leonardo DiCaprio), who is informed on the subject of phrenology and fancies himself French and sophisticated but cannot speak the language and lacks true gentlemanly manners. Candie's desire to connect with the vaunted European "culture" is also linked to an inauthentic "nostalgia" for class divisions and religious intolerance. Schultz's civilized behavior, which is based in enlightened education (multilingual and well-travelled) and finds no need to demonize or oppress the "Other" (e.g. racism) for his own sense of power, is met with suspicion by the brutal, illiterate slave traders or even a privileged man like Candie. In *Django*, the "language problem" is only a symptom of Tarantino's larger concern, the lack of an education and with it the failure of self-realization.

In 1784, Kant wrote that

> Enlightenment is man's release from his self-incurred tutelage. Tutelage is man's inability to make use of his understanding without direction from another. Self-incurred is this tutelage when its cause lies not in lack of reason but in lack of resolution and courage to use it without direction from another. Sapere aude! [Dare to know] "have courage to use your own reason!"—that is the motto of enlightenment.[6]

Kant further accuses "laziness and cowardice" as the causes for lack of empowerment and ease of oppression. Here is the basis of Schultz's education and the educating discourse he has with Django. It was this understanding of the power of education that may have guided him into the revolutions of 1848, and in a distant mirror in *Basterds*, it is this loss of enlightened education and self-realization that leads Tarantino's Europeans, specifically his Germans and Austrians, but also his Italians and French into the barbarism of the early to mid-twentieth century. Education, or rather the choice to learn and fight against what Kant feels is the "restriction on freedom" that hampers true self-realization (we live in an age of enlightenment not in an enlightened age, as Kant would say), is even more compelling as the ideological cornerstone of this film when one considers the filmmaker's own experience with rearing, education, and experience.

Tarantino's autodidactic education in cinema and cultural history (mostly through exploitation genres and foreign film as a video store employee) that followed his incomplete high school education is at the root of his blending of the Kantian education-as-enlightenment with his own experience in the character of Django. Again from Kant: "Which restriction is an obstacle of enlightenment and which is not an obstacle but a promoter of it? I answer: The public use of one's reason must always be free, and it alone can bring about enlightenment among men."[7] Tarantino replaced traditional education and a short stint in acting school with a form of public discourse.

As onetime video-store compatriot and filmmaker Roger Avary recalls, Tarantino immersed himself in discussing cinema culture and customer recommendations at length. That experience is credited as the inspiration for his writing and direction.[8] Tarantino simplifies this desire for self-starting experiential learning in a field with which he obviously found affinity and empowerment: "When people ask me if I went to film school, I tell them, 'no, I went to films.'"[9] It recalls the following quote from Lessing's "The Education of the Human Race" (1777): "Education gives to Man nothing which he might not educe out of himself; it gives him that which he might educe out of himself, only quicker and more easily."[10] How much of Tarantino's pride in his self-motivated and experiential education is projected into the educating discourse between Schultz and Django, and in the growth of Django as a critical thinker might be gleaned from the notion that like Tarantino's development as a filmmaker, Django did not go to school to learn the standards of the American society of his era. He simply went into it and survived against all odds.

Django, or the revolution and the education

Django's absurd satin "Blue Boy" outfit he wears as a demonstration of his first free experience in selecting clothing for himself is emblematic of both the German Enlightenment and cinema—and perhaps what Tarantino considers a form of "enlightenment" found in the vulgarized cinema of exploitation in the 1970s. The circa 1770 Thomas Gainsborough portrait of a merchant's son wearing the style from a century earlier, which Django's clothing suggests, relates the growth of the enlightenment from the end of the baroque era and the wars of reformation and counterreformation in Europe. The progress of the past hundred years is conveyed in the presentation of both the archaic opulence and the absurdity of it to a more rationalized society of the 1770s. Django's choice of a similar garment signals his own verbose fascination with the beginnings of education and self-realization, which is later discarded for more adult, contemporary, and rational clothing. It is also a comment on the emerging African American culture of the 1960s and 1970s, which surfaces in an anti-establishment, counterculture embrace of romanticized ethnic clothing.

With the fantasy projections of his characters as vague ancestors of the film figure Shaft and even Martin Luther King, Tarantino mashes historical facts in this film as a remark on the relative lack of a recorded black slave history, in the way that he attacked the inaccuracies of war films in *Inglourious Basterds*. Thus Django becomes the carrier of the "public use of one's reason"—the Kantian road to enlightenment given to him by the German "Forty-Eighter" dentist–turned-bounty hunter Dr. "King" Schultz, and represents the fictive, allohistorical *beginning* of the battle against slavery and racism in the United States. Schultz's actions perhaps even "trigger" the Civil War and the end of slavery by suggesting to slaves that survive his battle with traders in Texas, that they unshackle themselves, kill the surviving slave trader, bury him, and make their way to a more "enlightened" place in this county. It is a distant mirror of Hans Landa's more draconian destruction of Hitler, Goebbels, and other Nazi leaders, which places him on the same "historical" side with the self-sacrificing Shosanna and the martyred Bridget von Hammersmark, in ending the Third Reich and the war. The philosophies of enlightenment and individual self-realization, which in Tarantino's two-film dialectic begins in the German-speaking world, moves to America, and ultimately returns to a fascist Europe, are discourses that replace the concept of "history," which the filmmaker believes is impossible to depict accurately or with any objective value in cinema. For Tarantino, it is quite acceptable to get the so-called facts wrong, but the philosophical spirit right. As Kant would explain it, true cultural growth and human understanding comes from a reform "in ways of thinking"—or for Tarantino, fictive, allohistorical "revolutionary" pastiches that teach principles rather than reflect cinematic fictive-historical glory:

> But be it noted that the public, which has first been brought under this yoke by their guardians, forces the guardians themselves to remain bound when it is incited to do so by some of the guardians who are themselves capable of some enlightenment.... Perhaps a fall of personal despotism or of avaricious or tyrannical oppression may be accompanied by revolution, but never a true reform in ways of thinking. Rather, new prejudices will serve as well as old ones to harness the great unthinking masses.[11]

Schultz's "teaching" of the Germanic myth to Django in order to contextualize Broomhilda's name and the *Niebelungenlied*'s (the original and the later Wagner's opera cycle) value of love (Brunhilde and Siegfried) against the struggle for hegemony into the experience of Django and the search for his enslaved wife is also ambiguous in its dualistic representation. It ruptures the racist value that has been placed on these ancient sagas through the interpretation of the later Richard Wagner operas and those that would influence Hitler and Nazism. The founding of the German Empire, inflamed by nascent German patriotism during the Napoleonic era, the repressions of the Congress of Vienna "restoration," and the growth of German nationalism by the 1830s as a prelude to the revolutions of 1848, had been influenced by the romantic/mythic ideals of heroism and transcendence as well as neoclassical ideals of ambiguous social and cultural constructions (beauty = truth; truth = beauty) for the sake of "harmony." Walter Benjamin's analysis of fascism as the "aesthetization of politics" is the ultimate result. In Benjamin's *The Origin of German Tragic Drama*, the author finds a more truthful and accessible history in allegory than in the enshrinement of the ruins of the past. This is "valuable because it delves beyond the aesthetic of the ruin as an object, and reads it as a process, a means of demythologizing and stripping away symbolism—a means of approaching historical truth through reduction, at the *expense* of romantic aesthetics."[12] It counters the creation of mythological history, just as Tarantino counters mythological history in cinema by presenting deconstructions of it, and in the case of *Django*, smashing the American historical (and cinematic) myth of the South as a ruin worthy of any romantic salvation.

The dynast, or the echoes of Lessing and Beethoven

Schultz's business deal with Django allowing him freedom and money for assistance in finding the Brittle Brothers until they can have the opportunity to locate Broomhilda sets up a progressive economy based in need and rationalism. The pair also symbolizes an American nation of immigrants regardless of race, and pits it against the mythic American concepts of an Anglo-white "nativism" and imperialism— particularly in the ideology and the mission of the "frontier" (Tarantino has called his film a "Southern" in applying aspects of the Western film genre to the American antebellum South).

Arriving in a town in which both Schultz and Django are denied on the basis of difference, Schultz guns down the Sheriff, the romanticized and heroic representative of frontier law in the history of the American West and in the Western genre, in the way he may have shot reactionary representatives of the equally romanticized monarchical dynasties in 1848. He informs the stunned townspeople and the Marshall, who accuses him of being lawless for having "shot our Sheriff like a dog in the street," that this elected and apparently respected official was a wanted outlaw with a $200 price on his head. It obliterates simplistic binary images of "traditional" good and evil in the American cultural imaginary of national creation in the frontier. We return to Schultz's possible lessons from Kant, who posits, "It is freedom to make public use of one's reason at every point. But I hear on all sides, 'Do not argue!' The officer says: 'Do not argue but drill!' The tax collector: 'Do not argue but pay!' .... Everywhere there is restriction on freedom."[13]

Similarly, the linkage of this corruption of freedom and law to potential Marxist critique of class conflict and pre-capitalism is performed at Bennett's plantation, where Schultz and Django are only admitted (particularly repugnant to the plantation owner is a "nigger on a horse"), when Schultz flatters him with an offer of significant money for one of his female slaves. Django's status as a freeman is incomprehensible to the slaves, and particularly to the female slave who is ordered to show him around and treat him within the "boundaries of taste": Django is not to be treated as a slave, or a white man, but as something in between. The discovery of the Brittle Brothers leads to Django's memory of Broomhilda's vicious beating for having attempted to escape with him, and it is reflected in the present, with the whipping of a female slave that broke some eggs. The blood splattered on the white cotton plants with the execution of the Brittle Brothers becomes one of Tarantino's greatest visual symbols of the film, deromanticizing the plantation culture with a barbaric melodrama and countering it with symbols of revolution Schultz and Django—and the red of both Marxism and blood staining the system of white superiority. It is replayed when Schultz, expecting revenge by the plantation owner and his men, trick them into finding his "tooth" wagon, which explodes and Django's subsequent shooting of "Big Daddy" Bennett results in a wildly galloping white horse splashed with red blood (Figure 1.1).

The telling of the legend of Brunhilde, which follows this violence, becomes a lesson on the patriarchal oppression of women. Brunhilde is imprisoned by a magic fire by her father until an enlightened male (Siegfried) will slay a dragon and walk through the fire to rescue her "because Brunhilde is worth it." With Schultz referring to Django as a "real-life Siegfried" and maintaining that as a "German" he is "obliged" to help him on his quest, Tarantino breaks the expected image of the blonde Siegfried, which would be used later as a mythic symbol of "Aryan" superiority and hypermasculine warrior ideals. He "exposes" the mythic characters and their story as revolutionary allegory "before" it became so identified.

The relationship between the German Schultz and plantation owner Calvin Candie, who fashions himself a Frenchman who speaks no French, is a reversal of the German and French relationship in *Inglourious Basterds*. There, the German occupation manipulates and exploits the French, particularly in the relationship in which Hans Landa (as an Austrian understanding himself at that point to be a Nazi German) extorts the information about the missing Jews from a Frenchman that has hidden them. In *Django Unchained*, a German wants something again, but this time it is the pseudo-Frenchman

FIGURE 1.1 *The Emblem of the South*

Candie who shows prowess in manipulation. Having travelled to the Candyland plantation in Mississippi under the guise of purchasing a slave wrestler, but in actuality having traced Broomhilda to her owner, Schultz witnesses a barbarism that seems to overwhelm even his experiences in the 1848 revolutions, and the violence of his role as a bounty hunter in the United States. The use of the Mandingo wrestlers as animals who fight to the death is considered "a good bit of fun" by Candie in the same inhumane manner Landa first considers himself a Jew hunter, and then without any hesitation resolves his anger and frustration by strangling Bridget von Hammersmark to death for her involvement with the Basterds. But the nadir of Schultz's experience in *Django Unchained* is witnessing Candie order a runaway slave named D'Artagnan (Ato Essandoh) to be torn apart by guard dogs because his earning potential as a Mandingo fighter is waning. Schultz is willing to "reimburse" Candie for his losses to keep D'Artagnan alive, but Candie rejects this to reaffirm his superiority to Schultz and Django.

Schultz requests Broomhilda to be his comfort slave when he arrives at the plantation on the basis that she speaks German. When she is presented to him after being cleaned up from her sentence in the "hot box," Schultz speaks to her in respectful German, addressing her as *Fräulein* (literally translated as Miss, a title that was primarily used for unmarried young *ladies* in this century), asking permission ("*Darf ich?*") and expressing polite forms of excuse ("*Entschuldigen Sie mich*") with the formal pronoun "*Sie*." He clearly places Broomhilda on his own class level. In a reflection of *Inglourious Basterds* where Waltz's character dispels with both German and French for English so that the hidden Jewish family does not understand the plan he has for them, his character here uses German to keep Candie's people from understanding the reunion with Django he has planned for her. The dinner negotiations for a Mandingo fighter, which covers up the goal of liberating Broomhilda, pits Schultz's humanism and reason against Candie's commodification of human life and "scientific" racism—based in phrenology and craniometry. He attempts to convince Schultz of the growth of the "exceptional nigger" in an otherwise feeble population—which Django eventually "proves" to be during his bloody revenge: "that one nigger in ten thousand!"[14]

Schultz's intention to reunite the married couple brings two significant German Enlightenment texts to mind that can assist in understanding the character's convictions. Both are from the German playwright Gottfried Ephraim Lessing, whose class-clause development in flipping the traditional high-born tragedy and low-born comedy to a more humanized dramatic art, in which the aristocracy would be present in intelligent comedies and the middle classes would be understood through their moral strictures and social sacrifices—in the most influential structure in German dramatic writing, the bourgeois tragedy. This drama would most often present the plight of a victimized young woman, abandoned to desperation (often the character was with child) by the lover, who would return too late to prevent her death. Lessing's most notable bourgeois tragedies are *Miss Sara Sampson* (1755), which follows this pattern, and *Emilia Galotti* (1772), in which a capricious prince desires a young, innocent woman as an object of possession (marriage would be impossible due to class differences) and selfishly ignores the fact that she would be turned into a courtesan. The only solution, which also criticizes the middle-class moralist strictures, is the father's killing of Emilia, who ultimately has no control over her own life, to spare her a fate worse than death. The separation of Django from his wife, and her obvious sexual abuse as a house slave, suggests the destruction of young women's lives in the Enlightenment bourgeois tragedy, especially given Django's "education" as a freeman at the hands of Schultz, and Broomhilda's uncommon education in language and social manners by her obviously somewhat enlightened (or sympathetic) former German owner. They no longer represent the common slave image or mentality by the time they are reunited at Candyland. Education and learning, as particularly as the German Enlightenment would emphasize, is the key to freedom not only from oppression, but from class limitations.

Candie is the abusive "prince" of his own inherited fiefdom of Candyland, echoing the self-interested dynasticism Schultz would have fought in 1848. He would use Broomhilda in any way that would please him, including the threat of opening her skull to make his point on phrenology and force Schultz to admit that she is Django's bride, certainly echoes Lessing's condemnation of egotistic and amoral monarchs in *Emilia Galotti*, but some comparison to his

Nathan der Weise (*Nathan the Wise*, 1779) can also be made. This progressive plea for religious tolerance, set in Jerusalem during the Third Crusade, allows the Jewish merchant Nathan to become father figure of an extended family that includes his daughter, a Christian (Templar Knight) and a Moslem (represented by the enlightened Sultan Saladin). There is some of this "society as extended family" consciousness to be found in Schultz's bringing together of Django and his bride. As a father figure to Django and a "relative" to Broomhilda based in German-speaking kinship, the disparate trio form a family unit that would no doubt have strengthened if Schultz had not found his demise by Candie's racism, and desire for money and control.

The most compelling moment of the film is Schultz's reaction to Candie's sister playing Beethoven's piano bagatelle *Für Elise* on the harp (a typical Tarantino anachronism regarding historical accuracy in film, since the work was not published until 1867) in the salon after dinner. Schultz has just been forced to pay $12,000 for Broomhilda or Candie will kill her to "examine" her skull. Schultz's disgust at the inhumanity that surrounds him is brought to a turning point as he recalls D'Artagnan being torn apart by the dogs while he listens to the core of the German Enlightenment in music. Beethoven's inscription history for his Third Symphony "Eroica" (heroic) suggests music composed to battle tyranny: first dedicated to Napoleon, whom he admired in his role as High Consul following the French Revolution, Beethoven tore up the dedication upon learning that Napoleon had declared himself emperor.[15] With Beethoven as the immediate "motivation" for Schultz's inability to accept Candie's tyranny, resulting in both their deaths and setting Django on his path of avenging the barbarisms of Candie's world, Tarantino locates the German humanist spirit as a counterpoint to the pseudo-scientific and social ideologies of dehumanization in this era. Schultz's shooting of Candie returns him to the beginning of his own "revolutionary" life, which would have begun in earnest in "March Revolutions" of 1848, which spread from the revolts in France. But it is also a nod to Beethoven's celebration of the spirit of the French Revolution, and his anger at its ultimate corruption and failure. Moreover, Django's blood-bath execution of most of the plantation residents following their return from Candie's funeral, and his destruction of the manor itself, is allusive to the French Revolution and the killing of the king and his court, while it also recalls the 1848 February Revolution which brought down the monarchy of Louis Philippe. Unlike *Inglourious Basterds*, where his destruction of the cinema frees Europe from Nazism, Tarantino's annihilation of Candyland is only symbolic: "What Tarantino wants to see annihilated is Southern culture in total, a culture which he portrays as both incorrigibly corrupt and completely degenerate."[16]

Beethoven's influence in Tarantino's film might not end with what we hear. The composer's only opera, *Fidelio* (1814), comes to mind when considering Schultz's plot to present himself as a wealthy businessman interested in the profits of the (fictional) Mandingo fighting, in an effort to gain entrance into Candie's world and rescue the imprisoned Broomhilda. Based in part on a French opera, the 1798 *Léonore, ou L'amour conjugal* by Pierre Gaveaux, and thus a representative union of the French and German Enlightenment spirit (opposing the allo/historic and fictional/symbolic Franco-Germanic conflicts translated into *Inglourious Basterds* and *Django Unchained*), Beethoven's opera is positioned against the political injustices of its time. The story of Leonore, who plots to rescue her husband Florestan from political forces that have imprisoned him by disguising herself as a guard named Fidelio to gain access to the prison, provides a narrative thread that can be seen in its gender reversal in *Django Unchained*. Given Tarantino's anger against female exploitation and abuse throughout his oeuvre, the "idea" of the heroic Leonore countering patriarchal tyranny would be surely appreciated by the filmmaker, and the possible use of the opera's basic plot with the gender reversed makes the expected point regarding man's inhumanity to (wo)man.[17] Critical voices, however, find that while "Tarantino has a knack for presenting audiences with strong female characters who have a set place in his films, that's absent in *Django*.... Female characters get screen time but no life and rarely any lines, they instead are merely plot devices used to keep the story rolling."[18] Additionally, unlike the pragmatic choices and transient identities of Hans Landa in *Inglourious Basterds*, which posits that Hans Landas are possible anywhere at any time and among the highly educated,

> ...white villainy in the form of Calvin Candie is delineated along more unequivocal traditional lines.... This is problematic since

by removing any sense of realness from the most potent figure, namely the plantation slave owner, from the racist landscape and having him "perform" the role of the perfect villain works to disavow guilt.... Unlike the other white racist constructs which are ruthless, brutal and ugly, Candie's eloquent banter and relationship with Stephen does not make him altogether unsympathetic. In fact, Candie is charismatic, a professional and a good host but what makes him totally unappealing as a human being is an ancestral arrogance that Schultz is unable to fathom. This leads to Schultz shooting Candie and finally declaring his European political liberalism as the genuine article.[19]

Auf Wiedersehen, or the question of Romantic transcendence

There is a distinct pattern of oppositional forces, tensions, and synthesis that runs through the film in presenting the émigré Schultz, his education of Django, their actions in defeating Candie, and Django's decisive self-realization as a "revolutionary." Additionally, the extratextual relationships with the dystopic universe of *Inglourious Basterds* and its representation of the failure of European liberalism and intimation of ongoing racism in the United States (Brad Pitt's nearly lynched character that still bears the rope scar on his neck; the fantasy of organized Jewish American rage against anti-Semitism) offers perhaps a Tarantinonian dialectic, in which Wilhelm Wicki (Gedeon Burkhard), the Austrian Jewish member of the Basterds, has emigrated to the United States to escape Nazism (a presuggestion of *Django Unchained* or an "historical" repetition of Schultz) and returns to fascist Europe to "teach" the Nazis a lesson. Moreover, the characters of Shosanna and Bridget von Hammersmark, representing different aspects of Western European identity, French Jewish peasant/rural and German-Gentile aristocrat/urban *women*, are the true liberators of Europe from Hitler, and symbolically from historical male oppression conveyed to Django by Schultz in his tale about Brunhilde's imprisonment.

Schultz's final farewell to Candie sets up another Tarantino commentary on language: "Mr. Candie, normally I would say *auf Wiedersehen.* But since what *auf Wiedersehen* actually means is 'until I see you again,' and since I never wish to see you again, to you, sir, I say: good bye." The finality of this choice precipitates the bloodbath in Candie's inherited library full of books he has probably never read.[20] Following Django's torture and his rescue from castration by the orders of Candie's repressed but still somewhat more compassionate sister who sentences him instead to work the mines, he escapes. The term *auf Wiedersehen* is used once more by Django, addressing the crumpled body of Schultz he finds in a corner of Candie's barn. The Romantic transcendence this intimates is dualistic: Django hopes for more men like Schultz, a "return" of him as a pattern for the future. Perhaps more moving is Django's embrace of Schultz as a liberator, teacher, and father figure, and the suggestion that he has a metaphysical/spiritual hope of actually seeing Schultz again. The revitalization found in simple faith and love is placed in opposition to the misuse of religion in bigotry—in the historical American South or in the *Basterds* Nazi universe.

Despite the complexity of the historical/political/philosophical interactions and counterrelationships that run across both *Django Unchained* and *Inglourious Basterds*, the American South and its slavery are one and the same for Tarantino, and its malevolence cannot be "contained" or "removed" without the complete destruction of its host, even in the reductive fantasy of revenge cinema. *Django Unchained* functions intensely as eradication of previous cinematic imagery, particularly the iconic imprint of demonized slaves and heroic white moral crusaders against "black criminality" in D. W. Griffith's *Birth of a Nation* (1915), among other films. It also demolishes the sentimental memorial to an impossibly idealized slavery culture in *Gone with the Wind* (1939), which helped envisage America as an unquestioned moral leader in an approaching war against racist fascism. Django's victory over Candyland finds him backlit by the flames of its ruins, finely dressed and astride his horse with bride by side, the scene resolves his very visceral battle against racism and injustice with a "romantic" transcendence of different kind—back into types from cinema: Django as leading man; Django as man of mystery; Django as gentleman bandit; Django as impersonation of another fantasy of post-slavery African American triumph, Will Smith as Reconstruction-era James Bond in *Wild Wild West* (1999). His horse, which suddenly dances like a Lippizan stallion, mocks the heroism, gives him momentary superpowers, and recalls anthropomorphic cartoon animals, even the former/slave imaginary in Disney's *Song of the South* (1946). The moralistic revolutionary spirit of Dr. "King" Schultz is suddenly hard to recall; the Civil War seems impossible now, even unnecessary. The timeless ending is as eccentric as the conclusion of *Inglourious Basterds*, and far more dislocating. In shifting the powerful image of the self-sacrificing Shosanna and the annihilation of the Nazi leadership, to a swastika being carved into Hans Landa's forehead as a statement of the will of the pitiless and rather ignorant Bastards leader Aldo Raine, *Inglourious Basterds* is critical about its own ironic conclusion. It dissolves the concept of the history film while *Django Unchained* is Tarantino's protest against history.

Notes

1   The *Biedermeier* refers to the social and artistic styles and modalities that appealed to the growing middle class in Central Europe following the end of the Napoleonic era and the "restoration" brought about by the Congress of Vienna in 1815. The political oppression under Austrian Foreign Minister and Chancellor of State Prince Metternich that attempted to forestall revolt or a disruption of the balance of power led artists and society to reject Romanticism and praise domestic and nonpolitical values and at least publically, the status quo. The era ended with the 1848 revolutions.

2   *The Wall Street Journal* quoted in *Moviefone* http://news.moviefone.com/2012/12/16/christoph-waltz-django-unchained-interview/ (accessed November 27, 2013).

3   Michael J. Anderson, "New Film: *Django Unchained* (2012)," *Tativille: A Place for Cinema & the Visual Arts*, http://tativille.blogspot.com/2013/01/new-film-django-unchained-2012_25.html (accessed November 29, 2013).

4   See Hans L. Trefousse, *Carl Schurz: A Biography* (New York: Fordham University Press, 1998).

5   The 2011 study *Lincoln's Marxists* by Benson and Kennedy attempts to trace the election of 1861 and the policies of the Civil War, the decline of a "Christian America," and the continued sociopolitical influence (including feminism), which sets the "tone for today's Leviathan government," to an early Socialist/Communist infiltration of U.S. politics and government by German "Forty-Eighters."

6   Immanuel Kant, "What is Enlightenment?" The quote by Kant is from Horace, *Ars poetica*.

7   Immanuel Kant, "What is Enlightenment?", 1784. Internet Modern History Sourcebook. http://www.fordham.edu/halsall/mod/kant-whatis.asp (accessed March 3, 2014).

8   "An Interview with Danny Strong." *IGN*. http://www.ign.com/articles/2003/05/19/an-interview-with-danny-strong (accessed February 28, 2013).

9   "Quentin Tarantino," *Faces of the Week*, BBC. May 14, 2004 (accessed February 28, 2013).

10 Lessing, G. E., "The Education of the Human Race," in Gotthold Ephraim Lessing, *Nathan the Wise, Minna von Barnhelm, and Other Plays and Writings*, edited by Peter Demetz, foreword by Hannah Arendt (New York: Continuum, 2004), 316.

11 Kant.

12 Naomi Stead, "The Value of Ruins: Allegories of Destruction in Benjamin and Speer," *Form/Work: An Interdisciplinary Journal of the Built Environment*, No. 6 (October 2003), 51–64. http://naomistead. files.wordpress.com/2008/09/stead_value_of_ruins_2003.pdf (accessed November 27, 2013).

13 Kant.

14 Phrenology as set out by Franz Joseph Gall in his first lectures in Vienna and later in Paris at the end of the eighteenth century concluded that character and intelligence could be read by the size of bumps on (and in) the skull. Dismissed as fraudulent by many scientists and condemned by the Catholic Church, his theories, however, found interest in Victorian England, which applied it to colonialist racial classification and pre/post–Civil War United States as a justification for slavery. See van Wyhe's website which includes his article, "The authority of human nature: The *Schädellehre* of Franz Joseph Gall," *British Journal for the History of Science*, 2002, 17–42. Stephen Jay Gould offers an in-depth examination of the racial science of human measurement in the nineteenth-century craniometry, a measurement of the skull which was used to classify "inferior" beings. The collapse of this pseudoscience was due to the failure of it to actually support racist expectations. Moreover,

Gould also explores the attempts to measure the criminal human body as well as concepts regarding hereditary intelligence and the IQ testing, which has been utilized as a more sophisticated version of such older racial and gender theories. See *The Mismeasure of Man*, particularly "American Polygeny and Craniotomy before Darwin: Blacks and Indians as Separate, Inferior Species" 30–72.

15 *Sinfonia Eroica ... composta per festeggiare il sovvenire di un grand Uomo* ("heroic symphony, composed to celebrate the memory of a great man"). See Carl Dahlhaus, *Ludwig van Beethoven, Approaches to His Music* (Oxford: Oxford University Press, 1991) 19–29.

16 Quentin, "*Django Unchained* (Quentin Tarantino, US)," *Cinemascope* 54, http://cinema-scope.com/currency/django-unchained-quentin-tarantino-us/ (accessed November 1, 2013).

17 Robert von Dassanowsky, "Introduction: Locating Mr. Tarantino or, Who's Afraid of Metacinema?" in *Quentin Tarantino's Inglourious Basterds: A Manipulation of Metacinema*, ed. Robert von Dassanowsky (New York/London: Continuum, 2012), ix–xi.; See also Heidi Schlipphacke, "*Inglourious Basterds* and the Gender of Revenge," in *Quentin Tarantino's* Inglourious Basterds: *A Manipulation of Metacinema*, ed. Robert von Dassanowsky (New York/London: Continuum, 2012), 113–133.

18 "*Django Unchained*, December 30, 2012," *The Cinephiliac*, http://thecinephiliac.wordpress.com/2012/12/30/django-unchained/ (accessed November 1, 2013).

19 Omar Ahmed, "*Django Unchained*—Re-imagining Slavery," *Ellipsis: The Accents of Cinema*, http://omarsfilmblog.blogspot.com/2013/01/django-unchained-dir-quentin-tarantino.html (accessed November 27, 2013).

20 Schultz embarrasses Candie by commenting on his uninformed Francophila in naming the brutally killed slave, D'Artagnan, after the heroic character from Alexandre Dumas' novel, *The Three Musketeers*. Schultz tells him Dumas would never have approved what took place, to which Candie replies "Soft hearted Frenchie" and Schultz retorts: "Dumas is Black." Dumas father, Thomas-Alexandre Davy de la Pailleterie, was the son of a French nobleman and a black slave woman from the French colony of Saint Domingo.

2

Franco-faux-ne: Django's Jive

Margaret Ozierski

Quentin Tarantino's latest film, *Django Unchained*, has provoked a controversy among critics, professional and self-appointed alike. Indeed, the film provokes the viewer's visceral response to unmitigated violence, for example, but the latter, accompanied by moments of lyrical beauty evocative of contexts altogether foreign to the cliché of the South, ought also to elicit from the viewer a measured, thoughtful consideration. Another striking, related feature of the film is its insistent references to foreign languages and cultures, especially the French. Given that a swath of the South is permeated by francophone culture—a baroque, seemingly decadent Catholic influence whose locus is New Orleans—pretentions to French language and culture not only signify the plantation owner's cultured status at a time when speaking French held such cultural cachet, but could also be seen as representing a *faux*-gentility of the South that appropriates this culture in a minor register for its own ends. In this chapter, I propose to analyze the notable instances where the French language and phenomena of French culture make a programmatic appearance in the film, in an attempt to better understand the workings of *liberté égalité fraternité*, ideals espoused by the French Revolution whose echoes are clearly heard in the film in a very different context, the slave-holding United States.

Although the operative myth of the film is the German one of Siegfried and the *Nibelungenlied* (The Song of the Nibelungs), the ideal of liberation is one espoused by the French Revolution and others that swept Europe after it at around the same time as the setting of the film, and one way to understand this ideal as it is developed in the film is by locating it specifically within the speaker, the user of language in a minor register who accedes to the status of (liberated) subjecthood. In my discussion, I will consider the concepts and work of important French and francophone theorists and writers, such as Alexandre Dumas, who is mentioned in the film, as well as Franz Fanon, whose conceptualizations of the post-colonial subject help to understand Django's breaking through the chains of linguistic enslavement to become a new speaking subject.

The speech patterns and peculiarities of characters are a feature of the film that is cast in the foreground from the opening sequence. The first time the viewer encounters the character of Dr. "King" Schultz, the figure instrumental to Django's coming into liberated subjecthood, we are struck not just by his accented speech, but by the elaborate mannerism of what he says and how he says it. In this scene, we first see a chain gang of slaves and three slave drivers on horseback on a dark winter night in the woods somewhere in Texas. Dr. Schultz appears driving a carriage with a preposterous bobble-tooth atop it that communicates in no uncertain terms the profession that serves as his cover, itinerant dentist, but which might also be interpreted as extirpator of rotten elements from the body politic for monetary gain: bounty hunter. He asks for information about a certain slave whom he wishes to purchase, but the slave drivers will have none of his story. They instantly mistrust him, especially because he addresses a slave as equal:

Ace Speck: Hey, stop talkin' to him like that!
Dr. Schultz: Like what?
Ace Speck: Like that!
Dr. Schultz: My good man, I'm simply trying to ascertain
Ace Speck: Speak English, goddamit![1]

Schultz is clearly marked as a foreigner who simply does not talk like the rest of the figures who inhabit that same landscape. Compared to the slave drivers who speak with laconic economy to one another and snarl at the silent slaves, this man appears of a different class altogether. While they communicate to get from point A to point B and bark orders at what they perceive to be sub-human slaves, King Schultz does not just state his business; he speaks in an excessively wordy way marked by elegance, attention to social form, education, and cultured status that immediately captures the notice of those whom he thus addresses. Indeed, his manner of speaking is marked by features that one might deem extraneous European "frill" that only serves to perplex the ignorant or, as happens later at the Candie plantation, to oil the machinery of business transaction, but whose aesthetic or liberating value is lost on the Americans that King Schultz encounters.

What is also lost on the American speakers—and the slave drivers in the opening sequence are emblematic of this—is not just the human status of the slaves, but also, notably, the barely human status of the slave drivers themselves, as well as the humanizing power that language has to make this state of affairs come to light, and indeed, to reverse it. The slave drivers are white-trash emissaries doing dirty work for money that capitalist plantation owners like "Monsieur" Candie dispense to them the way they throw scraps, or the occasional slave, to the dogs. The system dehumanizes everyone caught in its mechanism. When Schultz addresses them in what they perceive to be a very peculiar manner, he does not simply "talk fancy" at them, but proffers a chance for them to relate to him in a humanizing fashion to which they are not accustomed. The crucial difference between Schultz, the European foreigner, and the slave drivers and their bosses is that the speech of Schultz possesses authenticity and a humanizing power in its aesthetic form of address, while for the others speech is simply a means to an end. Notably, he uses the polite form "Sie," when he speaks to Broomhilda in German.

Unfortunately, his attempt to politely address the slave drivers in the opening sequence—to dignify them with a human status—fails. The latter refuse his unique gesture and instead, out of mistrust, contempt, and sheer hatred for his extension of that same gesture in egalitarian fashion to a black slave, Django, they turn their guns on King Schultz. In so doing, they elucidate the real terms of "parlaying" operative in this business transaction: violence, the violent usurpation of power over another. In the end, King Schultz is a quicker draw, and being on the side of right and rights (his own self-defense and that of Django), they are no match for his own meting out of just violence. Or, to remain within the paradigm of language, they come to "understand" King Schultz through the language of his firearm, a tool of execution of his communicative as well as deadly intention. Language becomes a deadly act, the only form of communication with which they are willing to engage. As Frantz Fanon articulates it in his pivotal work, *The Wretched of the Earth*, violence is the only language that, in the end, the colonizer understands, and the colonized are justified in employing it to demand their right to self-determination, indeed, to their very status as fully fledged political, human subjects. As I argue in the following, the sequences with "Monsieur" Candie are a particularly pointed reminder to the viewer that, in this regard, the American slaveholder, no matter what his linguistic affectations might be, is no different from the European colonizer, and in the end, also only understands the language of violence.

At this point, Schultz takes up with Django, the slave he has just purchased from the now-dead slave drivers. Having purchased him, he declares him a freeman. Having obtained the information he asked for but could not get from the slave drivers, he makes a proposition to the freeman Django to join forces with him and become a partner in his profession, bounty hunting, which he defines as delivering corpses for cash. This profession, Schultz says, is in essence no different from slave-trading, except that what he deals in are defunct bodies of wanted, known criminals whose human subjects have departed this world, and whose inanimate *corpses* possess the monetary exchange value. There is, however, a crucial difference between the slave trade and bounty hunting as Schultz practices it: while slave traders trade in living flesh and deny the human subject that animates it, Schultz fully acknowledges the human subject, whom he duly dispatches to the next world in full consciousness of his action in order to secure the valuable corpse. While in both cases the flesh is valuable, it is noteworthy that Schultz's attitude to the flesh represents the ethical stance with regard to the human. He recognizes that the human subject has no exchange value as such and cannot, indeed must not, be bought and sold like a piece of meat. In this logical frame, it makes sense that he "gives" Django his freedom. Indeed, giving in this case is a perfect gift: it is the impossible giving of something that cannot be given, and the gift of poison (the word *Gift* in King Schultz's native German means just that). Indeed, the "gift" of freedom occasions a whole series of troubles for Django, who must now act as a moral agent, choosing to be duty-bound to his new partner and to set off to rescue Broomhilda, his wife.

Django's assumption of his free subjecthood is marked by choices, and is also linguistically loaded in that he leaves behind the sphere of the silence of slaves, who only obey and never talk back. At first, he remains silent and lets King Schultz "do the talking," as, for example, they execute their first bounty hunt together (the crooked sheriff of Daughtry, Texas). Increasingly, however, Django is required to speak and does so with the requisite boldness, offending all those who only see a slave who ought to be meekly following his master where the freeman proudly rides a horse. When Django and King Schultz lay their plan for seeking out and killing the notorious gang of three brothers at Big Daddy's plantation in Tennessee, Django plays the role of King Schultz's valet, a figure who is not a slave, but a paid servant. The striking blue outfit with white jabot that Django picks out for himself, reminiscent of the titular figure of Thomas Gainsborough's painting *The Blue Boy* (1770), and coming off as rather extravagant in the 1858 American setting, is remarkable and noteworthy. It reflects not only Django's foray into self-expression through sartorial taste, but also the wealth of his master, who is his employer, not owner.

The viewer should not confuse this relationship with that of master and slave in the American context, especially as this subtle reference to French culture invites the comparison with famous figures of the valet in French theater. For example, in Pierre de Marivaux, one of the most important playwrights of the eighteenth century working with the Comédie-Française and the Comédie-Italienne and known for such comedies as *The Game of Love and Chance* (1730) and *The Triumph of Love* (1732), the figure of the valet is a savvy character who often shows more spirit and wit than his master, and who woos the *soubrette*, or lady's attendant, on the side while saving the day in the end. Hardly the silent subservient type, he is rather the archetype of resourcefulness and linguistic boundary crossing. Moreover, the style of writing known as *marivaudage* that Marivaux popularizes is a kind of meandering in a pleasant, aesthetic way that involves mixing of metaphor, of high and low, of registers that normally do not coexist on one plane. The figure of Django as valet can certainly be said to engage in a sort of *marivaudage*: by his very act of speaking back to townspeople, figures of authority, or plantation hands, he is making two worlds collide—that of the silent black slave and the outspoken white master—that in the view of most of the figures he addresses should never coincide. Indeed, he is derided for his outfit, for riding a horse, and for speaking because in partaking of all of these things, the valet becomes a mirror of his master, in appearance no different from him, dangerously close to being *in essence* no different from him. Just as the figure of the valet in French eighteenth-century theater represents a kind of democratization—of theatrical subject, of theatergoer—taking root in French culture, in step with the rise of republican revolutionary values, the figure of Django as valet in the nineteenth-century American landscape announces a similar revolutionary current, recognizably foreign and belated though it might be. The brilliant travelling shot that shows Django walking along at Big Daddy's plantation, in his fancy livery with a bag slung over his shoulder, is a perfect example: on his way to kill two of the three wanted men who have sought refuge there, the backdrop to Django's *passage à l'acte* (he acts on his own initiative at that point) looks like a scene out of a pastoral French painting, complete with the figure of the idyllic swinging young slave girl, herself reminiscent of the figure in *The Swing* (1767) by Jean-Honoré Fragonard. While the swinging figure partakes of a forbidden pleasure, Django is the agent of a violent act normally reserved for a white man. The travelling shot registers the tension inherent in a place where idyllic scenes give way to scenes of sadistic violence (Django then sees a young woman slave being brutally whipped for having broken some eggs), while also registering a nascent democratization, the emergence of new subjects who are privileged as centers of the scene (Django as the focal point of brewing violent action; the swinging girl as new point of aesthetic interest). Through astute staging and mise-en-scène, Tarantino brilliantly captures the sheer displacement of these annunciatory figures, who at once belong to the scene and are utterly foreign to it (Figure 2.1).

The most pronounced foil to the authentic foreignness of both Django and King Schultz is "Monsieur" Calvin Candie, whose French

FIGURE 2.1 The Blue Boy *and* The Swing

affectation is pure façade, he not being able to speak any French and being totally ignorant about the French culture he pretends to admire. Before examining the overt references to French culture that abound in this part of the film, it is worth noting that at the point where Django and King Schultz encounter Monsieur Candie, first at the New Orleans Cleopatra Club, then on his own turf, "Candie-land," Django and King Schultz have operated another kind of *marivaudage*. The "valet" has now crossed over into the territory of expert on Mandingo fighters, no longer dressed up in frilly blue suit, but rather the sober clothing of the former bounty hunter and speaking with terse self-assurance. The "master" is now in the position of apprentice, having capital, manners, and the gift of gab, but no expertise, deferring to the (equally sham) superior knowledge and judgment regarding brute muscular vitality possessed by the free black man with whom he travels. King Schultz and Django have in a sense moved into similar positions, pretending to be something they are not but having to maintain the farce and project confidence, not unlike the *perceived* position of Django no matter what costume or confidence he might project, as a pretender to subjecthood.

The perceived pretense of Django to being a free subject, and the need for both Django and King Schultz to maintain a farce, must be considered in contrast to the un-avowed but patent fakery of the lover of French culture, Calvin Candie. There is an immediate incongruity legible in the name: his first name calls to mind one of the strictest, most austere reformers of Christianity, the French John or Jean Calvin (or Jehan Cauvin), seemingly at odds with the lavish slaveholder/ pimp persona of the owner of "Candie-land" or Candyland, a sweet fantasy place located in Mississippi. The obvious fakery of this fine gentleman with "Francophile" tendencies that have no substance beyond having a high-class prostitute from his New Orleans brothel for a mistress is an indicator of his privilege and power—he can be a fake, and no one will take him to task among those he frequents and who gain access to him. Thus, he can call one of his Mandingo fighters who runs off and is then torn apart by dogs at Candie's order "D'Artagnan," remaining ignorant of the fact that D'Artagnan is a hero out of a French novel written by a black French author, Alexandre Dumas, as King Schultz reminds him shortly before he fatally shoots him in his own library. The name of D'Artagnan is pure heroic façade: the slave has no subjecthood in Candie's eyes, and thus is nothing but a brute that fights to the death and has happened to win, which is what assures his exchange value and makes him an important piece in Candie's collection of valuable objects. D'Artagnan bears no resemblance to the D'Artagnan of Dumas, except in name and as a reminder of everything that the black slave will never be in the eyes of Monsieur Candie and others like him. His struggle will never achieve the noble contours of that of the D'Artagnan of fiction, or of history.

At the same time, Candie's fake Francophilia is an indicator of a deeper-seated fakery that animates his very being. To invoke his name once again, "Candie" pronounced with the French affectation so beloved by the holder of the name sounds very much like "Candide," the eponymous hero of Voltaire's highly satirical *Candide, ou L'Optimisme* (1759), one of the most famous works of the French Enlightenment inspired by current events and written in novella form to deliver biting satire in response to the German philosopher Gottfried Leibniz's religious optimism as expressed in his equally famous *theodicy* (which originates the term), *Théodicée*, a work written in French. The titular figure of *Candide* lives in an Edenic setting, firmly believing, despite empirical evidence to the contrary, that he inhabits "the best of all possible worlds," the "Leibnizian" mantra with which his teacher, Pangloss, has indoctrinated him. The novella follows the progress of Candide's slow but steady disillusionment and end in the resolutely circumscribed practicality of "cultivating his own garden." Having run rampant through Eden, Candide has some extraordinary adventures and learns important lessons. Like Candide, Candie lives in a fantasy world and has a preceptor, the head-butler slave Stephen, who has been instrumental in keeping up a certain ideology of racial difference that makes Candie's world go round. Candie, however, as the fore-shortened name suggests, is a "Candide *manqué*": rather than steadily becoming disabused of a pernicious ideology and moving to the solid though modest terrain of new ground based in evidence, as Candide does in settling in his "garden" at the end of the novella, Candie the plantation master of la-la "Candyland" never breaks through the illusion of the fantasy world he inhabits, maintained by a pernicious preceptor or "master" in the form of Stephen—himself a fake who benefits from his parasitizing of Candie's power—but rather runs unchecked until the bitter end. His end comes in the person of King Schultz, who out of frustration, trauma, and sheer disgust—and in refusal to be morally compromised by shaking the hand of the likes of Calvin Candie—shoots Candie in his own library, surrounded by books that he has never read. To bring up Frantz Fanon again, King Schultz seems to realize that only the language of a bullet might dislodge the fantasy which organizes Candie's worldview and underpins his racial superiority.

But the illusion that Candie lives seems to be one that not even a bullet through the heart is able to dislodge: the superiority of his race that, in his view, explains the servitude and submissiveness that keeps slaves like the exemplary Ben—whose skull he produces for his little lesson at the dinner table—in chains and unable to make any violent gesture that might end that servitude. This illusion leaves him vulnerable—and indeed, Monsieur Candie is always in need of proving himself, his wealth, his brilliance, his manhood, in the form of a beautiful mistress, a collection of Mandingo fighters, his affectation of French culture—to the fact of Stephen, the faithful old butler who is largely responsible for the continuation of the enslavement of black men and women. Unfortunately, the illusion is one shared by an entire nation for whom racial ideology at the time is like a religious creed.

This, however, does not make the act of killing Candie a futile or destructive self-annihilation. It should not be understood as nihilistic desperation on the part of a helpless King Schultz running amok in a tense situation, only making things worse for Django. Instead, it is the authentic and ethical response of this foreigner forced into an act he finds morally repulsive—the conciliatory handshake proposed as a "custom" of the South by Monsieur Candie—that would amount to becoming like the figure that King Schultz despises. The only way out is through the drastic, violent act of speaking in a language Candie understands, a firm "no" in the form of a bullet that also paradoxically humanizes Candie—because it takes his spoken request seriously, and no longer simply on the plane of fakery—in the very act of extinguishing his subjecthood. Moreover, it turns the deal that Django and King Schultz came to cement, acquiring Django's wife Broomhilda, into something more than a brute financial transaction, a dealing in human flesh, something that as bounty hunters they are not in the business of conducting. Like the "acquisition" of Django, in which there is a steep moral price to be paid in dead subjects (the slave drivers at the beginning of the film), the moral price here has been driven up a notch to include self-sacrifice on the part of King Schultz himself. It is also that self-sacrifice that makes Django ethically responsible to carry on the subjecthood he has assumed, a moral imperative to not turn back but rather finish what he started. The act of King Schultz drives home the subjective fact of Django that others would prefer to strip away or ignore, and which Django himself must face to choose to do what is right. In other words, Django must follow the path of subjective development, like Candide, and continue to strip away the illusion that powerful men like Candie, and nihilistic figures like Stephen, continue to uphold.

In going down this path, Django begins to resemble the very heroes of nineteenth-century French novels invoked earlier in the person of the misnamed Mandingo fighter, D'Artagnan. While the fighter D'Artagnan, a slave who is nothing but a thing to be disposed of by his master, resembles neither the fictionalized friend of the Musketeers nor the historical figure of D'Artagnan, the loyal servant, confidant, and stand-in of King Louis XIV as effective leader of the elite Musketeers, Django does begin to resemble another iconic figure of French legend and literature: the man in the iron mask. *L'Homme au Masque de Fer*, before being taken up by Alexandre Dumas in a sequel volume to *The Three Musketeers*, entitled *The Vicomte of Bragelonne: Ten Years Later*, is an historical figure whose identity has been disputed and widely speculated upon, making the enigmatic prisoner of the state the stuff of legend and perfect material for fictional narratives such as that of Dumas. Speculations aside, significant for my argument here is the narrative use to which Dumas puts the legend of the man in the iron mask, as this is specifically the line of thought the viewer is invited to take by Tarantino's own *auteurial* borrowing from Dumas when he shows Django imprisoned, after the shooting spree that leaves Candie and other members of the household dead, hanging upside-down and wearing an iron mask that obscures his features.[2]

For Tarantino, Django as man in the iron mask is not simply a graphic borrowing of Dumas' borrowed legend to drive home visually the excruciating pain of the physical punishment and the extreme threat that Django endures as he awaits his fate, literally suspended and being decided upon by Candie's surviving sister and Stephen. As in Dumas' account, what hangs in the balance is Django's identity and who will emerge from the iron mask when it is removed. In Dumas' account, the man in the iron mask is a prisoner whose identity must be closely guarded, as he is Philippe, the twin brother of Louis XIV and a pretender to the throne. His identity has been closely concealed his entire life, and he becomes part of a plot by one of the Musketeers to enrich himself by installing a new king in place of the old. Philippe is thus the specter of a power rivaling that of the legitimate heir Louis. In Tarantino's critique of the American power scheme, based not on the hierarchy of royal families but brute capitalist force, presenting Django as the specter of a rival power, in essence no different from the "legitimate" master of the plantation whose power he is perceived as wanting to usurp by the survivors, is a highly provocative act of representation. When presented with the image of Django as man in the iron mask, the viewer must see Django as essentially no different from the plantation master Candie. If Philippe is separated from power by pure chance of being born a moment later, or simply because he has been chosen by his parents to stand aside and let his brother rule—a pure accident of fate—the viewer must recognize that in essence, what separates the master Candie from Django, the nonexceptional slave who claims exceptional status, is also pure accident, that of skin color. Django is a human subject like Candie and capable of rebellion and the assumption of moral agency, despite the master's racist delusions that relegate Django to a permanent status of subservience. And the effective subservience and humiliation that the mask represents in fact do nothing to break Django's spirit, only making him stronger in the end, only making his casting off of slave status, for the second time, even more audacious and decisive than the first time.

"I AM that exception, that one in ten thousand," Django proclaims to Stephen as he proceeds to destroy Candyland and all it stands for in a final blaze of gunfire and dynamite. The nonexceptional human subject thus performs the exceptional in claiming "ownership" of his being—his very subjectivity—against established power that would strip him of his very humanity, of that being.

Notes

1 *Django Unchained Script*, http://www.imsdb.com/scripts/Django-Unchained.html (accessed November 30, 2013).

2 Such masks were in fact used to discipline slaves in the American South. The mask here is thus also a historically accurate basis upon which is grafted the intertextual "plant" that I discuss below.

3

Of Handshakes and Dragons: Django's German Cousins

Dana Weber

Crucial scenes in Quentin Tarantino's *Django Unchained* (2012) are formulated in a "Sekundenstil"[1] that renders even the minutest reactions of characters and reveals their perspectives. Indeed, the action may unfold so quickly that it appears insufficiently motivated or ambiguous within the larger logic of events. This happens especially in two cases: Dr. King Schultz (Christoph Waltz) and Django's (Jamie Foxx) conversation at a campfire and Schultz's heated dialogue with the plantation owner Calvin Candie (Leonardo DiCaprio) that results in a shoot-out. The ambiguity of these two scenes is echoed in the film: "Why you care what happen to me?" Django asks the dentist, "Why you care if I find my wife?"; Stephen (Samuel L. Jackson), Candie's house slave, expresses the same perplexity about Schultz's motivations: "Now, why that German gives a fuck who that uppity-son-of-a-bitch [Django] is in love with, I'm sure I don't know." Why does Schultz's position deviate so radically from that of white supremacy in the antebellum South? What is really behind his disinterested support considering that none of *Django Unchained's* characters—least of all he—are one-dimensionally pure, ethical, or romantic enough to convincingly justify such honorability?

In its search for answers to the ambiguity surrounding the dentist's figure, this chapter investigates the relationships among the four male leading characters by close readings of these two scenes. Partners in what Jacques Derrida in his *Politics of Friendship* calls "phratries," bonds of friendship and fraternization, they are antagonistically pitted against each other. In their volatile economy of fraternization, Django's wife Broomhilda (Kerry Washington) serves as the desirable object that they violently negotiate between them. As I argue, this web of fraternal and agonistic relations is marked by philosophical, cultural, and political parameters that inevitably lead to its demise and identify precisely the ambiguities of *Django Unchained* as contemporary statements about human relations that must leave behind a patriarchal past. As the chapter aims to uncover what Django eventually finds out and Stephen cannot understand, the analysis employs a philosophical concept of friendship whose history Derrida has outlined and expands it by including the institution of Germanic blood brotherhood in the discussion. By fashioning an intricate and problematic web of male bonding, and critiquing it, the argument contends, *Django Unchained* ultimately offers a politically lucid review of contemporary race relations in America.

Handshakes and fraternity:
The legend of Brunhilde

After successfully completing their first bounty hunting mission together, Django and Schultz share supper. Finding out that Django's wife Hildy is a German-speaking slave, Broomhilda von Shaft,[2] Schultz tells his partner the story of her Valkyrie namesake, "a character in the most popular of all the German legends."[3] In the dentist's version, Brunhilde was disobedient to her father Wotan, "God of all Gods," who has banished her on a mountain guarded by a fire-breathing dragon until a brave hero can save her. Siegfried, as the doctor narrates, indeed "scales the mountain because he's not afraid of it. He slays the dragon, because he's not afraid of him. And he walks through hellfire—because Brunhilde's worth it."

The direction and camera work used in this scene tell the emotional story of Django's affections in parallel with Schultz's speech. Django leaves his plate of food aside, paces around, sits down at the fire, watches the storyteller expectantly. His facial expression, listening position, and inquiries stand witness to his eager anticipation. In his turn, Schultz speaks calmly and slowly, lowering his voice and using large gestures to mark significant points of the story. Frequent cuts between medium shots of the two characters and the points of view of each indicate their intense involvement. As the scene presents it, Schultz's German tale conveys to Django an affective truth that both protagonists share beyond their distinct cultural determinations. At the same time, the dentist also realizes his human affinity with the man he has freed. When Schultz and Django agree to collaborate professionally a moment later, plot, direction, and camera work collude again to highlight how they cement their bond. By now, the camera has drawn closer and slowly moves from medium shots to close-ups of their profiles. The protagonists are positioned on the left (Schultz) and right hand (Django) of the screen and look at each other when Schultz offers Django a business partnership. At first, Django is incredulous about this proposition and cannot fathom why a wealthy white doctor would be interested in his fate. As thinly motivated as it may appear to the audience, Schultz's explanation that he feels responsible for a slave he has freed and, as a German, supportive toward a real-life Siegfried, nevertheless seems to persuade Django. He is the first to stretch out his hand for a handshake (Figure 3.1). This agreement is not purely economic: although Schultz promises Django a third of his profits,[4] the benefit that the freedman reaps is affective, cultural, and social: he rescues his lost wife, becomes involved in cross-cultural interaction, and experiences equality for the first time.

FIGURE 3.1 *The fraternal handshake*

Once the pair proceeds to Hildy's rescue, the enterprise demands more from them emotionally and economically than they had anticipated. And yet, neither Schultz nor Django steps back. The deeper, unspoken philosophical and cultural motivations underlying the loyalty between these two characters can be illuminated with the help of Derrida's study on the concept of friendship in Western culture. His deconstructive readings of historically varying fraternity models trace their conceptual history and uncover their major internal contradictions (*aporias*). While Derrida ultimately criticizes the obvious—the exclusion of women from androcentric relationship models that have come to constitute the canon of "authentic friendship"—he also calls for a new language that dispenses with "homo-fraternal" schemas in exchange for discourses of freedom, equality, and justice.[5]

As a western, *Django Unchained* relies on a basic premise of male cooperation against all odds, so that *The Politics of Friendship* offers a useful framework for approaching its discourse of fraternization and locating it in a Western philosophical tradition. However, Derrida's insights do not illuminate its transcultural dimensions. Instead, recent American historical studies on friendship discuss transracial and gendered narratives from American literature and culture precisely in view of how they productively emulate classical and modern European models of masculine amity to generate their own cultural perspectives about this relationship.[6] In this light, *Django Unchained*'s unlikely western heroes, the former African American slave and the German dentist, bespeak a transatlantic language of friendship politics, a contemporary one that transcends the narrative time of their story and identifies the film as political comment on present-day American racial relations. Though it draws from both classical and modern Euro-American models, the relationship between Django and Schultz reformulates these predecessors in a new discursive place that is far removed from both cross-racial American friendship notions and conventional western tropes.

To this end, the film uses the ambiguities of the friendship concept as productive spaces for refashioning interpersonal relations. For example, Derrida criticizes the narcissism of notions which stress equality as the recognition of the self in the other, arguing that this self-absorbedness ultimately exempts from the labor of friendship[7] when only active investment accounts for the political work that undergirds this relationship.[8] At the same time, the passage through an ordeal as action that constitutes and ratifies this bond identifies it as time-sensitive.[9] In *Django Unchained*, narrative and cinematography literally time Django and Schultz's work of friendship, terminating it in death. In the beginning, a self-interested Schultz frees Django because he needs him to identify the Brittle Brothers, wanted men for whose capture he hopes to receive a substantial bounty. Once Schultz achieves his goal with Django's help, the former slave and the doctor associate for one winter. Schultz's death during the attempt to rescue Broomhilda next spring ends their collaboration, limiting the time-frame of the plot to only a few months from 1858 to 1859. During this time, Django's personal identity morphs from that of an oppressed slave who has no control over his fate to that of a free subject who accomplishes his major goal (reuniting with his wife) and ascends socially in the process.

Remarkably, Django's personal and social trajectory is also performative, marked not only by a change of attitude but also by a theatrical one of outfits. In this, he initially follows Schultz's instructions that the two have to "put up an act" if they wish to gain access to the society of wealthy plantation owners where they hope to accomplish their goals. As action transforms into self-enactment here, the steps of Django's emancipation are marked by a series of fashion choices that range from the persona of a theatrical eighteenth-century "valet" clad in blue velvet—possibly an ironic allusion to both Thomas Gainsborough's painting "Blue Boy" (c. 1770) and Sambo's blue pants in Helen Bannerman's children's book *Little Black Sambo* (1899)—to the appropriation of Candie's stylish burgundy outfit. Historically, such self-stylization would have attracted attention at a time when a slave's "fancy clothes" could "induce suspicions of the direst sort"[10]—just as they do in the film. On a symbolical level, however, Django's fashion trajectory alludes to the modern history of trans-racial and male friendships that originates in the age of eighteenth-century sensibility.[11] His last appearance as affluent grand seigneur completes this development by a contemporary African American image that reaches beyond the film's historical context. This external change mirrors Django's inner development from a white man's dutiful companion to an independent and self-confident individual.

Django's point of origin is marked by a tossing away of garments, however. Rescued by Schultz from the slave trek in the first scene of the film, he casts away the blanket in which he had wrapped himself against the cold: we see a slave's back, naked to the waist, reborn. His skin is scarred by past whippings, revealing the signs of a vulnerability that he will later conceal underneath fashionable outfits. In their homological coincidence with the fateful mark on Siegfried's back that ultimately causes the demise of the Germanic hero, the marks embedded in Django's skin instead constitute the foundation of an exemplary heroic identity that the film develops from here on, thus inversing the course of the German heroic narrative in an American cultural context. As the emergence of Django's subjectivity also encompasses the historical trajectory of Afro-American self-definitions, the freed slave serves as a projection surface and a model, not a realistic personality in a meticulously reconstructed historical context. And it is precisely as a hero, a model available for emulation, that he appears to the slaves he encounters, for example to those owned by Big Daddy (Don Johnson) or to Candie's cruelly discarded former Mandingo fighters together with whom he is transported to the LeQuint Dickie mine.

While Django and Schultz's collaboration encourages this development, it also calls attention to the irreconcilability between the uniqueness claimed by exemplary (i.e., affective) male relationships and the dispassionate democratic community that is ideally based on their multitude.[12] In this regard, the bounty hunters' interactions dispense with the emotions that render friendship iconic in representations of literary and filmic male bonds after the eighteenth century.[13] Although Schultz recognizes Django's feelings as a basis for transcultural communication, they are not addressed to him, nor is he sentimental about his connection to his partner. Instead, the German's most intense emotional stirring is caused by the horrifying fate of an escaped Mandingo fighter whom Candie orders to be torn apart by dogs. In spite of his familiarity with the bloody business of bounty hunting, Schultz is culturally overwhelmed by an alien style of cruelty that haunts him to the point of blowing his cover. In his turn, while Django appreciates his freedom and the chance to earn money together with Schultz, Django's affections are directed at Broomhilda. Familiar with slave mistreatment, Django manages to remain stern and unmoved during the Mandingo fighter's gruesome execution. His cultural background allows him to suppress emotion in this critical moment, whereas he had been moved more than Schultz by Brunhilde's alien story. The protagonists' emotions are thus not only coupled with their cultural backgrounds, but—given that Django makes it clear to Schultz on the way to Candie's plantation that he is now in his (cultural) territory and the doctor accepts this fact—leadership shifts to the culturally and thus [un]emotionally most competent partner.

The absence of overt displays of fondness between Django and Schultz—as well as their differing goals—suggest that, as Derrida asserts, in their case too democracy is driven by the "political desire" to transcend the fundamental paradox between personal proximity and distance.[14] Schultz and Django's relationship is fundamentally democratic in this philosophical sense: as both maintain their cultural, personal, and even teleological singularity, they actively negotiate closeness and distance between each other at all times. In this regard, the pair comes close to a Kantian notion of friendship based on the modern distance required by fraternal respect and responsibility.[15]

Django's discovery of Schultz's body in Candie's barn is a case in point. The significance of this scene is indicated by its detailed direction: Django first pulls Hildy's papers from the dead man's back pocket and checks that they are complete. Only then does he concentrate on what is left of Schultz. His determined expression does not change and no tears well up in his eyes at the sight of the dead friend's back that is now also crossed by bloody slashes. Yet, in a brief, unexpected gesture, the freedman kisses his hand and puts it on the dead man's head, murmuring "Auf Wiedersehen." Though the scene clearly indicates that Django cares about his dead partner, nothing about his behavior displays the pathos of a tear-wrenching representation that one might expect conventionally in such a situation. As the film thus prevents insight into its character's privacy at a crucial moment, it suggests that—whatever affective bond Django and Schultz might share—the focus here is on the political, not the emotional dimension of their relationship.

Django Unchained thus maintains the male friendship between the dentist and the former slave wholly in its active investment and intradiegetically limited temporality. As philosophical and political discourse about amity along the lines discussed earlier, the film is successful because it does not offer sentimental prescriptions or pseudo-solutions for "real life" (as more moralizing films might do), but only an example of a lucid and ethical male friendship.

Handshakes and hostility: You really want me to shake your hand?

The political nature of Django and Schultz's bond moreover results from its contractual form. To Aristotle, political friendship—like marriage—belongs not to the category of ideal, but to useful friendship, one nevertheless based on equality and focused on both itself and what is accomplished with its help.[16] Moreover, pragmatic friendship is certainly more necessary socially than an aestheticized ideal one.[17] The fact that the German needs the freedman for his trade as a bounty hunter just as much as the former slave needs the German to help him rescue his wife reflects the equivalence of reciprocity that governs the characters' collaboration and underlines its contractual and egalitarian nature.

The relative detachment, distinct purposefulness, and restrained economy of emotion in the depiction of Schultz and Django's camaraderie identify it as a political, that is useful and necessary, relationship in the sense outlined earlier. Clarity in interactions and goals, the film seems to imply, is needed in cross-racial relations, not sentimentalism. The social, historical, and economical context of the antebellum South relativizes discourses of humanity, purpose, and value, considering that human beings were conceptualized there as commodities of assessable monetary worth: the slaves. In practice, social relations could therefore not be ethically ideal. Concepts of (white) "honor" over-compensated and obscured this inconvenient fact. As Bertram Wyatt-Brown observes, "Whatever we may think of [Southern] morality, slavery was considered an honorable institution indeed. The assumption of the rightfulness of ownership was a social fact built into the Southern way of life."[18] And yet, as Aristotle concedes, even a slave deserves friendship and can enter a legal and just community when he is regarded as a man, and not as a working tool.[19] In contrast to the Southern society depicted in the film, Schultz seems able to distinguish between race, the individual, and pragmatic interests. And once free, Django becomes a fellow man in an Aristotelian and Kantian sense.[20] Understood in this manner, both his and Schultz's racial markers remain signs of personal distinction. They account for the necessary nonidentity between partners, one that avoids the narcissistic presumptuousness of a friendship based on one's own recognition in the other, and thus also sidesteps an essentializing genetic outlook. By contrast, although they accept the legal fact that—although black—Django is a free individual and thus a viable business partner, Candie and his entourage continuously proclaim an African predisposition to servitude and justify it by a vulgarized racist-evolutionist-physiological Darwinism.[21]

Beyond the philosophical parameters of the friendship concept, the bond between the two bounty hunters can be interpreted with the help of a model of male association that Derrida does not emphasize: the oath or blood brotherhood. Discussing Carl Schmitt's notion of friendship, Derrida only touches upon this variant of fraternity. It is worth carving out a more detailed perspective on such allegiances in *Django Unchained* because they complement what has been said about Schultz and Django's bond so far, allow the meaningful integration of the Stephen–Candie duo into the film's narrative, and not least, offer a structural-cultural explanation for Schultz's seemingly inexplicable loyalty to Django.

Tarantino's familiarity with Richard Wagner's *Ring* tetralogy and his subsequent comments on this work's parallels to his film[22] substantiate claims of Wagnerian influence on *Django Unchained* easily enough. Comparatively seen, Siegfried's and Django's stories are similar indeed. Moreover, Samuel L. Jackson's remark that Leonardo DiCaprio's Candie and his Stephen form a "kind of double-headed monster"[23] explains this duo as the mythical dragon that guards the maiden Brunhilde in Schultz's tale. The fact that, after vanquishing the dragon, Siegfried advances beyond a ring of fire that surrounds sleeping Brunhilde and seduces her (in *Siegfried*) is moreover deconstructed in Django's discovery of Hildy in a shabby bed and the burning mansion at the film's end. These plot elements render Django's trajectory more spectacular narratively and visually and explicitly point at Wagner's music dramas. As Hildy applauds, on horseback, the flaming inferno that her husband has created, as she pulls out a rifle and rides at his side, the previously passive romantic character now starts to display traits of a potential Valkyrie. Not least, this end alludes to the finale of *Götterdämmerung*, the *Ring's* final act, where Brunhilde rides into the fire to follow dead Siegfried.[24] Wagner's firelit yet gloomy end thus mirrors the American couple's ride into an inscrutable night.

These parallels between Wagner's *Ring* and *Django Unchained* are insufficient to account for the fraternal narratives that mark the plot on a deeper level, however. And yet, just as in the medieval epic *Nibelungenlied* and in Wagner's *Götterdämmerung*, in *Django Unchained* doom is brought about by the complications of fraternal bonds gone sour. Tarantino's familiarity with Fritz Lang's version of the material, the silent film *Nibelungen* (1924),[25] allows one to suspect that, an auteur after all, he would be attentive to a film predecessor of this caliber in fashioning a Siegfried-story. To be sure, Lang's work compiles the best moments of all *Nibelungen* narratives throughout time.[26] It narrates major points of Siegfried's biography in a spirit of Wagnerian succession and establishes this iconic figure in film. More than in the *Ring*, however, the prominent narrative of Siegfried's blood brotherhood and its catastrophic consequences are of crucial importance in Lang's production.

Although historically, the knowledge of Germanic oath and blood brotherhoods[27] is indirect and vague, this male bond has seen a modern renewal in English- and German-speaking cultures since the nineteenth century. Formally and ideologically malleable forms of socialization, premodern blood brotherhoods were fictionally narrated rather than chronicled in historical documents. As ritual actions vouched for their value, structure, and efficiency,[28] the "friendships" they forged were political.[29] Premodern fraternities of oath and blood moreover surpassed marriage in importance and were so familiar to their contemporary audiences that they did not have to be explicated, hence the scarcity of descriptions about them.[30]

Siegfried's union with Gunther in Wagner's *Götterdämmerung*, its iconic film dramatization by Lang, and its adaptation to the American frontier in Karl May's adventure novel *Winnetou I* (1893) constitute crucial moments in the rediscovery of blood brotherhood in contemporary German culture. Anglo-American parallels appear, for instance, in Cooper's *The Last of the Mohicans* (1826). As Ivy Schweitzer argues,

> Cooper employs friendship discourses, and especially interracial friendship, to explore the types of affective bonds linking people of different backgrounds in the new nation. As a traditional republican, Cooper was attracted to the mixture of elite and egalitarian elements in the classical formulation of friendship as an intimate and ethical attachment based on notions of virtue, equality, personal sovereignty, rational choice, and generosity inherited and adapted by European culture from Greek, Roman, and humanist thought.[31]

In his text, cross-racial male bonding is promised in the handclasp between scout Hawk-Eye and Mohican Chingachgook.[32]

Thus, when Schultz and Django shake hands at the fire, they formally enter a democratic and political union of loyalty that has predecessors in American culture. Following the German tradition at the same time, the two consume shared physiological and cultural content: the evening meal and Schultz's story. While the temporality of the bond is forward-looking for Django, Schultz's involvement is marked by historical limitations. Thus, although in the historical context of the film's narrative this relationship is beneficial and forward-looking for Schultz, the dentist dies for its sake and with him a transcultural yet already anachronistic world of male loyalty. Only those who are able to learn from it and surpass it (Django and Hildy) survive.

The destructive potential of male bonding unfolds once Schultz and Django insinuate themselves into Candie's plantation in order to rescue Broomhilda under the pretext of wishing to buy a Mandingo fighter. Eventually exposed, the two are forced to purchase Hildy, a domestic slave of little monetary value for Candie, at the fabulous price they had offered for the wrestler. While Candie prepares Hildy's papers, the eerie malice of the situation is highlighted ironically by a harpist who plays Beethoven's *Für Elise*. Plagued by visions of the dismembered slave, Schultz tries to stop the music, then storms out of the room. Candie soon follows him to the library with the documents and two ironical slices of "white cake." Here, Schultz mockingly stuffs the papers into his back pocket and informs Candie that he won't bid him the German "Auf Wiedersehen" because the expression literally means that he wishes to see him again, which is not the case. Significantly, he does not touch the cake either, that is, does not share food with Candie as he had with Django. As Schultz and his friends turn to leave, however, Candie stops them. His hand outstretched, he walks toward Schultz and demands his compliance with a Southern "custom," a final handshake that must seal any business deal as a sign of good faith. Schultz refuses this confirmation of honor in the name of his different cultural background. Since Candie insists, Schultz shoots him: holding a gun, his outstretched hand signifies the breakdown of interaction, that is, death. As part of the minutely choreographed shoot-out that ensues, the film shows us a despairing Stephen holding dead Candie in a classical Pieta pose so familiar from literary and film scenes narrating the (earnest or lampooned) demise of a blood brother.[33]

The direction, acting, and camera movement of this scene situate spectators within a dense and volatile web of quickly shifting interpersonal relations. Rendered in the same "Sekundenstil" that the film has used for Django and Schultz's agreement (now enhanced by slow motion and acceleration), narrative and cinematography reach a compression and speed that critics have identified as specific for Tarantino.[34] The library scene constitutes the narrative core of the film because it summarizes and clarifies the relationships among all major characters and motivates the denouement of the plot. Formally parallel to Django and Schultz's agreement, it comes as no surprise that this scene also hinges on a handshake, simultaneously referencing (the perversion of) American fraternity and the destructive powers of its German predecessors. Thus, when the medieval Siegfried and his modern successors become involved in blood brotherhood, this is also for Brunhilde's sake and a moment when cultural, contractual, and physiological contents intersect in the oath. Winning the Valkyrie as a bride for his partner Gunther, Siegfried hopes to obtain the hand of Kriemhild or Gutrune (Wagner), Gunther's sister. In Wagner's version, for example, Gunther and Siegfried slash their arms, swear an oath, and drink drops of their blood mixed in a chalice with wine.[35] Lang adapts the scene yet again in *Nibelungen*. In light of Siegfried's former commitment to Brunhilde (as we learn from Wagner's *Siegfried* and Lang's film insinuates), one that he is made to forget, however, the hero's involvement in the bond with Gunther causes multiple betrayals and thus his inevitable death.[36]

In *Django Unchained*, the (naïve) Europhile Candie regards the educated German Schultz as a worthy partner for a male union. The cinematography suggests as much when it briefly superimposes Candie's and Schultz's close-ups. But this is also the dissonant moment when the plantation owner literally seals Broomhilda's fate by sealing her freedom documents with red wax, evoking blood, while Schultz is plagued by the tormenting images he had witnessed earlier. In spite of racial and social backgrounds that would seem to predestine them to a "fraternity within the privileged male elite,"[37] Candie and Schultz remain fundamentally incompatible with each other. Instead, they share the same political (conservative or liberal) agenda beyond racial distinctions with their "brothers" Stephen and Django. Candie and Stephen represent an older order of male chivalry, originally a "transatlantic phenomenon" that laid "the foundations for effective collaboration between citizens, thereby ensuring the very survival of the new nation" in the young American republic.[38] Eight decades after the revolutionary foundation of the new state, however, this nation was still defined solely as white. In spite of their numbers, Africans only served the economic and thus social survival of the white family and its lineage. Individuals such as the deceased slave Ben (whose anatomically prepared skull Candie breaks open mercilessly during a phrenological demonstration at the dinner table) verify this fact, serving, as he had, not only one master but an entire line of white male succession. If a genetic issue becomes apparent here, it is on the white side—something Candie overlooks. Yet, things are not so simple. Thus, in spite of his overtly racialized position as a house slave, Stephen turns out to be not only Candie's perfect domestic substitute, but he also dominates him in private, for example when— sipping brandy in the privacy of the library prior to the shoot-out—he informs his owner that Hildy is Django's wife. The overt and covert aspects of Stephen and Candie's bond confirm the two as a "two-headed monster," a dragon forged by antebellum Southern culture whose irrational powers result from violence, perverted Darwinism, and an opportunism motivated by fear. The narrative and personal impetuses of this relationship can only be surmised, given that the film never explicates them. To spectators, Stephen and Candie's bond remains as ambiguous as that between Schultz and Django is to the film's Southerners. So much can be suspected, however: that Candie and Stephen's collaboration is also driven by self-interest, one that comes to Candie in the form of inherited wealth and lifestyle and to Stephen possibly as a form of self-preservation. In other words, Stephen is not visionary enough to dare as Django does; perhaps he had been long ago, but his spirit of rebellion may have been stifled. His hobbling, perhaps a sign of a violently aborted escape attempt in a plot punctuated by such attempts, suggests as much. Instead, Stephen's pragmatic intelligence allows him to occupy a position of (socially invisible) power. An entity with two bodies and minds in their dual ruling of the house, Candie and Stephen have found a comfortable life situation that they aim to maintain at all costs.

The interweaving of male cross-racial relationships, the core theme of the film, uncovers dangerous ground in the conceptual history of male friendship. The clash between Django–Schultz and Stephen–Candie echoes Derrida's question about what happens to couples of brothers when they are not prepared to give up what they have in common: the adherence to a group and the claim to exemplary universalism,[39] which translate to irreconcilable political positions in the film. If the situation is complicated by adding Kant's meditation on the exponential expansion of friendship by each partner's second friends,[40] the question arises (for Kant, Derrida, and Tarantino) of how many friends fraternal friendship can accommodate at all.[41]

As a result, Candie's attempt to forge a new male bond threatens this institution. Since the legal deal is already closed at this point, the plantation owner aims to pull it into the symbolic realm when he endeavors to force his culture's codes of allegiance onto a foreigner. In doing so, he paradoxically provokes an answer in kind because the cultural parameters that dictate Schultz's beliefs and behaviors also surround the handshake with a powerful (and altogether not so different) meaning. Symbolically, the repetition of the handshake would cause the destruction of friendship for two major reasons. First, by inflation in a Kantian-Derridean sense, because it would have to be extended to each partner's partners, overburdening the allegiance structure. Secondly, in the Germanic sense it would destroy friendship by double treason. For Candie, forging a new fraternity would betray Stephen although his master seems ready to renounce him on racial grounds in exchange for the fraternity with a socially prominent white man. Likewise, Schultz's acceptance of the offer would "stab Django in the back." His refusal necessarily betrays Candie instead. Destruction follows as the only possible— and narratively already established—solution to such a conundrum.

The scene reveals a situation of failed cultural communication about male loyalty models which, while not that different from each other, are nevertheless both incompatible and outdated. The outcome of their clash leaves only Django and Hildy alive, actually inversing the story of the European template in which Siegfried and Brunhilde's love story in fact foreshadows and motivates subsequent catastrophic developments.[42] Django's trajectory after the deadly events at Candie's mansion can be taken as an approximate equivalent of the solitary journey that Siegfried undertook before his blood brotherhood embroilments in the German sources. The fact that Django is handed over to the LeQuint Dickie Mining Company, for example, alludes to his foil's entanglements with the Nibelungen, the dwarves, who mine the mountains.[43]

Django Unchained accomplishes two things by this adaptation of the German narratives. First, it adapts Siegfried's story to an American cultural context and reevaluates it as a meaningful modern heroic story. Although Django benefits a great deal from the old social order of chivalrous male allegiances, he leaves it behind in favor of a future of as yet unformulated, that is shapeable, social relations. Here, we hope as spectators, he will mold his own destiny as an emancipated forward-looking human being together with his partner Hildy. Nevertheless, the model that the two characters strive toward is not necessarily that of a patriarchal family, that is a mere replacement of the slaveholding one that Django destroyed. Equal to Django in loyalty, Hildy might very well become his equal in martial prowess, a real Valkyrie, thus performing an act of gender equalizing incompatible with a traditional family model. Yet, as noted earlier, neither the pair's destiny nor the world it will encounter or create is disclosed by the film. As *Django Unchained's* finale alludes to the western heroes' stereotypical ride into the sunset, in its parallels with Wagner's *Götterdämmerung* it also announces the demise of the fraternal universe. One can only speculate (not least for narrative reasons) that the newly forged pair will follow the "North Star" that Schultz had pointed out to the trek of slaves in the first scene of the film, and fulfill its promise of a dignified free life.[44]

Secondly, male fraternity does not perish. In Tarantino's filmography, it only aggravates into a worldwide conflagration seventy years later. It is my contention that *Django Unchained* and *Inglourious Basterds*, Tarantino's film that fantasizes the demise of the Third Reich's leadership, are connected to each other by the figure of the revenant brother.[45] In these two films, the two contrasting outcomes of the fraternal bond are signified by a doubling of Siegfrieds: if Django lives to become a positive model for contemporary African Americans (and not only them), a dead Siegfried becomes the blood brother who returns from the grave[46] as a ghost of fascist appropriation. As noted, Django bids deceased Schultz "Auf Wiedersehen." This might indicate his respect for a friend whom he greets for the last time in his own tongue; it also literally means "till I see you again," as Schultz had explained to Candie just before he died. And actor Christoph Waltz certainly returns as Hans Landa, *Inglourious Basterds*' diabolical SS officer (especially if we watch the films in terms of the chronology of their historical narrative, not of production). Not surprisingly, Schultz's first action reincarnated as Landa in *Inglourious Basterds* is to shake farmer Perrier LaPadite's (Denis Menochet's) hand, an emblematic gesture on which the camera dwells for no less than fifteen seconds, and his entrance is accompanied musically by an adaptation of Beethoven's *Für Elise*, the last tune the character had heard in his previous life. Landa then orders a carnage echoing the one that Schultz had caused and—again—destroys a family, the social unit to which Schultz had, in a sense, lost his brother Django. By letting Shosanna go, Landa moreover creates a solitary hero who will bring about the fiery demise of his current world, just as Django had destroyed his old one.[47] In a different historical context, then, Schultz proves himself as Candie's worthy foil after all. A devil in uniform—on a par with Candie's satanic appearance with goatee and a burgundy coat—he too is a cousin of Mephistopheles, the negative power that enters a contract of blood with Faust and dialectically enables his ambivalent deeds.[48]

Emerging from a single project,[49] Tarantino's two films offer a taut and coherent meditation on the historical and ideological shifts of the related concepts of heroism and fraternization. Read against each other, they reveal how cultural material is transferred in and through film and how it can be reevaluated ideologically in the process, also highlighting and critiquing precisely the material's dangerous readiness for flexible interpretation as a paradoxical result of its historical resilience.

Conclusion

Reading *Django Unchained* in terms of the bonds among its four male major characters and Hildy highlights the transmissibility of cultural narratives and their potential for political reevaluation. Through the cinematographic aesthetic of the two handshake scenes, the film points to the significance of such relationships and justifies their close reading. As it carves out yet questions models of male fraternization, however, *Django Unchained* does not fall into the trap of emotionalizing cross-racial friendships.

Popular in American culture since its incipience, the "brotherhood between all men" was often invoked "as a justification for emancipation and the admission of former slaves into full citizenship" although those "who already enjoyed membership in civil society had no intention of expanding their conceptions of fraternity to include even landless whites, let alone Africans."[50] Thus, the desire of a cross-racial handshake may have functioned in individual initiatives or on a private level, but it did not reform the social fabric as a whole. As Benjamin DeMott argues in his seminal study *The Trouble with Friendship*, the fact that "*[a]ll decent Americans [did] extend the hand of friendship to African Americans*" and that nothing was regarded as "*more auspicious for the African-American future than this extended hand*"[51] became a cultural theme that quickly spawned a wealth of friendship orthodoxy narratives in American popular culture.[52] However, such heart-warming cross-racial stories obfuscate the "institutional, historical, or political ramifications" of racism[53] thus removing them from public discourse.[54] The subsequent emergence of a new color-blind society in the second half of the twentieth century did little to encourage policy changes that would readily allow African Americans upward social movement.[55] Although DeMott admits that advances were made, there is no doubt that eighteen years after the publication of his book, his major thesis still holds strong: that American blacks and whites cannot yet be truly equal owing to their differing historical pasts, pasts that are not repairable by goodwill[56] and "self-congratulatory epic[s] of amity"[57] alone, but only by fundamental and wide-reaching social reforms. *Django Unchained* follows DeMott's call for political and democratic lucidity precisely by bringing forth a pair of emancipated heroes who can do without sentimental handshakes. Precisely shaping Hildy and Django's fate in this manner yet leaving it unresolved, the film identifies it as acutely contemporary.

Notes

1   Invented by Naturalists, the literary technique of "Sekundenstil" aims to copy reality in minute detail (Gero Von Wilpert, "Sekundenstil," in *Sachwörterbuch der Literatur*, 5th ed. (Stuttgart: Alfred Kröner Verlag, 1969), 700), thus anticipating filmic representations of real time and slow motion in prose and drama at the turn of the twentieth century. An iconic text that uses this technique is Gerhart Hauptmann's novella *Bahnwärter Thiel* (1888). The insistence and detail with which Tarantino focuses on his characters' actions and reactions in certain scenes of *Django Unchained* and the epic (i.e., novelistic) dimensions of the story he tells identify this particular literary technique as a useful concept for my structural and aesthetic analysis.

2   Consistent with his general eclectic and intertextual style, Tarantino borrows Broomhilda's last name from the title *Shaft* (1971), a Blaxploitation film and one of the most successful films at the box office in the year of its opening.

3   Owing to differences between the screenplay and the finalized film, I summarize the scenes on the basis of my own transcriptions of passages from the film.

4   The professional training in bounty hunting that Schultz gives Django probably makes up for the rest.

5 Jacques Derrida, *The Politics of Friendship*, trans. George Collins. (London: Verso, 2005), 278, 306.

6 See, for example, Caleb Crain, *American Sympathy* (New Haven: Yale University Press, 2001); Ivy Schweitzer, *Perfecting Friendship* (Chapel Hill: The University of North Carolina Press, 2006); and Richard Godbeer, *The Overflowing of Friendship* (Baltimore: The Johns Hopkins University Press, 2009).

7 Derrida, 178.

8 Derrida, 8.

9 Derrida, 14.

10 Bertram Wyatt-Brown, *Honor and Violence in the Old South* (New York: Oxford University Press, 1986), 186, 161.

11 See, for example, Godbeer, Crain.

12 Derrida, 22.

13 For example, Natty Bumppo and Chingachgook's union in James Fenimore Cooper's *The Last of the Mohicans* (1826) or the bond between the German scout Old Shatterhand and his Apache blood brother Winnetou in Karl May's *Winnetou* tetralogy (1893–1910).

14 Derrida, 22.

15 Derrida, 276. As Derrida explains, Kant regards affection as harmful for friendship.

16 Derrida, 203–204.

17 Derrida, 205.

18 Wyatt-Brown, ix.

19 Derrida, 197.

20 Derrida 197, 252.

21 Candie substitutes a questionable social argument for a purportedly irrefutable genetic one.

22 DW, "Tarantino ließ sich von Wagner inspirieren," n.d., http://www.dw.de/tarantino-ließ-sich-von-wagner-inspirieren/a-16524893 (accessed January 17, 2013); Kathrin Moser and Donya Ravasani, *Amerika's dreckige Geschichte*, 3 sat, January 8, 2013. http://www.3sat.de/page/?source=/kulturzeit/tips/166980/index.html (accessed January 10, 2013). This information is repeated in various articles and news pieces, especially in German media.

23 Video embedded in the article by Susan Vahabzadeh, "Warum Tarantino Sklaverei und Holocaust vergleicht," *Süddeutsche.de*, January 10, 2013. http://www.sueddeutsche.de/kultur/roter-teppich-fuer-neuen-tarantino-film-1.1568666 (accessed January 12, 2013).

24 Richard Wagner, *Götterdämmerung*, ed. Egon Voss (Stuttgart: Philipp Reclam, 1997), 110–111.

25 See Peter Körte, "Die Leute Sollen Django Applaudieren!" *FAZ. net*, http://www.faz.net/aktuell/feuilleton/kino/quentin-tarantino-im-interview-die-leute-sollen-django-applaudieren-12021769.html (accessed January 14, 2013).

26 Harbou, cit. David Levin, *Richard Wagner, Fritz Lang, and the Nibelungen* (Princeton: Princeton University Press, 1998), 13.

27 As Leopold Hellmuth explains, oath and blood brotherhoods can hardly be separated. Leopold Hellmuth, *Die germanische Blutsbrüderschaft* (Rudolstadt: Edition Roter Drache, 2010), 16. Following Schmitt's ideas about these conceptions, Derrida also disregards their difference, 138. Therefore, the current argument does not distinguish strictly between them either.

28 Klaus Oschema, "Das Motiv der Blutsbrüderschaft," in *Riten, Gesten, Zeremonien*, ed. Edgar Bierende, Sven Bretfeld, and Klaus Oschema (Berlin: Walter de Gruyter, 2008), 47–51.

29 Oschema, 53. The ceremonies establishing this union were marked by gestures of affiliation that ranged from cutting each other's wrists and hands and letting the blood mix, to occasionally drinking it. Schweitzer explains that this gesture originates in the worship of Mithra, an early Persian god whose name means both "friend" and "contract," 47.

30 Hellmuth, 14.

31 Schweitzer, 144.

32 James Fenimore Cooper, "The Last of the Mohicans. A Narrative of 1757," in *The Leatherstocking Tales* (New York: The Library of America, 1985), 877.

33 For two prominent German examples, see Winnetou's heroic death in May, *Winnetou III* (Freiburg: Fehsenfeld, 1909), 402. http://www.karl-may-gesellschaft.de/kmg/primlit/reise/gr09/kptl_7.htm (accessed July 20, 2013); or a spoofing of heroic death in Helmut Dietl and Patrick Süskind's comedy *Rossini oder die mörderische Frage, wer mit wem schlief* (1993).

34 Heidi Schlipphacke remarks that Tarantino's film aesthetic captures in a few minutes what other filmmakers develop for hours. See "*Inglourious Basterds* and the Gender of Revenge," in *Quentin Tarantino's Inglourious Basterds*, ed. Robert von Dassanowsky (New York: Continuum, 2012), 147.

35 Wagner, *Götterdämmerung*, ed. Egon Voss (Stuttgart: Philipp Reclam, 1997), 32–33. As Hellmuth shows, Wagner's explicit blood brotherhood aimed at theatrical effect rather than historical accuracy, 77–78 (footnote 142). Conflating this action with Cooper's sentimental bond, May transports this ritual to the Wild West in *Winnetou I*. Incidentally, Lang and Thea von Harbou, his wife and screenwriter for *Nibelungen*, were both ardent fans of both Wagner and May. See Peter Krauskopf, "Deutsche Zeichen, deutsche Helden," in *Jahrbuch der Karl-May-Gesellschaft 1996*, ed. Claus Roxin, Helmut Schmiedt, and Hans Wollschläger (Hamburg: Karl-May-Gesellschft). http://www.karl-may-gesellschaft.de/kmg/seklit/JbKMG/1996/365.htm (accessed December 26, 2012).

36 Lacking a serious female component, only the blood brotherhood narrated by May remains free of moral and ethical complications, thus adhering to Cooper's model of a pure male union. Precisely the insistence on purity distances it from the other German versions.

37 Godbeer, 171.

38 Godbeer, 12.

39 Derrida, 164.

40 Derrida, 260.

41 This, in fact, is the major idea that Derrida theorizes in *The Politics of Friendship*. The logic here is that the quantity of agreements also indicates their quality, pointing to the aporia at the basis of democracy.

42 For a concise summary of the *Ring's* plot, see Wagner, "Der Nibelungen-Mythus (1848)," in *Gesammelte Werke und Dichtungen*, 3rd ed., vol. 2 (Leipzig: Fritzsch, 1897). Although the actual *Ring* does not follow this narrative line faithfully, the text nevertheless explains the powerful web of loyalty and treachery that drives forth the music dramas.

43 In the medieval epic, Siegfried defeats the Nibelungs and their allies and thus obtains a fabulous treasure. See *The Nibelungenlied*, trans. Cyril Edwards (Oxford: Oxford University Press, 2010), 13–14. Wagner's *Ring* and Lang's *Nibelungen* each adapt this plot element in line with their own aesthetic and ideological aims.

44 The brightest light in night sky, the North Star guided fugitive slaves to freedom on the Underground Railroad. See *North Country Underground Railroad Historical Association (NCUGRHA): Our Logo*, n.d., http://www.northcountryundergroundrailroad.com/our-logo.php (accessed October 3, 2013).

45 The historical and ideological truth narrated by *Inglourious Basterds* is the Nazi preference for bonds of male allegiance and a monstrous culture of the *phratry*. Needless to say that all versions of the *Nibelungenlied* were favorite narratives of this regime and its aesthetics of monumentalism and solemnity. For readings of Lang's *Nibelungen* in a fascist context, see Tom Gunning, *The Films of Fritz Lang* (London: British Film Institute, 2001); Lotte Eisner, *The Haunted Screen*, trans. Roger Greaves (Berkeley: University of California Press, 1969); Anton Kaes, *Shell Shock Cinema* (Princeton: Princeton University Press, 2009); or Siegfried Kracauer, *From Caligari to Hitler*, ed. Leonardo Quaresima (Princeton: Princeton University Press, 2004).

46 This is the belief in German folklore. See Heino Gehrts, "Der Sinn der Blutsbrüderschaft," in *Märchenspiegel* (Braunschweig: Märchenstiftung Walter Kahn, 1993), n.p.; or Dean A. Miller's treatment of the Norse trickster, the unreliable partner of the hero and a figure with connections to the Netherworld, *The Epic Hero* (Baltimore: The Johns Hopkins University Press), 244–260.

47 In fact, Shosanna's revenge reestablishes the Jewish characters disavowed and elided according to David Levin by Lang's and Wagner's versions of the Nibelung material.

48 The scenes representing the respective deals between Schultz and Django, and Schultz and Candie are visually parallel: we observe each character from the perspective of the potential partner, the other's back in the foreground. However, the handshakes are formulated differently: we do not gain access to the full perspective of the other in Schultz and Django's case, because we only see them in profile. This careful guarding of the friendship's privacy is missing in Schultz and Candie's case. By allowing us to see the perspective of each partner in the moment of the second handshake, the film forces us to reflect on what we would do in this situation: enter a friendship of convenience with the South's devilish system of slavery or risk a dangerous refusal. Unlike Goethe's doctor Faustus, Tarantino's doctor chooses the latter and thus immediate death.

49 See, for example, Henry Louis Gates' interview with Tarantino, "'Tarantino Unchained,' Part 1: 'Django' Trilogy?," *The Root*, December 23, 2012. http://www.theroot.com/print/68766 (accessed December 28, 2012). The third part of Tarantino's planned trilogy of historical revenge and recuperation fantasies remains to be made.

50 Godbeer, 170.

51 DeMott, 48 (emphasis added). See DeMott, *The Trouble with Friendship: Why Americans Can't Think Straight About Race* (New York: The Atlantic Monthly Press, 1995).

52 DeMott, 45. His examples include Michael Jackson's hit "Black or White," movies such as *Philadelphia* (1993), *Forrest Gump* (1994), and *The Cosby Show* (1984–1992) on television.

53 DeMott, 22.

54 DeMott, 27.

55 DeMott, 36.

56 DeMott, 143–144.

57 DeMott, 180.

4

Django and *Lincoln*: The Suffering Slave and the Law of Slavery

Gregory L. Kaster

Released in a season of Civil-War sesquicentennials—of the war itself, the Emancipation Proclamation, the Gettysburg Address, and the Thirteenth Amendment—Quentin Tarantino's *Django Unchained* and Steven Spielberg's *Lincoln* inevitably invite and indeed merit comparison.[1] For all their obvious differences of style, story, and tone, when viewed from the standpoint of antebellum American slavery and its abolition, *Django* and *Lincoln* complement one another in interesting and historically illuminating ways. This chapter focuses on two of those ways in particular, while also glancing at some related others. Set in 1858 on the eve of the Civil War, *Django* can be viewed both literally and interpretively as prelude to *Lincoln*. It captures certain essential realities—above all the pain and suffering violently inflicted on slave men and women—of the slavery whose abolition, which is the central theme of *Lincoln*, set in early 1865 near war's end, came not through Union victory alone but through that victory in tandem with Congressional passage and state ratification of the Thirteenth Amendment to the Constitution. More than this, the two films are instructively complementary in confronting American audiences with an uncomfortable truth about U.S. history: that slavery at the local, state, and national levels was the law, including the highest law of the land, the U.S. Constitution.

Little noticed amid all the emphasis on *Django Unchained* as Spaghetti and Blaxploitation Western is its cinematic iterations of antebellum abolitionism's emphasis on the horrible cruelties slavery daily inflicted on the bodies of slave women and men.[2] Indeed, abolitionists white and black would instantly recognize many of the film's images as their own. As Elizabeth Clark has shown, beginning in the 1830s as their movement emerged, abolitionists marshaled in their speeches and writings the "the story of the suffering slave" to arouse white northerners' sympathy and support. "Two of the most influential antislavery works of the 1830s," Clark notes, "were classics of this genre"—Lydia Maria Child's *An Appeal In Favor of That Class of Americans Called Africans* (1833) and Theodore Dwight Weld's *American Slavery As It Is: Testimony of a Thousand Witnesses* (1839). The latter from the start outsold other antislavery tracts until publication of *Uncle Tom's Cabin* in 1852.[3] In the 1840s and 1850s, the story was told as well in the popular and compelling autobiographical slave narratives of those who had formerly lived its suffering before being freed or escaping. Typically these narratives sought "to portray slavery as a brutalizing institution designed to annihilate the slave's very self." And thus they featured "formulaic scenes: the whipping or mutilation of family members and of the narrator; the auction block where slaves had to perform to demonstrate their value and where they were separated from other members of their families, most for the last time; and the transportation of slaves in coffles, or chain gangs."[4]

The trope of the suffering slave pervades *Django*, which reflects these formulaic scenes of slave narratives and includes still others depicting slavery's brutalizing cruelty. The film establishes the violence and pain of slavery from virtually the start, when we see the severely whip-scarred backs of Django and four other slave men chained together at the ankles in a coffle "somewhere in Texas," having been sold, we learn, at the Greenville, Mississippi, slave auction. Their suffering is echoed in subsequent scenes in which Django's wife Broomhilda screams in agony as she is brutally whipped, after Django's desperate pleas that she be spared are ignored (she and Django had run away); another slave woman is nearly whipped for breaking eggs (her whipping thwarted at the last minute by a now-armed Django); and a second, larger coffle of slave men and women, some in iron collars and muzzles, fills the screen when the action shifts to Mississippi.

In the course of the film, at times via flashbacks, we also see a close-up of Django muzzled with a slave mask and wearing a spiked iron collar; a close-up of Broomhilda branded on her cheek with an "r" for "runaway" (Django from the start is marked by the same); a male slave torn to pieces and eaten by dogs after sobbing to his master that he cannot go on as one of the latter's Mandingo fighters; Broomhilda's removal from a sweltering hot box into which she has been crammed, naked, for running away again; the forced exposure by her master of Broomhilda's whip-scarred back to Django and his partner, Dr. "King" Schultz; and Django's near castration as he hangs naked, upside down, hands bound and face muzzled again.

By comparison to these scenes of cruelty and suffering, the film's glancing references to the pervasive sexual exploitation of slave women are tame. We see slaveholder Calvin Candie's concubine, elegant and cool in "The Cleopatra Club," and Broomhilda, whom Django earlier tells Schultz is going to be made "a comfort girl," escorted to Schultz's room at Candyland plantation for his pleasure—Schultz's ruse to reunite her and Django.

Much has been made of the film's fanciful Mandingo-fighting story line, with commentators pointing out that slaves were too valuable for their owners to pit them one-on-one in sporting fights to the death.[5] True, though Aisha Harris has noted that "Slaves were sometimes sent to fight for their owners; it just wasn't to the death," and Theodore Weld included in his compilation of slavery's "atrocities" the account of a witness who had "known Negro boys, partly by persuasion, and partly by force, made to strip off their clothing and fight for *the amusement of their masters*. They would fight until both got to crying."[6] Viewed in light of the trope of the suffering slave, *Django*'s references to and one actual scene of Mandingo fighting serve to underscore the power masters exercised over slave bodies, in this case slave male bodies—specifically the power to inflict pain. That the film's Mandingo fighters inflict the pain upon each other directly themselves, as Mississippi cotton planter and Mandingo businessman-aficionado Calvin Candie urges one of them on to the deadly finish, only highlights Candie's power as master to make slaves suffer his violent bodily cruelty, even, tellingly, without himself lifting a finger.

Django not only vividly depicts some of the physical violence (actual and threatened) on which slavery daily depended, it also cleverly highlights another recurring cruelty central to the institution and, as suggested earlier, prominent as well in the story of the suffering slave—the antebellum domestic slave trade. With the rise of the cotton kingdom across the Deep South following Eli Whitney's invention of the cotton gin came "a massive forced migration from the Upper South of more than 1 million slaves," with transfers (as Old South planters relocated with their slaves or gave them to their children moving west) accounting for some 40 percent of that migration and sales for the rest. Indeed, "the domestic slave trade became a great business between 1800 and 1860." In the process, it broke up about one quarter of slave marriages (which never had legal standing to begin with) and "separated almost a third of all slave children under the age of fourteen from one or both of their parents."[7] The trade sets in motion the plot of Harriet Beecher Stowe's famous antislavery novel, *Uncle Tom's Cabin*, when the benevolent but indebted Kentucky planter Mr. Shelby must, to his extreme distaste, come to terms with the slave trader Haley, over the sale of Eliza's child Harry and Uncle Tom. To his distraught wife, Shelby describes Haley as "not a cruel man, exactly, but a man of leather,—a man alive to nothing but trade and profit,—cool, and unhesitating, and unrelenting, as death and the grave. He'd sell his own mother at a good percentage—not wishing the old woman any harm, either."[8]

In an echo of Stowe's novel, the slave trade also launches the plot of *Django*. And like the novel, the film makes clear from its opening moments that slave bodies are not only scarred but also commodified. As already noted, Django himself first appears as part of a coffle of slaves auctioned in Greenville, he and Broomhilda having been sold there "separately" at their master's order as punishment for their running away. Marching the coffle from atop their horses are the slave-trading Speck Brothers, and in the ensuing action Dr. "King" Schultz unexpectedly arrives seeking Django from among what he calls the traders' "inventory." "I'm simply a customer trying to conduct a transaction," Schultz explains when one of the brothers objects to his interaction with Django. "I don't care," says the trader, "no sale"—to which Schultz dismissively replies, stating as given the commodification critical to turning human beings into slaves, "Don't be ridiculous. Of course they're for sale." Aided by his gun and deadly quick shot, Schultz purchases Django for 125 dollars, taking care to write his own bill of receipt.

Slavery's commodification of human beings is underscored subsequently in the haunting scene of a slave coffle in Greenville, and in Django and Dr. Schultz's effort to purchase Django's wife, Broomhilda, from the notorious Calvin Candie. Fittingly, their effort involves pretending to be interested in trafficking with him for a Mandingo fighter.

More pointed is bounty hunter Schultz's succinct explanation of his work to Django: "Well... the way the slave trade deals in human lives for cash, a bounty hunter deals in corpses.... So, like slavery, it's a flesh for cash business." The matter-of-fact irony of his explanation cleverly throws into sharp relief the awful buying and selling of *living* human beings that was an essential everyday occurrence of slavery.

"We will prove that slaves in the United States are treated with barbarous inhumanity," Weld promised in the introduction to *American Slavery As It Is*, and for all its parody and pulp, *Django* brilliantly does exactly that. It is the cinematic echo and elaboration, more than 175 years later, of Weld's damning assertion that "SLAVEHOLDERS TREAT THEIR SLAVES WORSE THAN THEY DO THEIR BRUTES."[9] Those who have criticized the film as lurid[10] would do well to scan even just the index of Weld's book, with its enumeration of violent cruelties against slaves, shocking still in their methods and scope: "Chopping of slaves piecemeal," "branding, breeding, ... burning," "starvation of, teeth of knocked out, tied up all night, toe cut off, ... travelling in droves," "Whipped, Whipped and burnt, Whipped to death," "Slitting of ears, Smoothing iron on girl's [sic] backs," to mention only some of the brutalities indexed.[11] The same critics would do well also to read former slave and abolitionist leader Frederick Douglass's sanguinary description near the start of his famous narrative of his half-naked Aunt Hester's torture by whipping, which he devastatingly witnessed as a child. Disobeying her master's orders, the attractive Aunt Hester had gone out at night and, worse, been caught in the company of a male slave her master had warned her against seeing. For this, Douglass recounts, her master "stripped her from neck to waist, leaving her neck, shoulders, and back, entirely naked." He next made her stand on a stool and tied her bound hands to "a large hook in the joist" above

> so that she stood upon the ends of her toes. He then said to her, 'Now, you d----d b----h, I'll learn you how to disobey my orders!' and after rolling up his sleeves, he commenced to lay on the heavy cowskin, and soon the warm, red blood (amid heart-rending shrieks from her, and horrid oaths from him) came dripping to the floor.[12]

Her screaming and bleeding, Douglass vividly remembered, only intensified the master's fury. "The louder she screamed, the harder he whipped; and where the blood ran fastest, there he whipped longest. He would whip her to make her scream, and whip her to make her hush; and not until overcome by fatigue, would he cease to swing the blood-clotted cowskin." It was a "terrible spectacle" Douglass would never forget, and a most ominous foreshadowing of "the blood-stained gate, the entrance to the hell of slavery, through which I was about to pass."[13]

Compared to Douglass's luridly horrifying account, Tarantino's staging and filming of Broomhilda's whipping—her dress remains pulled up, at least in front, and we see neither the blows landing on flesh nor the blood they draw—is remarkably restrained. The focus, in keeping with the trope of the suffering slave, is on the screaming Broomhilda's harrowing and heartrending pain. Tarantino has said, "what happened in slavery times is a thousand times worse than I show," and the historical record bears out the essential truth of his remark (Figure 4.1).[14]

Boldly revivifying "the pornography of pain"[15] in abolitionist moral suasion exemplified by Douglass's passage, *Django* graphically renders the torturous suffering of enslaved people that, though invisible in *Lincoln*, was implicitly and inextricably bound up with the political battle the latter film depicts.[16] Screenwriter Tony Kushner focuses *Lincoln* on the politics surrounding passage of the Thirteenth Amendment by the House of Representatives (which had previously defeated it) in January 1865, as the Civil War nears its end. Having

FIGURE 4.1 *Broomhilda's whipping*

won reelection in November 1864, Lincoln (Daniel Day-Lewis) sees a brief window of opportunity to move quickly and successfully to passage by securing, through his patronage power, the votes of twenty lame duck members of the opposition Democratic Party. He appreciates, as his cabinet and wife Mary (Sally Field) do not, that now, between his reelection and imminent Union victory in the war, is the auspicious moment to destroy slavery decisively by an amendment to the Constitution which will render moot any doubts about the legality of his Emancipation Proclamation two years earlier. Thanks to his own superb political skills, crucially aided by his political right-hand man, Secretary of State William Seward (David Strathairn), and Radical Republican Congressman Thaddeus Stevens (Tommy Lee Jones) of Pennsylvania, Lincoln succeeds. The film shows us the behind-the-scenes maneuverings of Lincoln and Seward (and of the men Seward retains to procure votes), along with the verbal sparring on the House floor between Stevens and his Congressional opponents that together culminate in victory. *Django* reminds viewers of both films that slavery was no mere abstraction; it was a quite tangible evil dependent on inhuman violence and pain, an evil that made passage of the Thirteenth Amendment abolishing slavery the political and *moral* triumph *Lincoln* celebrates.

Django and *Lincoln* are complementary in other, more specific ways as well. Viewed together, they arrestingly convey the revolutionary import of the Civil War.[17] Thus the suffering sold slaves of *Django*'s opening, and the avenging Nat-Turner-like slave-rebel Django of its conclusion, have become, as *Lincoln* begins, uniformed and armed African American Union soldiers engaged in muddy and deadly hand-to-hand combat with Confederate troops. Following the battle scene, a white Union soldier begins reciting before Lincoln his address at Gettysburg two years earlier in 1863, followed by a black soldier who recites its stirring conclusion—"that we here highly resolve that these dead shall not have died in vain—that this nation, under God, shall have a new birth of freedom—and that government of the people, by the people, for the people, shall not perish from the earth."[18] Lincoln's address, like his Emancipation Proclamation almost eleven months earlier, reflected that a war for the Union had become the emancipation war abolitionists had pressed for from its start, a war toward which Django's dynamiting of the big house on Candyland plantation dramatically, satisfyingly, and prophetically gestures.

Where the insurrectionist Django has become in *Lincoln* part of a revolutionary army organized by the state, the rebellious Broomhilda has been domesticated in the film's "Mrs. [Elizabeth] Keckley" (Gloria Reuben), the former slave who is First Lady Mary Todd Lincoln's dressmaker. Keckley in real life was also her confidante and companion, a relationship the film only hints at.[19] In an exchange with Lincoln, who tells her "I don't know you Mrs. Keckley. Any of you," she tells the president, "my son died fighting for the Union, wearing the Union blue. For freedom he died. I'm his mother. That's what I am to the nation, Mr. Lincoln. What else must I be?" In contrast to Broomhilda, riding off on her own horse with Django as the dynamited Candyland big house burns behind them, the onscreen Keckley has circumscribed, chiefly maternal agency—sacrificing a son for the cause of freedom in an emancipationist war; asking Lincoln as he exits Mary's boudoir, "Did you tell her a dream?" which we have just seen him do, upsetting Mary whom Keckley will presumably comfort; and sitting next to Mrs. Lincoln in the gallery as the House debates and later passes the Thirteenth Amendment. Broomhilda defies both her master's authority and, at least momentarily if also imperfectly, the conventions of true womanhood, as a repeat runaway and then emancipated woman, smilingly and confidently riding into freedom with her rescuer-husband, gun in hand. *Lincoln's* Keckley, by contrast, is basically conventional.

The principal protagonists of these two films are, of course, even more obviously different than Broomhilda and the onscreen

Mrs. Keckley. Most important, aside from their different skin colors and backgrounds (slavery versus freedom), is the difference in their relative positions of power: an avenging individual with dynamite and a gun, and the elected President of the United States and Commander-in-Chief of the Union's military now at war to ensure that the oath he has sworn to "preserve, protect and defend the Constitution" is upheld, and the Union created by that document maintained. Yet Django and Lincoln have in common a steely resolve that marks them both, in nineteenth-century terms at least, as manly and heroic, while simultaneously raising the matter of means and ends in the quest of each. When a repelled Schultz unexpectedly intervenes to save, by purchasing, the Mandingo runaway slave who tells his master Calvin Candie he can fight no more, Django, acting the part of the black slaver earlier assigned him by Schultz as part of their ruse to rescue Broomhilda, says no to the transaction—"we ain't payin' a penny for that pickaninny"—thereby dooming the slave to the dogs. Allowing Schultz to proceed would have undermined his and Django's credibility in the eyes of Candie, endangering (perhaps fatally) their mission. For the sake of Broomhilda, Django sacrifices another of Candie's slaves and watches unflinchingly as dogs brutally destroy him.

Lincoln, for his part, will not be dissuaded—not by his cabinet, his wife Mary, nor anyone else—from pursuing quick passage of the Thirteenth Amendment by the House of Representatives. After explaining to his cabinet that the uncertain legality of the Emancipation Proclamation could result in freed slaves being returned to slavery, Lincoln, holding up a pen, his voice rising, declares, "And come February the first, I intend to sign the 13th Amendment!" To ensure that he does, Lincoln unabashedly uses his patronage power to procure the twenty votes necessary for passage. When William Seward protests that the amendment is "too important" to be purchased, Lincoln responds, "I said nothing of buying anything. We need 20 votes was all I said. Start of my second term, plenty of positions to fill." Without consulting Seward, Lincoln accedes to conservative Republican Preston Blair's demand that he undertake peace negotiations in return for Blair and his son Montgomery securing the support of the party's conservative wing. Shrewdly, he orders that the Confederate peace commissioners be brought only as far as Hampton Roads, Virginia, which allows him to later deny to Congress rumors that a delegation offering peace is in Washington. Technically true, his denial of course is also highly disingenuous, which enables voting on the amendment to proceed, ultimately successfully (119 to 56). Like Django, Lincoln never loses sight of his larger goal and does what he must to attain it.[20]

Though in different ways, then, both films endorse an end-justifies-the-means approach to the respective emancipation work of their eponymous heroes (limited work in Django's case if viewed literally rather than symbolically, focused as it is on Broomhilda individually). Moreover, notwithstanding their attention to the individual agency of Django and Lincoln, both make clear that the success of each man's quest is a collaborative effort, thanks above all to Schultz, Seward (and his and Lincoln's vote procurer, W. N. Bilbo), and Stevens. Neither hero goes it alone.

More important than these connections, *Django* and *Lincoln* are fundamentally complementary in that the law and its relationship to slavery are at the heart of both films.[21] In the former, bounty hunter King Schultz scrupulously abides by the law. He explains one of his killings by first announcing, "I'm a servant of the court," and then summarizing the warrant he holds for the dead man. The onscreen Lincoln, reflecting the historical Lincoln's "attachment to Euclid's principles of reason,"[22] rehearses for his cabinet all the ways the Emancipation Proclamation could be construed as illegal, after which he observes, "I hoped it was legal to do it. I'm hoping still." Subsequently, when Seward meets with the men who will do the actual work of procuring votes, he instructs them, "nothing strictly illegal."

These story lines about the law form a backdrop to the films' shared larger crucial point that slavery was inscribed in law—that it was, significantly, a constitutional regime.[23] In arguably the most chilling scene of *Django*, Calvin Candie without hyperbole thunders, "under the laws of Chickasaw County [Mississippi], Broomhilda here is my property. And I can choose to do with my property whatever I so desire!" Candie's assertion of his absolute property rights in his human chattel, coupled with his earlier patting of Broomhilda's belly as he asks Schultz if he had seen her naked when she was brought to him, recalls the haunting words of Harriet Jacobs in her searing

1861 account of the psychosexual torments she endured as a young female slave. There was, Jacobs wrote, "no shadow of the law" to protect her from a master "who met me at every turn, reminding me that I belonged to him, and swearing by heaven and earth that he would compel me to submit to him."[24] She was, in short, the property of her master—"He told me I was his property; that I must be subject to his will in all things"[25]—and his ownership of and power over her body were at once enabled and enforced by the law.

Thus, while it is Django's violence that physically rescues Broomhilda from Candyland plantation, it is her freedom papers, signed and sealed earlier by Candie in a transaction with Dr. Schultz, that formally—legally—liberate her from slavery. In a key scene, Django himself underscores this point by removing the papers from the dead Schultz, carefully folding them, and placing them in his own coat pocket.

Here is where *Django* is more than simply chronological and substantive prelude to *Lincoln*. At one level, to be sure, the Thirteenth Amendment represents Broomhilda's freedom papers writ large, achieved legislatively, through the realpolitik of Lincoln, Seward, and their Congressional allies, through procuring votes rather than through purchasing the freedom of a commodified body. More than this, however, the films together teach and mutually reinforce the same discomforting lesson for Americans today—slavery in the United States at every jurisdictional level from the local to the national was upheld by the twinned pillars of violence and the law. In their own ways, *Django* and *Lincoln* cinematically affirm recent scholarship by historians highlighting the Constitution's proslavery nature. Though the word "slavery" appears nowhere in the document, slavery was indeed underpinned by the highest law of the land. "Of its eighty-four clauses," David Waldstreicher points out in his important book on the subject, "six are directly concerned with slaves and their owners. Five others had implications for slavery that were considered and debated by the delegates to the 1787 Constitutional Convention and the citizens of the states during ratification." "In growing their government," Waldstreicher inescapably concludes, "the framers and their constituents created fundamental laws that sustained human bondage."[26]

Slavery's codification in law, its constitutionality, is why the great activist and scholar W. E. B. Du Bois considered it one of those wrongs made "especially heinous, black, and cruel when it masquerades in the robes of law and justice and patriotism."[27] And it is why, as these two films together remind us, the end of slavery in the United States came not only violently, in civil war, but necessarily and decisively, legislatively as well. In this sense, both movies are about a new birth of republican freedom, grounded too ultimately in the law and encompassing black and white people alike—with *Lincoln* carrying forward in time, finishing and extending legislatively, the emancipation work begun in *Django* by means of violence and freedom papers. Django's acts of emancipatory vengeance are thus elevated into something grander when viewed against the backdrop of Spielberg and screenwriter Tony Kushner's tribute to the post-Emancipation-Proclamation-Gettysburg-Address   Lincoln,   and the principled, hard-nosed, even unsavory politics he, Seward, and Stevens pursue onscreen and pursued historically in midwifing the new birth of freedom Lincoln at Gettysburg had so eloquently evoked.

The *Congressional Globe* reported "an outburst of enthusiasm" in the House of Representatives when it passed the Thirteenth Amendment on January 31, 1865. Members "wept like children" while spectators in the packed galleries, among them black residents of Washington, signaled their joy as well.[28] One imagines Django and Broomhilda cheering the news too, while also concurring with Frederick Douglass's warning that the work of abolitionists was not yet finished,[29] and expressing no surprise that Calvin Candie's Mississippi would be the last state to ratify the amendment, unofficially in 1995 and formally in 2013.[30]

Notes

1   This chapter is a revised and expanded version of an op-ed written for and distributed by the History News Service (HNS). See Gregory L. Kaster, "The Law of Slavery Lies at the Heart of the Movies 'Lincoln' and 'Django Unchained,'" January 2, 2013, http://historynewsservice. org/2013/01/the-law-of-slavery-lies-at-the-heart-of-the-movies-lincoln- and-django-unchained/. I wish to thank HNS editor David P. Nord for accepting and improving the op-ed, my Gustavus colleague Kate Wittenstein for helping me clarify my thinking about the two films, and Oliver Speck for making this book happen.

2 An important exception is historian Stephen Kantrowitz's essay
   "'Django Unchained's' White Abolitionist Vision," HNN: History
   News Network, January 28, 2013, http://hnn.us/article/150272.
   Kantrowitz acknowledges that because of the film's "abolitionist
   representation of slavery as despotic, unbridled cruelty" it "does
   something no American film has done before: it places the
   experience of terror—as a structural, daily, lived reality—at the
   center of the experience of slavery." However, he argues, that same
   vision means *Django* reduces slave lives "to horror stories," thereby
   replicating "white abolitionism's skepticism about black people's
   desire or capacity for freedom." I agree with both of Kantrowitz's
   points; yet I would also note that the film is not intended, any more
   than abolitionist works were, including slave narratives, as a study
   of the complexity of slave lives and, further, contra Kantrowitz, that
   it powerfully and cleverly conveys "the annihilation, in the name
   of commerce [abetted, I would add, by the law], of human ties
   and joys" that he rightly notes was the "true monstrousness of
   slavery." See my discussion below of how the film captures the
   commodification essential to slavery. Steve McQueen's important
   film *12 Years a Slave* (2013), based on Solomon Northup's 1853
   narrative, was released just as I was finishing this chapter and
   there was no time to incorporate comparisons of it to *Django* here.
   Judging from the early commentary, it mostly, if not completely,
   avoids the shortcomings Kantrowitz finds in Tarantino's film.

3 Elizabeth B. Clark, "'The Sacred Rights of the Weak': Pain,
   Sympathy, and the Culture of Individual Rights in Antebellum
   America," *Journal of American History*, 82 (September 1995), 463,
   466–467.

4 Clark, "'The Sacred Rights of the Weak,'" 468. Clark's discussion
   of slave narratives draws on and cites (469 n. 14) two important
   works by literary scholar William L. Andrews: "The Representation
   of Slavery and the Rise of Afro-American Literary Realism,
   1865–1920," in *Slavery and the Literary Imagination*, ed. Deborah
   E. McDowell and Arnold Rampersad (Baltimore: Johns Hopkins
   University Press, 1989), 62–80; and *To Tell a Free Story: The First
   Century of Afro-American Autobiography, 1760–1865* (Urbana:
   University of Illinois Press, 1986).

5 See, for example, Henry Louis Gates, Jr., "Did Dogs Really Eat
   Slaves, Like in 'Django'?," *The Root*, January 14, 2013, http://www.
   theroot.com/articles/history/2013/01/how_accurate_is_ django_
   unchained_on_riding_horses_mandingo_fighting_and_dogs_eating_
   slaves.html.

6 Aisha Harris, "Was There Really 'Mandingo Fighting,' Like in *Django
   Unchained*?," *Slate*, December 24, 2012, http://www.slate.com/

blogs/browbeat/2012/12/24/django_unchained_mandingo_fighting_
were_any_slaves_really_forced_to_fight.html; testimony of Mr. F.
C. Macy, quoted in Theodore Dwight Weld, *American Slavery As
It Is: Testimony of a Thousand Witnesses* (1839; repr., New York:
Arno Press, 1968), 107. Weld uses the word "atrocities" in his
"Advertisement to the Reader," *American Slavery As It Is*, iii.

7 James A. Henretta, Rebecca Edwards, and Robert O. Self, *America:
A Concise History* 5th ed., vol. 1, *To 1877* (Boston: Bedford/St.
Martin's, 2012), 355, 358.

8 Harriet Beecher Stowe, *Uncle Tom's Cabin; Or, Life Among the
Lowly*, in *The Oxford Harriet Beecher Stowe Reader*, ed. Joan D.
Hedrick (New York: Oxford University Press, 1999), 106.

9 Weld, *Slavery As It Is*, 9, 111.

10 For example, David Denby, "'Django Unchained': Put-On, Revenge,
and the Aesthetics of Trash," *New Yorker*, January 22, 2013,
http://www.newyorker.com/online/blogs/culture/2013/01/django-
unchained-reviewed-tarantinos-crap-masterpiece.html, called the
film "luridly sadistic."

11 Weld, *American Slavery As It Is*, 212, 217, 218.

12 David W. Blight, ed., *Narrative of the Life of Frederick Douglass,
an American Slave, Written by Himself: With Related Documents*
2nd ed. (Boston: Bedford/St. Martin's, 2003), 45–46.

13 Blight, ed., *Narrative of the Life of Frederick Douglass, an American
Slave, Written by Himself*, 45.

14 "Quentin Tarantino, 'Unchained' and 'Unruly,'" interview with
National Public Radio's Terry Gross, January 2, 2013, http://www.npr.
org/2013/01/02/168200139/quentin-tarantino-unchained-and-unruly.

15 The phrase is from Karen Halttunen, "Humanitarianism and
the Pornography of Pain in Anglo-American Culture," *American
Historical Review*, 100 (April 1995), 303–334.

16 As Elizabeth Clark has observed, "the Thirteenth Amendment and
the Civil Rights Act [of 1866] in particular—the high water marks of
abolitionist sentiment—show clear intent to regulate, not just state
action, but violence between private individuals bound together by
legal status, specifically the systematized violence of slavery." Clark,
"'The Sacred Rights of the Weak,'" 491.

17 More than twenty years ago, James M. McPherson cogently and
concisely stated the case for the war as a revolution in his essay
"The Second American Revolution" in *Abraham Lincoln and the
Second American Revolution*, ed. McPherson (New York: Oxford
University Press, 1991), 3–22.

18 For the full text, see http://www.abrahamlincolnonline.org/lincoln/
speeches/gettysburg.htm.

19 The real-life Keckley was also an activist who organized the
Contraband Relief Association, which provided aid to refugees
from slavery crowding into Washington, D.C. For an overview of
her life, see the entry for Keckley by Gertrude Woodruff Marlowe
in the *American National Biography Online*, http://www.anb.org/
articles/20/20-00530.html.

20 Sean Wilentz has pointed out in "Lincoln in Hollywood, from Griffith
to Spielberg," *New Republic*, December 21, 2012, http://www.
newrepublic.com/article/books-and-arts/magazine/111242/the-lost-
cause-and-the-won-cause, how "nonsensical" is the view of the
film "as a brief for compromise in American politics delivered at a
time of stalemate in Washington…. Lincoln," he stresses,
was never prone to compromise; he was willing to lead the
nation into a civil war rather than compromise on his and his
party's fundamental purpose, which was to halt the extension of
slavery. Lincoln fought as hard as he could to get his way, even if
it required deviousness in strategy as well as tactics. He did not
always prevail, and he sometimes had to settle for partial victories.
But the idea of Lincoln, or any great American president, going
into political battle with compromise on his mind is outlandish,
a disservice to the practice as well as the history of American
democracy.

21 Stephen Marche, "*Django Unchained* Is a Better Movie about
Slavery than *Lincoln*," *Esquire*, December 24, 2012, http://
www.esquire.com/blogs/ culture/django-unchained-lincoln-
slavery-14895534, stresses that unlike the latter film the former
"knows that America's relationship to slavery was not merely
through legal institutions; it was a physical reaction to black
flesh—a potently horrific mixture of abjection fused with desire."
Unlike Marche, as should be clear from this chapter, I believe that
an essential part of *Django's* achievement is precisely its reminder
that the violence inflicted on enslaved black bodies, and the
"horrific mixture" that stoked it, were crucially and systemically
inscribed in an sanctioned by the law of slavery.

22 Wilentz, "Lincoln in Hollywood."

23 I am indebted to David Nord for suggesting this phrase.

24 Harriet Jacobs, *Incidents in the Life of a Slave Girl, Written by
Herself*, ed. L. Maria Child (Boston: Published for the Author, 1861),
45, 46.

25 Jacobs, *Incidents in the Life of a Slave Girl, Written by Herself*, 45.

26 David Waldstreicher, *Slavery's Constitution: From Revolution to Ratification* (New York: Hill and Wang, 2009), 3. See also George William Van Cleve, *A Slaveholder's Union: Slavery, Politics, and the Constitution in the Early American Republic* (Chicago: University of Chicago Press, 2010).

27 W. E. Burghardt Du Bois, *John Brown* (Philadelphia: G. W. Jacobs, 1909), 340.

28 On the "spectators" and celebration in Congress when the amendment was passed, see Eric Foner, *The Fiery Trial: Abraham Lincoln and American Slavery* (New York: W. W. Norton, 2010), 313–314; *Globe* quotes on 314.

29 Douglass warned in a speech in May 1865 that "while the black man is confronted in the legislation of the South by the word 'white,' our work as abolitionists … is not done." "Slavery," he insisted, "is not abolished until the black man has the ballot." Quoted in David W. Blight, *Frederick Douglass' Civil War: Keeping Faith in Jubilee* (Baton Rouge: Louisiana State University Press, 1989), 191. As this suggests, Douglass believed that the enfranchisement of women could wait. One imagines Broomhilda, if not also Django, dissenting from that part of his warning.

30 Because of a procedural oversight following its vote to ratify in 1995, official ratification by Mississippi did not occur until 2013, after two academics, prompted by *Lincoln*, discovered the mistake, which the state then corrected. "Mississippi Ratifies 13th Amendment Abolishing Slavery … 147 Years Late," http://www.theguardian.com/world/ 2013/feb/18/mississippi-us-constitution-and-civil-liberties.

PART TWO

Philosophy Unchained: Ethics, Body Space, and Evil

5

Bodies In and Out of Place: *Django Unchained* and Body Spaces

Alexander D. Ornella

Introduction

"**T**here's a nigger on the horse" marks the beginning of Quentin Tarantino's most recent violation of filmic style, language, and good taste other directors might not get by with. As offensive as language and images might be, the film's *mise-en-scène*, its language, and its dialogue express that the encounter between bodies is always shaped by a politics of bodies in/out of place and ideas about whose bodies might inhabit which spaces or what spaces are off-limits for whose bodies. The "nigger on the horse" in *Django Unchained* shows that skin color, body, and space are intimately related. Skin and skin colors are often markers of difference and surfaces subject to identity politics and boundary processes. They grant bodies access to or prohibit them from inhabiting certain spaces. If bodies violate their ascribed spaces, social actors have measures in place to express this dislocation and restore the boundaries.

In his study of topless beach culture, Jean-Claude Kaufmann describes the production and demarcation of social space through social actors, behaviors, and rituals. He shows that even a "natural" space such as the beach is never mere natural but shaped by boundary processes to fit and make space for or discard certain bodies. Similarly, bodies do not just transform the makeup of space through their presence/absence or them entering/leaving, but space boundaries leave an imprint on bodies and their behaviors to make them fit into specific spaces producing bodies that fit. Drawing on Kaufmann's study of space-body-boundaries and boundary processes, this chapter analyzes the production of space in *Django Unchained*. It argues that the film is all about space dynamics, that is subverting, opening, closing, and securing space. In fact, the production of space and bodies that (do not) fit are an important part of the film, its audiovisual style, and its narrative. Space, however, is not just constructed within the film and for the characters on screen, but the words and gestures on screen have immediate effects on how the audience demarcates space, places or displaces bodies, and thus ultimately participates in the creation of (other) bodies. In a first step, therefore, I will introduce Jean-Claude Kaufmann's sociology of space. It then analyzes the production of space from the perspective of imaginary/material spaces and looks at access strategies to space and violation of space, and power struggles within spaces. This chapter is not a study of American slavery and as such not overly interested whether or not the film is historically accurate. While this is an important question, it is a question in its own right and scholars of slavery have commented on that aspect already. Rather, this chapter is informed by research of slavery and looks at the film as such, that is the film as work of (popular) art given to and speaking to a contemporary audience.

Bodies of space—Jean-Claude Kaufmann's beach bodies

Body, in a way, is space, is in space, acts upon space, and is acted upon by the surrounding space. When a person enters a space, it affects the makeup of space and we can look at the relationship between body and space from at least four perspectives: physical, visual, affective, and cognitive. Physical, because objects and bodies always change the physical/material makeup of spaces. Bodies change the material landscape of space because bodies themselves are physical. Bodies entering, leaving, or simply being in space reconstitute and transform existing spatial structures. Similarly, the space a body is about to enter can have a material impact on how bodies prepare, clothe, and present themselves or where bodies place/are being placed within space. Visual, because bodies, matter, or objects in general contribute to how the space is seen and perceived. Bodies, then, contribute to an aesthetics of space. Often, it is the visual or the aesthetics of both body and space that dictate—or at least contribute—to the way body is present in space. The physical itself can have a visual/aesthetic quality and the structuring of bodies and spaces can follow aesthetic, visual, or ideological ideas that find expression and are being incarnated in the visual. Affective, because the physical relationship between body and space is always also an experienced, a felt one, both by others and by one's own body. When a person enters a room, their presence can go unnoticed by others inhabiting the same space or their presence can literally be felt (positively or negatively) by other "inhabitants." Similarly, when a person enters a space, the very space they enter can be experienced as inhibiting or enabling. In short, how we perceive space and bodies in space depends on various factors: bodies themselves, the kind of bodies we allow or disallow to be in certain spaces, entering/exiting bodies, as well as the way we create and shape spaces. Finally, cognitive because the way bodies and space are structured (or the way we structure them) provides a frame through which we look at the world and at others. Spatial structures, then, can foster or inhibit awareness of unjust or inhumane relationships. That is, how bodies are recognized and the role they play within group dynamics depend at least to some extent on bodies and the makeup of space. Analyzing the relationships between bodies and spaces we can thus learn something about social, cultural, religious, or political ideas. Yet, we always need to be aware of the frames we find ourselves in. As Peter Brown in the introduction to his study on sexuality in early Christianity points out, "societies can lay their codes across the body"[1] in a variety of different ways and these codes are intimately related to the perception of body as/in space and space itself. Peter

Berger and Thomas Luckmann point out that "society sets limits to the organism, and the organism sets limits to society."[2] As such, how bodies behave in and in relation to space, how bodies imprint themselves on space can be seen as an analytical framework to better understand social and political codes at work.

In *Corps de femmes, regards d'hommes. Sociologie des seins nus*,[3] Jean-Claude Kaufmann analyzes the social construction of space and the relationship between body and space in the context of French topless beach culture. On first sight, topless beach bodies do not seem to have anything to do with racial stereotyping and the atrocities of slavery in *Django Unchained*; it might even seem inappropriate to use a study on beach nudity and leisure space as a framework to look at a film that uses slavery as an excuse to indulge in on-screen violence. Kaufmann's observations, however, show that the production of bodies and spaces are inherently governed by social imaginations of a body's proper place in regard to social and spatial boundaries while also always subverting them.

In Kaufmann's analysis, both the beach and beach bodies are socially constructed. Today, we usually think of the beach as a natural, idyllic, and harmonious space.[4] It is a sublime, liminal space, a space whose aesthetics and awe-inspiring characteristics can cause ecstatic experiences.[5] In our imagination, we often construct the beach as natural space that invites the stressed and overworked individual to relax and leave one's cares behind. During summer high-season, when bodies are packed next to each other like sardines in brine, for example at Adriatic beaches, not much of the natural look and feel is left and one has to make some extra effort to get to a part of the beach slightly less inhabited. This notion of a natural and idyllic—or a naturally idyllic—beach is the result of a sociocultural process rather than a realistic description of our encounters with beach-nature. Or, as Jean-Didier Urbain puts it, we never really long for "pure" or untouched nature, but a particular version of nature, an imaginary nature: nature is "already a chosen, selected nature. Not nature for nature's sake, but a particular version of nature: comfortable, welcoming, predisposed to human habitation, inflicting on visitors neither aggression nor challenge."[6]

Martin Döring argues that the beach is always also a sociopolitical space because it is embedded in social and political negotiation processes.[7] As sociopolitical space, it is marked by bodily practices which, in turn, are shaped by the space they find themselves in. That is, the beach space, personal space within the beach space, and spatial boundaries are marked and established through ritual practices. Socially established boundaries shape how individuals and groups act and interact while maintaining the illusion of beach space as natural space, as space of freedom, free of social constraints. The social beach space is also created and marked by geographic boundaries which are never mere physical but always also heavily invested with meaning transcending the mere physical.[8]

Spatial boundaries are marked and established through rituals. The way individuals choose and mark their spot, for example, can be a sophisticated and elaborate process. And while the decision process can be a very deliberate process, good manners usually dictate not to be too obvious that the beach is scanned for an appropriate spot. Rather, one is expected to behave as if the spot was really randomly selected and thus avoid the impression of deliberately choosing one's beach neighbors.[9] More provocatively, one could argue that the impression the beach community is aiming for is that (beach) body does not choose its space but spaces choose their bodies contributing to a naturalization of the body-and-space relationship. Once a spot has been chosen, the space needs to be appropriated and marked, not only to fit one's body but also to safeguard one's body. This personal safe space is created with the help of rituals and objects that are carefully—but often unconsciously—placed. Rituals can include putting on a thick layer of sunscreen giving an additional sense of security in face of penetrating gazes.[10] The way body inhabits its space, too, can contribute to boundary processes. Lying down, for example, can create a peculiar form of intimacy. It is a simple process that protects the still exposed topless body from penetrating gazes.[11]

Body-politics shape the behavior on the beach as bodily-political space as well. Beach bodies create the space of the beach but the space of the beach and its boundaries not only mark bodily behavior but classify and judge it. Kaufmann argues that beach boundaries, in particular for topless sunbathing, are quite solid and normative rather than blurry or negotiable. The beach is negotiated as legitimate space to be topless and what is acceptable behavior or appearance immediately becomes improper and indecent behavior the moment boundaries are crossed. Trespassers are singled out and judged as being bodies-out-of-place or bodies in the wrong space. As example, Kaufmann uses a pharmacy just hundred meters from the beach and a bakery right next to the beach. Even though these two spaces are adjacent to the beach and frequented by beach bodies, entering these spaces topless is considered unacceptable, even by other topless women:

> But the boundary (where the beach ends) is a strict one and uncrossable. Once one leaves the beach, the ban of the nude bosom becomes effective again. One has to understand the normative force of this boundary. The banalization of topless culture would not work if it was not marked by and did not belong to a specific space, a space that is separated and distinct from ordinary life in a similar way vacation is separated and distinct from the every day. It is exactly the idea that being topless is only possible at the beach that allows for and amplifies the possibility to practice it.[12]

And yet, the confined space of the beach, the space of topless beach practices, is not an anything-goes space. The banality of the nude bosom, for example, is not without complications, for example when the hand touches the bosom even if only to put on sunscreen. Too fast or slow a movement over the bosom can easily bring about wrong impressions and thus has to be carefully controlled.

The beach rules, then, are not natural features of the beach but are—often naturalized—social constructs. Some rules might have to do with safety concerns, while the origin of other rules might be less clear.[13] And while practices, rituals, rules, and bodies construct the beach as sacred and social space, the beach as space safeguards those very rules and practices through which it is constructed, as Urbain argues: "The beach [...] indeed protects and isolates this ritual demand. Thus it enables the restoration of elementary physical and social relations, based on sensory experiences, primitive coenesthesias, and convivialities."[14] The beach is (or better has been) an empty space, a "space without social or cultural reference points"[15] and social relations always have yet to be invented but they are, in a peculiar way, always already there.

Bodies in space—Body/space politics in *Django Unchained*

Django Unchained has caused a huge controversy among commentators with questions ranging from the film's historical accuracy,[16] its violence,[17] or whether or not Tarantino uses slavery as convenient medium to enact his own "racial cross-dressing fantasy."[18] From its very beginning, however, *Django Unchained* is fundamentally a film about *messy* spaces: spaces and bodies, bodies and/in spaces, space-body politics, and the question of whose body is allowed to inhabit which space. In particular, the film creates spaces only to ridicule those who defend their boundaries.

The visual culture of and imposed on the slave body, the visual exploitation of slave bodies, is not independent of the construction of space, but creating slave/free bodies and creating slave/free spaces are intimately and problematically intertwined. Bodies embody space and provide space with a rich, stubborn, and messy texture. Through bodies and their relationships we can recognize and analyze the hierarchical and power structures of a specific space. Yet, not only bodies act in and upon space, but space, too, acts upon bodies. Space embodies bodies by providing—or better imposing—a framework to view, experience, sense, feel, and read bodies. Spaces and their boundaries place and displace bodies, enable or limit bodies. Setha M. Low describes the interaction between body, space, and sociocultural contexts as "embodied spaces":

> The concept of embodied space […] [underscores] the importance of the body as a physical and biological entity, lived experience, and a center of agency, a location for speaking and acting on the world. […] Embodied space is the location where human experience and consciousness take on material and spatial form. […] Embodied space is presented as a model for understanding the creation of place through spatial orientation, movement, and language.[19]

The visuality and materiality of space and body mean that the kind of body someone is and the way body is marked, created, and part of or set apart from a community is codependent on which spaces a body is allowed or supposed to inhabit.

The social construction of bodies and spaces means in the context of film that the audience is never mere spectator but they share in the production of space and the visual/imaginary world that unfolds before their eyes. In her blog entry on *Django Unchained*, Susana M. Morris, an African American feminist, points out that the crowd she found herself watching the film with in Atlanta was almost exclusively black probably contributing to a very different cinematic space and viewing experience compared to a mixed, almost exclusively white, or even racist crowd.[20] Social actors, in a way, are the "makeup" of social and meaningful space. Their co-presence contributes to and alters the individual's experience of space *in* space.

Imaginary and material spaces

Space is never just material but always also has an imaginary component. As Kaufmann showed in his analysis, material space is always shaped and bound by the imaginary, by what is envisioned. Similarly, imaginary space does never solely exist in one's imagination but can have concrete material effects. It can imprint itself into the material world or become embodied through the physical.

We can observe the relationship between material and imaginary space in the beginning of *Django Unchained*. The film opens with the opening credits and a view on empty and rocky desert space. As the camera pans and the title of the film, "Django Unchained," is inserted, the tortured black bodies of a group of slaves comes into the frame. The physique of one body in particular stands out, Django's (his scarred muscular back which we see again a few minutes later allows us to identify him). The aesthetics here establish a link between the "rocky" (read: muscular ripped) bodies and the rocky space of the desert: surviving in the desert space under harsh conditions can bear witness to one's strength of will to survive, one's endurance. Linking the muscled rocky bodies with the rocky desert space can also give a sense of the hostile conditions and spaces many slaves had to endure: to survive in extreme and inhumane conditions. Even though the desert hosts a variety of life and desert nomads have been living in these extreme conditions probably ever since the history of humanity, to a spoiled Western audience the imagery of almost naked bodies in the desert speaks of endurance and suffering. Similarly to the way the desert is shaped and transformed by forces it is exposed to, such as wind, heat, or rain, the slave body is shaped, sculpted, and bears marks of external, social, or hostile forces. Yet, the imagery that external social forces are always forces that shape, subjugate, and enslave bodies, and inscribe themselves quite literally onto bodies presented to us here, is also a worrisome one. The desert space is, for the most part, "natural" space. Linking this natural desert space with slave bodies on an aesthetic level through these natural forces that might shape both does not only make it obvious that they are outcast in a way, but one might wonder if the underlying aesthetics suggests that the natural and proper space of these slave bodies, bodies that seem to be adapted to these hostile conditions, is this outcast-space. I am not suggesting that Tarantino intended to produce a racist iconography. Rather, we need to be aware that the remembrance and representation of slavery and its history always remains problematic, not only in a popular culture setting but also in other context, for example in museums.[21] The production and visual representation of space and bodies in space is always an expression of power relations as well as our, the audience's, perception of space. Seen from this perspective, we need problematic images, but not problematic in the sense of worrisome but in the sense of troubling. These problematic/troubling images would not cover up but problematize, stir up, uncover, and subvert, make visible hidden stereotypes and shame, and denounce oppressive and racist ideologies. In this sense, the representation of slavery always must remain problematic and we need to ask what kind of problematic images—worrisome or troubling—we are presented with in Tarantino's film.

The relationship between material and imaginary spaces can also be observed when Dr. Schultz hands the key to the foot shackles over to the other slaves giving them two options: either to bring their wounded overseer to the nearest medical station or to unshackle themselves and enjoy their newfound freedom. But he does not leave it at these two options. Rather, he creates this imaginary space poignantly telling them to unshackle themselves and make their way to the north, to a more enlightened part of the country. With imaginary I do not want to suggest here that Schultz creates a mere immaterial or unreal space (as problematic as "unreal" might be in this context), a space that solely exists in imagination. Rather, Schultz creates and classifies space by suggesting that there is a space, the "more enlightened part of the country," that is different from the space relations these slaves are used to. He does not leave it at this vision but makes this imaginary space almost tangible not only enabling them to leave their space (whether or not their escape could have been successful or not is a different story) but opening up this wholly other space. Before he leaves them to their decision, he remarks (though in a somewhat derogative way): "Oh and on the off-chance there are any astronomy aficionados among you, the North Star is that one." Even with this element of ridicule, the way the scene is set up and the way the actors react suggest that this simple gesture incarnated the imagined, virtual space as something real and reachable.

Granting access to space

In his beach analysis, Kaufmann observed that certain appearances, behaviors, or rituals are required in order to gain access to and be accepted in a specific space. Gaining or granting access to space are part of strategies of access and control. Often, these strategies are related to the question of who grants or subverts access to space and they require that a body is made fit to be allowed into a specific space. In the film we can observe access strategies in relation to a variety of spaces: the space of the slave, the "free" space, the space of the field, or the household space. These various spaces are intimately tied to strategies of demarcation through visual representations, material objects, and embodied power relations.

Django Unchained portrays these various access/control strategies through filmic techniques and material objects. Throughout the film, we encounter several "slave-spaces" with ambiguous meaning. In the beginning of the film, slave-space and white/privileged space are easily recognizable. We see white people in a position of power, on an elevated level, riding horses, while slaves have to drag their bodies by foot through day and night, heat and cold. While one could argue that this is a single space with a clear hierarchy, we can also look at this scene arguing that there are at least two distinct spaces interacting and competing with each other: the space of slaves and white space. White space is easily recognizable as space "up-high." It is the space on the horses giving those inhabiting the space, that is riding the horses, a superior position. The slave-space, on the other hand, is "grounded" space marked by the tortured slave bodies and the distinction between the space "up-high" (on the horses) and "down-below" (on the ground). On a filmic level, the boundaries between slave- and white space are further emphasized through attention to various details, such as the close-up shots of the chained feet, the attention to the difficulties of walking with chained feet, the sound of the chains, or evidence of torture by showing strained backs or brand marks. This attention to details as technique to create spatial boundaries does not seem to be a coincidence. In the visual traditions of pro- and anti-slavery movements, the body of the slave was usually marked with its objects of domination and control, for example shackles, whips, or other mechanical devices. In fact, as Anuradha Gobin argues, the relationship between torture tools and the slave body became codependent, naturalized, and one could not be thought of without the other.[22] In addition to these tools of dominance, we also need to pay attention to more bodily marks. Brand marks were often used to literally inscribe and burn difference into someone's body.[23]

Physical attributes have often been naturalized as characteristic that distinguishes between the body of the free and the slave. These naturalized markers, however, are by no means universal. In ancient Greece, for example, skin color was not necessarily related to one's social status as slave or free person. In eighteenth and nineteenth-century America, however, skin color became the marker of superiority and inferiority, a lifelong and unchangeable marker of difference.[24] Visual culture contributed to the production of the slave-body, appropriating marking and boundary techniques and thus appropriating the slave body itself. *Django Unchained* draws on and plays with this visual production of the slave throughout the film. Early on we see an example of a naturalized relationship between skin color, torture tools, and the body. After Dr. Schultz unchained (but not necessarily freed) Django, he has gained access to space high-up as he, too, now rides on a horse. Yet, Django inhabiting the space on the horse (or other spaces that are introduced to us as reserved for white people) remains problematic. Even though the tools of domination and control are now visually absent theoretically rendering invisible his slave past, Django cannot escape from being "Othered" based on his skin color. That is, he cannot leave his skin, his body, and his embodied past behind and while unchained, his body and his skin always tie him to spaces others construct for him and would like to contain him in.

Space, body, and personal history find themselves in a peculiar relationship. Space is not only something that is socially constructed but spaces themselves become active social agents. They are social agents not only because they prompt us to adapt our behavior: they are created by various social actors and socioreligious, cultural, political, and economic factors, but they also create their very own agents, present us with their very own value and power system, and they can inhibit or foster change. This means for Django that he continually has to defend, negotiate, and reclaim his freedom because in the film (and in our world, too) whiteness aims to defend and secure its spaces. The struggle for access to free/white space is also reflected in how the film portrays the process of manumitting Django and his wife. The many references throughout the film to the bill of sales pose an interesting question for the interpretation of space.[25] For Django and his wife, despite him blowing up everything in the end, it seems that space never becomes truly free space but always remains endangered depending on whether or not being free can be proven with the bill of sales. I am not suggesting that space determines Django, but requiring some bodies to carry the proof of their freedom with them but not others pushes them toward and beyond spatial boundaries.

Invading and violating spaces

Politics of access to space are often tied to the notion of invasion, violation of space, and subversion of spatial boundaries, and we can observe such subversion strategies in different scenes in *Django Unchained*. In the scene where Dr. Schultz unchains Django, the social hierarchy seems to be quite clear between the two spaces, slave-space and white space. And yet, if we look at the characters and the way they behave carefully, it also becomes clear that the space the slaves occupy is their space, or more provocatively: their safe space. What I mean here is as long as everyone stays in their own space (or is allowed to stay in their own space), the slaves have a sense of security and safety (at least as far as a sense of safety is possible given the circumstances).[26] While they are oppressed, as long as the "white folks" stay within their spaces, they know they are sort of "ok" for now. However, if "white folks" invade their space, usually no good comes from it. When Dr. Schultz gets down from his carriage and starts looking for Django, the black characters avoid eye contact; they express a feeling of insecurity not knowing what is going on or what might happen to them. Similarly, Dr. Schultz leaving high-up-there white space and almost transgressing into grounded space without any immediate purpose is seen with suspicion, or at least surprise, by the two overseers on the horses (Figure 5.1).

A violation of established space also happens when Dr. Schultz and Django enter the village. Having been unchained by Dr. Schultz, Django has been freed from the tools of his oppression, yet remains marked as the inferior Other through his skin color. When Dr. Schultz and Django ride into the little village, the characters realize that something is not quite right here, something happens that is not supposed to happen. When we see Dr. Schultz and Django riding into the city, the scene is Tarantinesque unsettling/amusing. But it is not (black) Django on the horse who is unsettling or draws our attention. It is more the whole "texture" of the image, the aesthetics, the

FIGURE 5.1 *Django draws the villagers' attention to him because he violates the privileged space on the horse*

music, and last but not least Dr. Schultz's carriage with its squeaky wiggly giant tooth replica on top. In a way, the scene is set to ridicule whatever comes next. And yet, it is not the squeaky tooth that draws the villagers' attention but the reality of the impossible, or as the village doctor observes with disbelief: "There's a nigga on a horse." This "nigga" on the horse disrupts and subverts the existing social space; he presents not just a mere intrusion but he is the unthinkable, he is that what cannot be but is.

How some of the villagers might have perceived this violation of their established, white, supremacist space is also portrayed on a filmic level. In the bar scene, for example, a villager's disorientation is expressed in the way the scene is shot, the characters behave, and audio effects are put to use. The innkeeper is busy refilling his lamps when the bounty hunter and Django walk into his establishment. Only when he turns around, the innkeeper realizes that the doctor's travel companion is black. Standing on a table, he is about to lose his balance, the camera quickly zooms in (with a zooming sound effect) expressing this experience of disorientation. The bar owner yells, "Wow, wow, wow, what the hell you think you doing boy? Get that nigga outta here!" Similar to what we see when Django rides into the village, this marks the violation of social space through a constructed Other (blackness in this case). Neither is a black person allowed into the space up-high (the horse), nor is she/he permitted into the realms of entertainment and alcohol. Rather than accepting these politics of space, Dr. Schultz and Django kick the innkeeper out of his own place. Yet, I am not fully convinced that we can interpret this scene as Django reclaiming space, at least not just yet. Technically, Dr. Schultz has agreed to give Django his freedom only after he helped him to find the Brittle Brothers. Django's appropriation of space is also questioned by the local sheriff's attitude. Dr. Schultz and Django have not committed any major offence, but the mere presence of a black body among white bodies causes consternation: "[Sheriff:] Now, why ya'all wanna come into my town and start trouble. And scare all these nice people [pointing towards the nice, read: white, people of the village surrounding him]?" On the one hand, we can understand "all these nice people" that Django successfully disrupted the village's naturalization processes; on the other hand, we witness strategies to close the boundaries that were disrupted and get rid of the intruder.

When interpreting this scene, however, we need to keep in mind that real life and real social space was often more messy and blurry than the clean and naturalized space Tarantino presents us with. While some areas might have enforced a strict segregation of the entire bar space or within the bar space, in many areas of America boundaries were often more blurry and people of different color drank and gambled together.[27]

The scene with the "nigga on the horse" and the scene in the bar also seem to be tied to a scene halfway through the film where Dr. Schultz and Django ride through the snow to deliver dead bodies to the local sheriff Don Gus and collect their bounty. If we compare the texture of this scene to the one in the village, the look and feel is quite different. Set in winter in a snowy landscape, here too, Django rides on a horse but it seems that he has now both successfully claimed and been given access to this space up-high. The sheriff welcomes them in an amicable way: "Doctor, Django, how the hell are you?" The way he interacts with the doctor and Django suggests that he knows them (and the screenplay suggests so, too) complicating simplistic assumptions about body-relationships. In fact, this scene is a crucial moment in the film, according to Tarantino himself:

> **QT** [Tarantino]: It's the only time in the movie (that) a white man
>   has addressed him, aside from Schultz, who has not even
>   mentioned his color and treats him with respect. Not even
>   just respect—he treats him as a professional. It's obvious
>   they have become a true team. They are both invited to come
>   inside and partake of the man's birthday cake.
> **HLG** [H.L. Gates]: You did that, not to say something about the
>   sheriff, but to say something about Django's maturity.
> **QT**: Three months were wrapped into one exchange. And you
>   see now that he's a professional. And he's invited inside. He
>   doesn't wait outside with the horses. And that's one of those
>   really important things.[28]

These scenes at the beginning and halfway through the film show how social spaces are always subject to transformation. And while Gates suggests that the scene is more about Django than about the sheriff, I would argue that this scene fundamentally articulates a transformed social space. Yet, what Tarantino says in the interview addresses the ambivalence of this transformation: Has Django appropriated white space, made it his own? Has he become one of them? Has he been granted access, invited to this space that he was formerly excluded from—as opposed to appropriating space and making it his very own?

Struggles over and within white spaces, or: The power of Stephen

A rather peculiar character we come across later in the film is Stephen, Calvin Candie's house slave in his mansion at Candyland. Critics have debated the relationship between Django and Stephen. Jelani Cobb argues that the true conflict in the film lies not in slaveholders versus abolitionists or slaves insurrecting against their masters, but between Django and the house slave Stephen. We could in this context, as Cobb does, discuss the impact this relationship has on the audience's racial perception, an important question.[29] At the very least, the character of Stephen teaches us, albeit in a problematic way, that slavery was a complex practice and phenomenon not only characterized by power relationships but economic interests, cultural rhetorics, or ideas of purity.[30] The experience of house slaves such as Stephen was often very different than those of field slaves, and female house slaves often had to pay dearly for being allowed into a more privileged space. No depiction of slavery can properly represent the slave experience, the violence, and the humiliation. What I am concerned here with, however, is how Stephen fits into the creation and transformation of space.

In *Django Unchained*, (skin) color is an important marker of Otherness and qualifier that determines who has access to which space. Yet, the idea of whiteness is not necessarily tied to biological characteristics. In his analysis of the 2013 George Zimmerman verdict, a mixed Latino/white man who shot a black teenager and was found not guilty,[31] Brian Bantum makes an even more provocative argument about how we create and imagine race: "To lose sight of Zimmerman's racial self-identification is to lose sight of how race has worked in this country, how whiteness was never about biology.

Whiteness has always been about a presumption of innocence, a power to judge, the freedom to exist and to be who you declare yourself to be."[32] It is of course difficult to apply Bantum's argument to the long history of slavery. Yet, it can help us better understand the character of Stephen in the film. Stephen has not only created some sort of safe space for himself, but he perceives himself as having access to and being part of privileged white space. This is expressed in the way he—often quite disrespectfully it seems—talks to Candie or the way he interacts with the other slaves. In particular, what he perceives to be his very own privileged access to white space is all of a sudden challenged by Django. When he first sees Django riding on the horse, he is shocked and asks Candie, "Who this nigger up on that nag?" And when Candie tells Stephen to get the rooms for Dr. Schultz and Django ready, it seems like the end of the world for Stephen: "[Stephen] He gonna stay in the big house? [Candie] Stephen, he is a slaver, it's different." Stephen is shocked about Django being granted access to the big house, a space reserved for whiteness in Bantum's sense, a space of perceived innocence (even though Stephen is far from the innocent handicapped victim as we later find out), superiority, or power to judge others. Similar to white folks who at the beginning of the film find Django's presence in privileged space something that cannot be, Stephen, too, thinks of Django having access to a space in which power over others is exercised and a space that exercises power over other spaces as that which cannot, that which must not be.

A slave was often subordinate and subject to their owner's (almost but not quite) unlimited power, something the film *Django Unchained* expresses very well when Candie orders his Mandingo-fighter to brutally murder his combatant for nothing but his own entertainment. To secure whiteness and white space, slaves were not only contained in separated spaces but they were denied access to the various legal and power frameworks to gain freedom.[33] We could therefore argue that Stephen, in a way, participates in, performs, and executes whiteness, that is power over others. One might object saying that Candie gives Stephen some leeway but that Stephen's power is ultimately limited by Candie. And yet, at the end of the film we get to know Stephen as a master of manipulation. He uses one of the most effective strategies of resisting a master's power, manipulation,[34] to consolidate his own power and achieve his aim: survive and in the context of the film to uncover and thwart Dr. Schultz's and Django's plan to free Django's wife. For Stephen, Django becomes the element he must but cannot contain because despite his bodily marks of Otherness, Django already acts from a position of power (the space up-high, on the horse) when the two first meet.

Stephen in all his ambivalence and evil traits, then, is an example that some house slaves did, in fact, participate in white privileged spaces. They exercised power over other slaves or restricted their social relationships exclusively to white people.[35] Looking at the screenplay, it seems that Tarantino might have had something like that in mind:

> Stephen has been Calvin's slave since he was a little boy. And in (almost) every way is the 2nd most powerful person at Candyland. Like the characters Basil Rathbone would play in swashbucklers, evil, scheming, intriguing men, always trying to influence and manipulate power for their own self-interest. Well that describes Stephen to a tee. The Basil Rathbone of House Niggers.[36]

At the end of the film, when the family returns from the funeral before Django blows up the big house, Stephen shows his evil character. Freed from his master, London Palmer writes, "the enduring servant continues to speak the language of the oppressor after Candie's death."[37] Stephen shows his true face it seems as the evil manipulator who planned intrigues and played the character of a handicapped person. He does not—at least not that we know of—intercede on behalf of any of the other slaves like some others at least sparingly did, such as Phibbah, the house slave of slave owner Thomas Thistlewood in eighteenth-century Jamaica. And yet, despite the manipulative and evil nature Tarantino might have had in mind for the character of Stephen, I argue that his character might be best understood as a mixture of "collaborator," victim, and "accommodator."[38] Unlike Phibbah, however, Stephen is unable to transcend slavery: "Indeed, she [Phibbah] accommodated herself so well to slavery that in the end she transcended it."[39]

Whether or not Stephen is an utterly evil character or not, whether or not his character could have more "character," his character can tell us that a plantation was a complex social space featuring complex social relationships. A plantation was not a coherently structured space with a clear power structure. There was, of course, the master–slave relationship, yet this relationship was not solely enforced through violent means but can be understood as a "negotiated relationship"[40] that was subject to ongoing renegotiations and in which master and slave were mutually dependent.[41] Similarly, the slave population was not a homogenous community. Rather, different slaves engaged differently with enslaved life or processes of resistance.

Planters' attempts to control the enslaved population and to put down rebellions did not rest solely on force. One of the intriguing aspects of slave rebellions involved the attitudes of those of the enslaved who did not rebel. In the midst of rebellions, some of the enslaved carried on working as usual. Others were armed by the authorities to help them defeat the rebels. In many outbreaks, members of the slave community themselves provided advance warnings of the plots to overthrow the system. Slave rebellions provide further evidence, then, of the complexity of a system that lasted for hundreds of years in the Americas.[42]

While I do not want to justify Stephen's behavior by any means, he is an example that slaves created spaces and roles for themselves within the space of the plantation. Steven Hahn argues that slaves continuously "battled to constrain the reach of slaveholders, define relations and activities subject to some of their own control, and turn privileges that owners may have conceded into rights they could embrace and defend. Slaves looked, that is, to carve small spaces of freedom in a large world of slavery."[43] While not legally entitled, some slaves, for example, appropriated land as their own or negotiated other aspects of their work or conditions of their private spaces with their masters.[44] For all we know Stephen carved out this privileged (or safe) space for himself without, as far as we can tell, caring about anyone else who is enslaved like him. I do not want to suggest that slavery brought out the worst in Stephen because slavery was too complex a practice of oppression for such a judgment. Two things seem to be striking though when looking at Stephen's relationship to spaces: his access to and role in white space and Candie's relationship to Stephen within privileged white space.

Stephen also exemplifies that the master–slave relationship was a complex and ambivalent one and often, as Trevor G. Burnard argues, "highly personal. Masters' power over slaves was never absolute. It was always contingent on slaves' recognition that masters had to be obeyed. Slaves did not always give that recognition, although the consequences of not obeying masters were extraordinarily severe."[45] Thus, the master–slave relationship can be seen as spaces relating to and being in constant tension with each other. The relationship of Stephen and Django, therefore, complicates our understanding of slavery. While Stephen was not free and accommodating to or complicit in the atrocities, Django shows that being a free person of color did not automatically put someone outside the space of slavery. In fact, free people of color, too, owned slaves and benefited from unfree and unpaid labor.[46]

The blurring and enforcement of spatial boundaries on the plantation in *Django Unchained* is probably most noticeable in the often intimate relationships between slaves and free people: the relationship between Stephen and Candie seems almost amicable with a paternal touch; when we meet Django's wife Broomhilda von Shaft at Candie's plantation, she is prepared for an intimate (though involuntary) sexual encounter with Dr. Schultz; Dr. Schultz introduces Django as freeman to Candie allowing him to stay in the big house. It seems that spatial boundaries are not as stable and impenetrable as they appear to be after all, in particular in the beginning of the film. As the film progresses, the crossing of boundaries seems not only possible without the danger of being punished, but the very crossing raises questions over the impact of these close encounters on racial, cultural, group, and personal identities both of masters and slaves.[47] In the context of Jamaican slavery, Burnard argues that eighteenth-century Jamaica had become a slave society with the majority of the population being slaves. Slavery, in Jamaica, not only changed all sociocultural traditions, including white-European ones, but also had an impact on all social relations between slaves, between slaves and whites, and within the white community itself. This minority situation whites found themselves in posed the questions why there were not more attempts to overthrow the master class and contributed to a strong loyalty within the white community—despite differences in class. It also fostered white supremacy thinking which was initially based on biological racism. With the spread of the notion that black people are as human as white people and thus should enjoy the same rights and freedoms, biological racism slowly turned into a cultural racism.[48] From the perspective of space, this means that master classes put strategies into place to safeguard white supremacist space. They found new markers of difference to replace eroding ones and justify master–slave relationships and as well as secure their access to unfree and unpaid labor.[49] These negotiations can also be observed in *Django Unchained*. After uncovering—with the help of Stephen—the true aim of Dr. Schultz's and Django's visit, Candie places the skull of old Ben, a house slave who watched over his father and his father's father for decades, on the dinner table asking his guests why Ben never attempted to kill his masters even though he had multiple opportunities to do so.[50] The space Candie describes having grown up in reflects some of the features, questions, and anxieties Burnard describes in his discussion of Jamaican slave society.

> [Candie] This is Ben. He's an old Joe that lived around here for a long time, and I do mean a long damn time. Old Ben here took care of my daddy and my daddy's daddy. Till he up and keeled over one day, old Ben took care of me. Growin' up the son of a huge plantation owner in Mississippi puts a white man in contact with a whole lotta black faces. I spent my whole life here, right here in Candieland, surrounded by black faces. Now seeing them every day, day in and day out, I only had one question: why don't they kill us? Now right out there on that porch, three times a week for fifty years, old Ben here would shave my daddy with a straight razor. Now, if I was old Ben, I would've cut my daddy's goddamn throat, and it wouldn't have taken me no fifty years to do it neither. But he never did. Why not? See, the science of phrenology is crucial to understanding the separation of our two species. And the skull of the African here? The area associated with submissiveness is larger than any human or any other sub-human species on planet Earth. If you examine this piece of skull here you'll notice three distinct dimples. Here, here and here. Now, if I was holding the skull of an Isaac Newton or a Galileo, these three dimples would be found in the area of the skull most associated with creativity. But

this is the skull of old Ben. And in the skull of old Ben, unburdened by genius, these three dimples exist in the area of the skull most associated with servility. [Addressing Django] Now bright boy, I will admit you are pretty clever. But if I took this hammer here, and I bashed in your skull with it, you would have the same three dimples, in the same place, as old Ben.

The message here seems clear: Django might be clever, he might be a freeman, he might have been granted (i.e. given!) access to privileged white space, but ultimately, Candie does not have to fear Django inhabiting the same space because his sole purpose is to serve. Slavery here occupies a naturalized state, not only something someone is born into but born as.[51] This Othering of Django is ultimately a desperate attempt to uphold boundaries that are literally falling apart in front of Candie's eyes as Django has invaded his space only to trick him.

Conclusion: The "nigga on the horse" as redemptive space?

Django Unchained ends with the blowing up of oppressive space, Broomhilda—in Tarantinesque theatrics—applauds, she draws and shoulders her rifle, and she and Django ride off happily ever after, leaving the burning big house behind. To give Django—or better the whole film—a religious connotation, in the post-credits scene one of the slaves Django freed while he was transported to the mines, asks, "Who was that nigga?" Redemption at last? Can Tarantino's *Django Unchained* even provide a redemptive space in all its moral ambivalence? Or, does Tarantino's film—with all its problems—stand for the moral ambivalence of life itself? In his interview with Tarantino, Henry L. Gates Jr. argues,

I'm a scholar of slavery, and one of the things I notice in my classes (that I teach) is that we've become inured to the suffering and pain of slavery, that we've distanced ourselves enough from it, that people can't experience the terror, the horrible pain, the anxiety, the stress, et cetera, that came with the slave experience.

I thought that in *Django* you really began to reinsert contemporary viewers into that pain, particularly through the scene when the dogs tear Candie's slave D'Artagnan apart.[52]

How, then, does the notion of space help to better understand the film, in particular with the striking religious reference at the very end, and what can we, as audience, learn from paying attention to the construction of space when watching the film?

Spaces are constructed by social agents but they themselves are/ become social agents in their own right. Social spaces are messy but we often develop practices to "clean" up this messy spaces and engage in practices of Othering that justifies our presence in a specific space but not someone else's. In his study of beach culture, Kaufmann argues that "sun worshippers" develop their own (often magical) rituals to justify their presence and their practices by denouncing someone else:[53] "Those with a dark tan advise those with a light or no tan to be cautious, the regulars in the Bretagne criticize those who appreciate the south."[54] Spaces and bodies within spaces always undergo naturalization and purification rituals. Whatever is unwanted or does not seem fit is expelled and only readmitted after purification. For the beach space, this means that anything that disturbs our imaginary natural space, such as seaweed or unfit, suffering/sick/disabled bodies, is not wanted and needs to be eliminated from this naturalized-imaginary space. Only after sick bodies, for example, have become healthy again—ironically often with the unwanted seaweed—they can be readmitted. And Urbain calls these purification processes "a desire for an unnatural purity":

There is a certain symmetry at work: what happens with fishermen also happens with seaweed. Rejected, expelled, or eliminated from the shore, these elements are reintroduced into the vacation universe only when they have been transformed into exotic curiosities, that is, literally, into external realities [...] These realities are henceforth foreign to the beach world; they are no longer natural but naturalized.[55]

The notion that spaces are far from natural but that we shape them according to our ideas of nature is helpful in the context of *Django Unchained*. Whiteness has become our default gaze obscuring our own Western complicity in this gaze. Similarly, racial labels altogether need to be seen as social constructs that depend on time and space.[56] Spaces, in this context, are always both imagined spaces rooted in sociocultural, economic, and historic experiences expressed in narratives and real spaces, that is, imaginary spaces incarnate.

To liberate ourselves from oppressive spaces, the symbolic deconstruction of imaginary and real spaces is sometimes necessary. Tarantino creates spaces only to destroy them. With his aesthetics and filmic techniques, he ridicules social boundary processes and shows that some people might experience the questioning of boundaries as if their world was turned upside down. Moon Charania criticizes that *Django Unchained* is "black on black violence, constructed by and for the white fetishistic gaze" asking the important question "At the very least, we sociologists should ask, can slavery and human depravity ever be objects of humor, of entertainment?"[57] Earlier, I argued that the audience participates in and often is complicit in the creation of filmic and cinematic space. Taking seriously Charania's critique and drawing on the beach/seaweed/fishermen imagery, we need to ask ourselves if we as white Western audience do not replicate the space we witness at some point in the film? When we meet Candie the first time, we witness him gazing at and enjoying a brutal Mandingo fight ordering his fighter to brutally murder his opponent at the end of the fight. Watching and enjoying the film, as I did I must confess, are we (and I mean here being white and Western) not like Candie safeguarding what we perceive as our Western civilized space creating and gazing at the violent savage Other? In other words, are we not complicit in granting and allowing the Other into what we perceive as our own space only under the condition that we can contain the alien Other? Tarantino argues that portraying the relationship between Dr. Schultz and Django, he relied on the Western trope of the experienced gunfighter showing his younger and inexperienced sidekick the ropes. Once he is ready to go his own way, the teacher has to give space to the actual hero.[58] Yet, if we look at the film as part of white spatial practices, we could argue that the violation of white bodies through black bodies is not just an expression of a racial fetish, but is only allowed into white space because the film itself contains strategies of containing the Other. If a white man, Dr. Schultz, kills white people, then there must be a reason for it and so Django, too, gets away with it and is granted access to this white space we create when engaging with the film. Dr. Schultz, then, is not the experienced gunfighter, but the containment field for black vengeance, the antidote that keeps us safe.

We should therefore ask if *Django Unchained* is a redemptive space. A common element of narratives of freed slaves is the element of emancipation, how they themselves, actively rather than passively, worked toward their emancipation and achieved freedom.[59] Charania, however, argues that Django's "sympathy for his enslaved counterparts is laced with a disgust for the black passivity he works rigorously to shake off (it ties him, in his mind, to the white masters). In this regard, Tarantino, his creation Django, and their enamored audiences are, well…All-American."[60] If we understand white space to mean a space of power that rules and dominates all other spaces, is Django, the "nigga on the horse," the black guy in white space being whitened in order to be accepted in white space while also being kept at a safe distance?

Leaving the question of *Django Unchained*'s historical accuracy aside, the film links past politics of space with today's spatial strategies. Or in other words: how we envision past spaces today in historiography, fiction, and popular culture might tell us more about the makeup of our very own spaces rather than the past. Ultimately, "the nigga on the horse" becomes a symbol that bodies, in a way, always are both at the same time in and out of place because however commodified or adapted they might appear, they always also are stubborn, messy, and resistant.

Notes

1   Peter Brown, *The Body and Society: Men, Women, and Sexual Renunciation in Early Christianity*, 2nd ed. (New York: Columbia University Press, 2008), xxiii.

2   Peter L. Berger and Thomas Luckmann, *The Social Construction of Reality: A Treatise in the Sociology of Knowledge* (Garden City, N.Y.: Doubleday, 1967), 182.

3   For this chapter, the German translation of *Corps de femmes* has been used as the English translation is not yet available: Jean-

Claude Kaufmann, *Frauenkörper—Männerblicke: Soziologie des Oben-ohne* (Konstanz: UVK Verl.-Ges., 2006). All translations in this chapter are mine unless otherwise noted.

4   For a history of the transformation processes and the different meanings ascribed to beaches, see Martin Döring, "Die narratologische Küste. Küstenbilder in zwei Romanen und Kurzgeschichten Guy de Maupassants," in *Küstenbilder—Bilder der Küste. Interdisziplinäre Ansichten, Ansätze und Konzepte*, ed. Martin Döring, Wolfgang Settekorn, and Hans von Storch (Hamburg: Hamburg University Press, 2006), 182–183; Kaufmann, *Frauenkörper—Männerblicke*, 38–39; Martina Löw, "The Social Construction of Space and Gender," *European Journal of Women's Studies*, 13, 2 (May 1, 2006), 121; Jean-Didier Urbain, *At the Beach* (Minneapolis: University of Minnesota Press, 2003), 28, 157. For a discussion on the fallacy of utopian beach space, see Kaufmann, *Frauenkörper—Männerblicke*, 121–122.

5   See Döring, "Die narratologische Küste," 181; Jürgen Hasse, "Küste als Raum der Erholung und der Freizeit," in *Küstenbilder—Bilder der Küste. Interdisziplinäre Ansichten, Ansätze und Konzepte*, ed. Martin Döring, Wolfgang Settekorn, and Hans von Storch (Hamburg: Hamburg University Press, 2006), 312–313.

6   Urbain, *At the Beach*, 136.

7   See Döring, "Die narratologische Küste," 183: "Die Küstenlandschaft, so hat es den Anschein, hat eine gemeinschaftstiftende Funktion, steht immer in einem gesellschaftlichen und politischen Zusammenhang, sie ist eine politische Landschaft": "The coastal landscape, it seems, can bring about community, is always embedded into a social and political context, it is political landscape."

8   See Kaufmann, *Frauenkörper—Männerblicke*, 119.

9   See Kaufmann, *Frauenkörper—Männerblicke*, 118–121.

10   See Kaufmann, *Frauenkörper—Männerblicke*, 49.

11   See Kaufmann, *Frauenkörper—Männerblicke*, 123.

12   Kaufmann, *Frauenkörper—Männerblicke*, 61: "Doch die Grenze (dort, wo der Sand aufhört) ist strikt und unüberschreitbar. Sobald man den Strand verläßt, tritt das Nacktheitsverbot für den Busen wieder in Kraft. Man muß die normative Macht dieser Begrenzung verstehen. Die Banalisierung des Oben-Ohne könnte nicht funktionieren, wenn sie nicht durch einen bestimmten Ort gekennzeichnet ware, der abgetrennt ist und sich vom normalen Leben wie Urlaub vom Alltag abhebt. Genau diese Vorstellung, daß das Oben-Ohne nur am Strand möglich ist, verstärkt gleichzeitig die Möglichkeit, es zu praktizieren."

13 See Urbain, *At the Beach*, 198.

14 Urbain, *At the Beach*, 198.

15 Urbain, *At the Beach*, 200.

16 See Stephen Marche, "Django Unchained Is a Better Movie About Slavery Than Lincoln," *Esquire*, http://www.esquire.com/blogs/culture/django-unchained-lincoln-slavery-14895534 (accessed June 27, 2013); Jelani Cobb, "How Accurate Is Quentin Tarantino's Portrayal of Slavery in Django Unchained?" *The New Yorker*, January 2, 2013, http://www.newyorker.com/online/blogs/culture/2013/01/how-accurate-is-quentin-tarantinos-portrayal-of-slavery-in-django-unchained.html.

17 See Hendrik Hertzberg, "Djangled Nerves," *The New Yorker*, March 7, 2013, http://www.newyorker.com/online/blogs/hendrikhertzberg/2013/03/djangled-nerves.html.

18 David J. Leonard in: David J. Leonard and Tamura A. Lomax, "Django Unchained: A Critical Conversation Between Two Friends," December 31, 2013, http://thefeministwire.com/2012/12/django-unchained-a-critical-conversation-between-two-friends/.

19 Setha M. Low, "Anthropological Theories of Body, Space, and Culture," *Space and Culture*, 6, 1 (2003), 10.

20 See Susana M. Morris, "Django Unchained and Why Context Matters," January 6, 2013, http://www.crunkfeministcollective.com/2013/01/06/django-unchained-and-why-context-matters/.

21 See Anuradha Gobin, "Technologies of Control: Visual Arts and the African Slave Body from the 18th Century to the Present," *Research and Practice in Social Sciences*, 2, 2 (2007), 126; Douglas Hamilton, "Representing Slavery in British Museums: The Challenges of 2007," in *Imagining Transatlantic Slavery*, ed. Cora Kaplan and John Oldfield (New York: Palgrave, 2010), 131–134.

22 Gobin, "Technologies of Control," 140.

23 See Gobin, "Technologies of Control," 126.

24 See Niall McKeown, "Seeing Things: Examining the Body of the Slave in Greek Medicine," *Slavery & Abolition*, 23, 2 (August 2002), 29; Frank M Snowden, *Before Color Prejudice: The Ancient View of Blacks* (Cambridge, Mass.: Harvard University Press, 1983); Steven Mailloux, "Re-Marking Slave Bodies: Rhetoric as Production and Reception," *Philosophy and Rhetoric*, 35, 2 (2002), 106.

25 For a discussion about free people of color required to carry proof that they are, in fact, free, see John Garrigus, "Free Coloureds," in *The Routledge History of Slavery*, ed. Gad Heuman and Trevor Burnard (London: Routledge, 2011), 237–243.

26 Slaves in different sociocultural context experienced different degrees of oppression or autonomy. In the context of Jamaican slavery, Trevor G. Burnard argues that the slaves had to deal with a quasi omnipresence of the masters. See Trevor G. Burnard, *Mastery, Tyranny, and Desire: Thomas Thistlewood and His Slaves in the Anglo-Jamaican World* (Chapel Hill: University of North Carolina Press, 2004), 254.

27 See Timothy J. Lockley, "Race Relations in Slave Societies," in *The Routledge History of Slavery*, ed. Gad Heuman and Trevor Burnard (London: Routledge, 2011), 256f. For the many spaces of interaction between slaves and free people slaves have appropriated for themselves over time, see Lockley, "Race Relations in Slave Societies," 250–251.

28 Henry L. Jr. Gates, "Tarantino 'Unchained,' Part 3: White Saviors. Interview with Quentin Tarantino by Henry Louis Gates Jr.," *The Root*, December 25, 2012, 2, http://www.theroot.com/views/tarantino-unchained-part-3-white-saviors.

29 See Cobb, "Tarantino's Portrayal of Slavery."

30 See Gobin, "Technologies of Control," 127.

31 See Lizette Alvarez and Cara Buckley, "Zimmerman Is Acquitted in Killing of Trayvon Martin," *The New York Times*, July 14, 2013, http://www.nytimes.com/2013/07/15/us/george-zimmerman-verdict-trayvon-martin.html.

32 Brian Bantum, "We Should All Be Terrified," *Brian Bantum*, http://brianbantum.wordpress.com/2013/07/14/we-should-all-be-terrified/ (accessed August 7, 2013).

33 See Antony Honoré, "The Nature of Slavery," in *The Legal Understanding of Slavery. From the Historical to the Contemporary*, ed. Jean Allain (Oxford: Oxford University Press, 2012), 15.

34 See Burnard, *Mastery, Tyranny, and Desire*, 211.

35 See Burnard, *Mastery, Tyranny, and Desire*, 231.

36 Quentin Tarantino, "Django Unchained. Screenplay," http://www.imsdb.com/scripts/Django-Unchained.html (accessed August 9, 2013).

37 London Palmer, "Why 'Django Unchained' Is Subversively Complex and Disappointingly Simple," *FilmSchoolRejects*, December 29, 2012, http://www.filmschoolrejects.com/features/why-django-unchained-is-subversively-complex-and-disappointingly-simple-lpalm.php.

38 Burnard, *Mastery, Tyranny, and Desire*, 240.

39 Burnard, *Mastery, Tyranny, and Desire*, 240.

40 Burnard, *Mastery, Tyranny, and Desire*, 252.

41 See Burnard, *Mastery, Tyranny, and Desire*, 253.

42 Gad Heuman, "Slave Rebellions," in *The Routledge History of Slavery*, ed. Gad Heuman and Trevor Burnard (London: Routledge, 2011), 220.

43 Steven Hahn, "Forging Freedom," in *The Routledge History of Slavery*, ed. Gad Heuman and Trevor Burnard (London: Routledge, 2011), 298.

44 See James Sidbury, "Resistance to Slavery," in *The Routledge History of Slavery*, ed. Gad Heuman and Trevor Burnard (London: Routledge, 2011), 208.

45 Burnard, *Mastery, Tyranny, and Desire*, 177. See also p. 210, where Burnard argues that "a master's power was close to absolute," or p. 240, where he argues that realities of power, freedom, or what slaves/owners could and could not do were often quite messy.

46 See Garrigus, "Free Coloureds," 238, 241.

47 See Jennifer L. Morgan, "Gender and Family Life," in *The Routledge History of Slavery*, ed. Gad Heuman and Trevor Burnard (London: Routledge, 2011), 147.

48 See Burnard, *Mastery, Tyranny, and Desire*, 244–245, 249, 256–258.

49 See Grace E. Hale, *Making Whiteness: The Culture of Segregation in the South, 1890–1940* (New York: Vintage Books, 1999), 4–6.

50 Unlike Candie's depiction, slaves did more or less successfully rebel against oppression throughout the history of slavery. See Heuman, "Slave Rebellions."

51 See Burnard, *Mastery, Tyranny, and Desire*, 258. Hale argues that in the United States up until the 1850s, slave status was more a legal/political difference than a naturalized one. See Hale, *Making Whiteness: The Culture of Segregation in the South, 1890–1940*, 4.

52 Henry L. Jr. Gates, "Tarantino 'Unchained,' Part 2: On the N-Word. Interview with Quentin Tarantino by Henry Louis Gates Jr.," *The Root*, December 25, 2012, http://www.theroot.com/views/tarantino-unchained-part-2-n-word.

53 See Kaufmann, *Frauenkörper—Männerblicke*, 49.

54 "Die Dunkelhäutigen raten den Hellhäutigen zur Vorsicht, die Stammgäste der Bretagne kritisieren die Anhänger des Südens." *Frauenkörper—Männerblicke*.

55 Urbain, *At the Beach*, 138.

56 See Garrigus, "Free Coloureds," 234.

57 M. Charania, "Django Unchained, Voyeurism Unleashed," *Contexts* 12, 3 (August 12, 2013), 58.

58 See Gates, "Tarantino 'Unchained' Part 2."

59 See Paul E. Lovejoy, "'Freedom Narratives' of Transatlantic Slavery," *Slavery & Abolition*, 32, 1 (March 2011), 95.

60 Charania, "Django Unchained, Voyeurism Unleashed," 59.

6

The "D" Is Silent, but Human Rights Are Not: *Django Unchained* as Human Rights Discourse

Kate E. Temoney

Life, liberty, and the pursuit of vengeance
—*Django Unchained* (2012), promotional materials tagline

We hold these truths to be self-evident, that all men are created equal, that they are endowed by their Creator with certain unalienable Rights, that among these are Life, Liberty and the pursuit of Happiness
—*United States Declaration of Independence* (1776)

Introduction

Auteur filmmaker Quentin Tarantino's latest mash-up, *Django Unchained* (2012), is a film about slavery that is part Spaghetti Western, part Blaxploitation, part romance, and part revenge but entirely spectacle. Like his previous acclaimed films, *Reservoir Dogs*

(1992), *Pulp Fiction* (1994), *Kill Bill, Vols. 1 & 2* (2003 & 2004), *Jackie Brown* (1997), *Death Proof* (2007), and *Inglourious Basterds* (2009), *Django Unchained* is an unabashed display of Tarantino's all-too familiar cinephilic tendencies, preoccupation with the macabre, ad nauseam use of the "n-word," and masterful use of droll dialogue and hip music. However, *Inglourious Basterds*, a World War II film, and *Django Unchained*, his most commercially successful film to date, exemplify Tarantino's foray into new territory—historical storytelling— which runs the risk of offending those who deem treating dark periods of history as sacrosanct, and thereby their solemnity diminished by embellishment or blithe handling. Jamie Foxx plays the titular role in *Django Unchained*, a slave in 1858 Texas. The film follows *Django* and his eventual liberator—a purported German dentist who turns bounty hunter, Dr. "King" Schultz (Christoph Waltz). Schultz purchases Django and agrees to free him upon the successful collection of a bounty on the Brittle Brothers, whom Schultz cannot identify without Django. True to his word, Schultz grants Django his freedom, but the two choose to continue to collect bounties together, with Django under the tutelage of Schultz. A gun-slinging adventure morphs into a story of love, rescue, and bloody revenge upon Schultz feeling compelled to assist Django in finding and freeing Django's wife, Broomhilda von Shaft (Kerry Washington), from bondage. Their quest leads them to the doorstep of Candyland and the plantation's owner Calvin Candie (Leonardo DiCaprio) as well as his furtive house slave Stephen (Samuel L. Jackson)—then the real carnage ensues.

One of the most high-profile comments about the film was made before the film's wide release and by a director who did not even see the film: Spike Lee and his assailing statements about the film's impertinent treatment of slavery sparked a volley of retorts from other black influential artists. In a December 2012 interview with *Vibe* TV, Lee said, "I can't speak on it 'cause I'm not gonna see it. All I'm going to say is that it's disrespectful to my ancestors. That's just me...I'm not speaking on behalf of anybody else," followed by the Tweet, "American slavery was not a Sergio Leone spaghetti western. It was a holocaust. My ancestors are slaves. Stolen from Africa. I will honor them."[1] Lee also took issue with Tarantino's excessive use of the "n-word," which is invoked over 100 times in *Django Unchained*—an overuse that Tarantino insists is commensurate with the racial epithet's casual use in the mid-nineteenth-century Deep South. As for those who actually screened the film, most reviews[2] of *Django Unchained* centered on the film's indulgent 165 minute-running time, over the top violence, irreverent humor, and revisionist retelling of history. For example, Rex Reed of the *New York Observer* found the film to be "overlong, raunchy, shocking, grim... and so politically incorrect it demands a new definition of the term. It is also bold, original, mesmerizing, stylish and one hell of a piece of entertainment."[3] Still other reviewers, while acknowledging the film's outrageousness, commented on the serious moral implications and cultural repercussions of filmic depictions of slavery. Roger Ebert wrote in the *Chicago Sun Times* that Tarantino's "films challenge taboos in our society in the most direct possible way,"[4] and Scott Foundas of *The Village Voice* puts an even finer points on Ebert's sentiment when he writes, "Like all the best of pop art, Tarantino's film is both seriously entertaining and seriously thoughtful, rattling the cage of race in America on-screen and off,"[5] while the *New York Times'* A. O. Scott similarly reiterated that *Django Unchained* is "brazenly irresponsible and also ethically serious in a way that is entirely consistent with its playfulness."[6] These reviews recognize the profound implications of portraying slavery on film, even in a Spaghetti Western format, and this provides an opening for considering the film as more than gory amusement but as a conduit for thoughtful conversation, and in fact, the film ignited national debates about race, violence, and the moral limits of allohistory (revised history).

In many ways, *Django Unchained* is an exemplar of the artistry that epitomizes Tarantino's directorial signature style, but the film also differs from his earlier endeavors. Commensurate with his previous films, *Django Unchained* is punctuated by moments of shockingly barbarous violence, inappropriate humorous interjections, and craftily devised, if not at times ridiculously amusing, confabulations. Yet, the film departs from his earlier works in squarely fixing a human rights atrocity in the middle of a narrative (here, one must recall that the backdrop of *Inglourious Basterds* is World War II and not the Holocaust, per se), unfolding the action in a largely linear fashion—which lends a "historical" quality to the film—and a more conventional manipulation of music that is synchronous as opposed to asynchronous with the action. The overall argument of this chapter is that by way of an inductive extension of Tarantino's explicit engagement of slavery and racism, it can be averred that Tarantino's aesthetic, in tandem with the film's text, gesture toward contemporary issues in human rights discourse by treating a controversial subject matter and by providing an imaginative and bearable space for grappling with the complex, incongruous, and seemingly inscrutable phenomena of atrocities in unorthodox ways. Before pursuing this thesis further, definitional clarity is warranted. Regarding human rights, it is sufficient to regard them to be universal protections against certain kinds of treatment (e.g. torture and seizure of property) as well as guarantees of certain kinds of benefits (e.g. education and the freedom to change religion) for no other reason than by virtue of the inherent dignity that is constitutive of being human. Human rights discourse, broadly speaking, concerns both scholarly and activist perspectives on the content of human rights, human rights violations, and the protection of human rights. "Aesthetic" is understood here as the stylistic/ artistic choices that dictate the manner in which a scene is filmed and experienced, and "text" is delineated as the content of the film, the information that is imparted to the viewer. The aesthetic techniques of film, then, dictate the experienced reception of the text, and synergistically, the two promote a species of "knowing" that is not bound by intellect and is beyond the capacity of the text to bring to fruition alone.

More specifically, it is argued that in an unexpected, inventive (and most likely unintended manner), the text of *Django Unchained* discloses complications regarding notions of the "truth" of human rights abuses and victim representation—which have typically been the purview of documentary film or more sober accounts of slavery (Steven Spielberg's 2012 *Lincoln* comes to mind) and are thereby considered more "factual" than a film like *Django Unchained* and escape the same kind of scrutiny regarding the "truthfulness" they convey and the stereotypes they may perpetuate. Second, the film informs a holistic approach to human rights study by both confronting the dark potential in all humans to act atrociously—which is an important component of seeing the stake we all have in addressing human rights violations and understanding the psychology and sociology of abuse in order to prevent it—and, third, tapping into a trend in human rights scholarship to empower and not merely essentialize victims of human rights abuses by including victim resistance and rescue behavior (translated as righteous revenge in Tarantino's films). Tarantino's text is complimented by his aesthetic methods of the disjunctive pairing of humor with disquieting moments, and attending despicable behavior with genteel discourse. Both techniques functionally replicate a dissonance and intensity for audiences, tempered by levity, which evokes a visceral reaction of something "not being quite right," a notion adopted from Patrick McGee, which may create an investigatory disposition guided by human rights discourse. As one may recall, the tagline of the promotional materials for *Django Unchained* is: "Life, liberty, and the pursuit of vengeance," an allusion to the Declaration of Independence that invites or at least does not object to human rights discourse.

To support these claims, the auteur's expressed intentions regarding the film's production and desired reception will be provided, but to be sure, although *Django Unchained* may be construed as conducive to human rights discussions, it should be understood that the film is primarily designed to entertain (including the director's self-amusement)—not to promote a human rights agenda. This point notwithstanding, this project is an exercise in exploring how Tarantino's artistic vision can be extended, interpreted, and appropriated as a meaningful contribution to human rights discourse. This approach is enabled by a perspicacious observation by Paul Gormley, who notes that critics James Wood and Derek Malcom have found Tarantino's films to be morally vacuous and apolitical, but in agreement with Gormley, these judgments are "in terms of *direct* discursive and narrative content."[7] However obliquely, *Django Unchained* can provide a fruitful avenue for human rights talk. Moreover, Sonia Tascon notes, that "Lisa Downing and Libby Saxton suggest that *all* films have an ethical dimension. Many Hollywood films, they state, are constructed within a moral framework, deploying notions of virtue to both unfold and resolve the narrative."[8] Nonetheless, if it is ceded that *Django Unchained* has an "ethical dimension," the question still remains as to whether the presented "moral framework" is a desirable one, and it does not impugn the quality of the film, or its discursive potential, to argue that the film is morally problematic. Tarantino's recycling of familiar, and sometimes controversial tropes, such as his problematic representation of "blackness," conflation of violence with heroism, and use of excessively "fun" brutality juxtaposed to the historicized brutality of the slave trade, run the risk of undermining, rather than emphasizing, the gravity of the latter.

Truth and consequences

It is generally accepted that the realm of the celluloid is one that can affect audiences in a potentially profound manner, reflecting and amplifying the afilmic world (the ordinary reality external to the film) within the profilmic world (the cinematic reality created by the film) back to us in compelling, vivid, and visceral ways. Since the late 1980s, when the first Human Rights Watch International Film Festival (HRWIFF) was held,[9] human rights movements have embraced the potentials of cinema and used the medium of film to expose human rights abuses, promulgate human rights protections, and mobilize activists. As one might expect, these festivals are dominated by documentaries—not of the genre of Spaghetti Westerns meets historical narrative in Hollywood splendor—yet each style must attend to what it means to impart "truth" and take responsibility for how the human subjects of their films are portrayed. Henry Louis Gates, Jr., offers a poststructuralist perspective that collapses the creative distinction between documentaries and narrative films when he writes that "Feature films are about what *could have* happened, while documentaries ostensibly are about what *did* happen ... all works of art, are in some sense fictions, because even works of history and documentaries are imaginative creations that are invented, in the sense of having been made ... the process of recreation inevitably is subject to all sorts of influences and factors, whether these are fictional or nonfictional recreations."[10] Joseph Conrad, whose 1899 *Heart of Darkness* is regarded as an influential piece of literature in discussions on human rights, goes so far as to argue the superior adeptness of fiction in conveying "truth" when he writes, "Fiction is history, human history, or it is nothing. But it is also more than that; it stands on firmer ground, being based on the reality of forms and the observation of social phenomenon, whereas history is based on documents, and the reading of print and handwriting—on secondhand impression. Thus fiction is nearer the truth."[11] Succinctly summarized, "truth" is not circumscribed by what is "true." Tarantino, too, touches on the benefit of nondocumentary styles of storytelling in an NPR (National Public Radio) interview:

> I mean not to sound like a brute, but one of the things, though, that I actually think can be a drag for a whole lot of people about watching a movie about either dealing with slavery or dealing with the Holocaust is just—it's just going to be pain, pain and more pain. And at some point, all those Holocaust TV movies, it's like, God, I can't watch another one of these. But to actually take an action story and put it in that kind of backdrop where slavery or the pain of World War II is the backdrop of an exciting adventure story, that can be something else.[12]

It is within the room created by the possibility of Conrad's "more than that" and Tarantino's "something else" that this project operates, within extra-factual ways of knowing.

Tarantino references *Heart of Darkness*, a fortuitous link that finds some purchase in comparison. For *TheRoot.com*—an online magazine dedicated to providing diverse black perspectives on contemporary issues—the Editor-in-Chief, Harvard professor, and culture critic, Henry Louis Gates, Jr., conducts an interview, a segment titled "On the N-Word." In the interview, Tarantino likens a scene from *Django Unchained* to a passage in Conrad's novella *Heart of Darkness* as "that almost *Heart of Darkness* section."[13] Presumably, Tarantino is referencing Conrad's description of the journey of his dubious protagonist, Marlow, who is making his way to the Company station. En route, Marlow witnesses the egregious mistreatment of the black "moribund shapes,"[14] African slaves, who are chained six-men deep and defeated in spirit, not unlike the indignities the audience witnesses of American slavery and plantation life following Dr. "King" Schultz and Django on their trip to Candyland. Both Tarantino and Conrad's accounts are fictional in the purest sense, but are their accounts any less "true" or powerful than nonfiction in imparting the actual horrors of slavery?

In numerous interviews, Tarantino relays his intention to depict the cruel practices of the American slave trade in the antebellum South in *Django*, and to this extent, he does not shrink away from slavery's brutalities: Django's whip-scarred back, Broomhilda's hotbox imprisonment, slaves being ripped apart by dogs, and the imposition of metal masks.[15] However, he also takes liberties with the facts, both through distortions of history and fabrications. For example, despite several outbursts of surprise by several different characters in the film at the sight of seeing Django on a horse, to see a slave on a horse was not an unusual sight[16] (presumably, the astonishment was at the social status conferred upon Django as ostensibly equal to the white Schultz). Interestingly, Tarantino's mixing of fact with fiction had viewers and the cast alike questioning what they thought they knew about slavery, a line that is further blurred by Tarantino's decision to tell the story in an uncharacteristically linear fashion (the above-mentioned *Jackie Brown* being an exception). Both of these techniques give the film a historic aura and along with it a modicum of the credibility such a characterization affords, risking miseducating the audience, but it can also galvanize efforts to separate fact from fiction. Not unlike how Jules' quoting of Ezekiel 25.17 in *Pulp Fiction* had some moviegoers reaching for a Bible, one of the most widely reported disturbing scenes in the film is the fabricated practice of Mandingo fighting (the fighting of slaves to the death for sport and for the amusement of their white slave owners), which had viewers surfing the Internet asking, "Is Mandingo fighting real?" Perhaps, ironically, this counterfact conveys a "truth" about the sadistic practices of the slave trade in a manner that no singular depiction of an actual abuse could—the utter dehumanization, the violence, and the implication of victims in their own victimization.

As documentary film is viewed as the least mediated medium of truth, Sonia Tascon raises an important concern of human rights documentaries, which is the potential transmission of unquestioned ideologies and social assumptions because documentary films are often immune to the kind of cultural interrogation to which narrative films are subject because documentary films enjoy a presumed veil of truth:

> I suggest that human rights films, by virtue of their documentary-style form, evoke a connection to truth that attempts to circumvent the difficult questions and critiques that may be raised, and would be raised, were they not human rights documentaries...the

genre's allegiance to the social problem category, very likely (although there is little research in this area to date) perpetuates audience perceptions that the films are to be taken seriously, accepted as truth, and acted upon in their entirety.[17]

Given that elsewhere in her essay, "Considering Human Rights Films, Representation, and Ethics: Whose Face?" she expresses concern about how people who are victims of human rights abuses are represented. Tascon relies on the work of Susan Sontag when she worries about the exotic representation of the "other."[18] Tascon and Sontag's worry is that this othering reinforces a cultural consciousness that believes that atrocities happen to people "over there," to the poor, to the backward, reinforcing stereotypes about who is typically the "face" of human rights abuses and distancing ourselves from victims as so unlike "us," and nascent human rights discourse on this point would benefit greatly by engaging in the longstanding debates in film criticism about fictionalized stereotypes and coded messages in feature films.

A "festival of cruelty": The dark side of humanity

The penultimate point of concern of human rights talk and the text of *Django Unchained* is the trend in human rights not only to honor and convey the tragedies of people who have endured human rights abuses, but also to understand the mind of perpetrators and probe the circumstances and psychology that produce perpetrators, not the least of which includes victims who become perpetrators and the potential for any one of us to become violent. Jonathan Glover, in *Humanity: A Moral History of the 20th Century*, insists that scholarship on atrocities "involves thinking about the implications of some things we now know civilized people are capable of doing to each other…. A consequence of this is to produce a darker account [of reality]. There are more things, darker things, understand about ourselves than who share this hope [that a more peaceful and human world is possible] have generally allowed."[19] Glover's chapter title, "The Festival of Cruelty," says it all. Seminal works in this area include Hannah Arendt's then controversial book *Eichmann in Jerusalem* (1963),[20] which asks how such an "ordinary" man like Eichmann could, without compunction, arrange the train schedules that led Jews to their deaths and did so because of his desire to do a good job. It is this work that contains the famous concept of the "banality of evil" or that the most pedestrian of people, and for the most innocuous of reasons, can commit depraved acts. Other titles, such as *When Victims Become Killers: Colonialism, Nativism, and the Genocide in Rwanda*[21] and *The Lucifer Effect: Understanding How Good People Turn Evil*,[22] further illustrate this strand of thought in human rights discussions, for if we recognize that the any of us can become murderous under the right circumstances, we can guard against the corrosive factors that potentiate violence and understand that to dismiss all human rights violators as "monsters" is unrealistic and dangerous.

Tarantino certainly exposes the dark side of humanity in *Django Unchained* by choosing the institution of slavery for his Spaghetti Western homage. He also provides faces of moral evil in Candie, the proto-Klansmen, and Candie's conniving but fiercely loyal house slave, Stephen. Moreover, Tarantino implicates his audience in violence through the Mandingo fight scene. Tarantino does so through his use of brilliantly written dialogue (which is often marked by a gentility that belies its subject matter), interjections of humor, and scenes of sometimes cartoonish violence. During Candie's dinner side "speech," a disjuncture is created by presenting Candie's case, based on the pseudoscience of phrenology (which has historical fidelity) for the barbarous act of slavery in overly refined language, and the presence of the imposing bleached, white skull of a beloved slave perched in front of him that he mercilessly hacks into to prove his "three dimple" theory visually reinforces this disjuncture between propriety and vileness.

Another illustration of this disjuncture is the much talked about exchange among a cadre of bumbling proto-Klansmen who argue about the impracticality of their hoods that have poorly cut and placed eyeholes and threaten their ability to conduct a raid and "kill a nigger" (Django), which is no laughing matter. Yet the finely crafted dialogue of an odious, racial theory and the pairing of jocularity with ill-fitting hoods and villainous proto-Klansmen, rather than detracting from their immense bigotry, exposes bigotry for what it is: absurd, and in this way, the film makes a compelling moral declaration against such evils.

One of the most nefarious characters in the film, Stephen, and to some degree, Django's brief assumption as a "slaver" call attention to another unsettling aspect of slavery: the implication of victims in their own abuse and the abuse of their victim group—a betrayal that feels particularly evil. This is not a circumstance specific to slavery, as during the Holocaust, *Kapos*, Jewish inmates entrusted with overseeing and disciplining their fellow Jewish captors as well carrying out various concentration camp tasks, could be just as cruel if not more cruel than their Nazi captors. Stephen is the hyperbolic embodiment of a *Kapo*, the ultimate and nightmarish house nigger, who enjoys the comforts his status affords him, which translates to a fidelity to his master. Tarantino's decision to include a character like Stephen in the film and to insert him in scenes of levity bordering on buffoonery (his exchange with Django upon first meeting him and his resentment over setting Django up in the "Big House"), as well as in chilling contexts (like Stephen's cognac swirling fireside parley with Candie when Stephen reveals Schultz and Django's true business with Candie), vividly and scarily, convey Stephen's duplicity, and one cannot help but wonder about the psychology behind it all and appreciate the complexity of the dynamics of victimization.

The aesthetic choices in shooting the Mandingo scene are particularly effective for creating the opportunity for audience members to not only witness but experience cruelty, a trauma that Tarantino fully admits he engineered but did not wish to do to the extent that the viewer could no longer enjoy the film.[23] He accomplishes this through several techniques and one is by leaving to the imagination the image of a man's skull being crushed by a hammer (as the audience hears a percussive hit and squish). Similarly, in the *Reservoir Dogs* torture scene of the undercover police officer, we hear the police officer's ear being severed but do not see it, which makes the scene all the more terrifying. Such intimate, off-screen moments of violence are eerily more unsettling than bloodbath shoot-outs. But more importantly, being amused by the violence in the Mandingo fighting scene in *Django Unchained* creates a vicarious, even if not fully acknowledged, experience of delving into the dark side of our humanity by having our enjoyment of watching a violent scene reflected back to us in watching slave owners take pleasure in watching slaves savagely fight and kill each other; far from encouraging us to avert our gaze or assume the role of voyeur, Tarantino implicates us in the violence, exposing a portion of our dark nature. Referring to *Inglourious Basterds*, Patrick McGee readily confesses that it may very well be the case that these kinds of connections that the director intends or that scholars detect may very well not be apprehended or appreciated by the viewer, but at the very least "the subtextual resonances that Tarantino carefully constructs produce a dissonance that makes it almost impossible for the spectator to walk away from the movie without the feeling that something wasn't quite right, even for a fantasy."[24] In Django, this disjuncture is conjured through the discomfort that arises from witnessing violence, overly civil dialogue about the most uncivil of matters, and making fun of that which is not typically deemed as an appropriate object of humor, which tempers the anxiety that attends directly dealing with uncomfortable issues. It is these methods that do the heavy lifting in *Django Unchained* as opposed to the tandem use of brutality and cheerful music that typifies the asynchronous texture of his scenes.

Counter to Tarantino's typical inclusion of music, in *Django Unchained*, the soundtrack works to fill out the persona of Django and sets the tone of scenes by reinforcing the action with music that appears in sync with the action as opposed to disjunctive with the action. For instance, the opening song, "Django," establishes the credibility of the genre of the film as a Spaghetti Western, not only in its reminiscent musical composition but also in its performance, Luis Bacalov and Roberto Fia, respectively, of Spaghetti Western soundtrack fame, as well as foreshadows Django as the true hero of the film. The bloodiest scene of the film, if not the bloodiest scene of all of Tarantino's films, is the shoot-out in the "Big House" in Candyland. Such a scene is ripe for Tarantino's signature *Reservoir Dogs* treatment: the upbeat "Stuck in the Middle With You" paired with the torture sequence of an undercover police officer. Instead, Tarantino ramps up the kinetic energy of the shoot-out by overlaying it with a rap song, 2Pac's amped up "Untouchable," just as he pairs the befitting male/female duet of the slow tempo and melancholic piece "Freedom" as we see Django helplessly watching the lashing of Broomhilda. Perhaps this more conventional use of music, coupled with the anachronistic use of modern songs in an antebellum film, connects the past of slavery to the present, pointing to the current legacy of slavery as well as to its continued practice in the form of human trafficking and slave labor, as cinema creates and recreates realities, or as Gilles Deleuze argues, cinema is "the organ for perfecting" a "new reality,"[25] and in doing so can make the past present and alter how we perceive our world.

"Bloody satisfaction"

In retelling the suffering of people, films reinscribe the identity of the abused as "victims," and this status may lead to "othering" or unchecked stereotyping. A counter to this tendency is the strand of human rights discourse committed to acknowledging not just what was done to victims but what victims did to deliver themselves from their abusive circumstances, what in human rights discourse is referred to as "rescue behavior" and "resistance"—typically, armed resistance. Paradigmatic illustrations include the Virginia slave insurrection led by Nat Turner in 1831 during American slavery and the 1943 Warsaw Ghetto Uprising in Poland during World War II. Tarantino's *Kill Bill, Vols. 1 & 2*, *Death Proof*, *Inglourious Basterds* and *Django Unchained* take victim "resistance" to a new level: "retribution" and "revenge." Although the first three films are not historically inspired, their protagonists represent a segment of the population that is often vulnerable and victims of abuse: women. The horribly wronged women in these films—to quote the central female protagonist of the *Kill Bill* volumes, the Bride—get "bloody satisfaction," and bloody satisfaction is also secured by the nine-man squad in *Inglourious Basterds*, comprised of eight Jewish-American infantrymen led by a non-Jewish Lieutenant who successfully hunt and kill Nazis, and Django's killing spree of slave owners and their associates. Yet, it is a satisfaction of a profound kind that transcends fantasy and the retribution of each film's protagonists—it is an exercise in catharsis,[26] a catharsis that only such an extravagantly bloody and outrageously funny allohistory can deliver.

Conclusion

During a *Vibe* interview, Jamie Foxx rhetorically asked, "When was the last time you seen a movie about slavery?" and Foxx's fellow actor Kerry Washington chimed in, let alone … "a movie about slavery where a black man frees himself?"[27] Good point. In addition, Reginald Hudlin, one of the producers of *Django Unchained* recounts asking Tarantino, "'Is this the first time in cinematic history that we've seen a slave master beaten with his own whip?' Quentin goes quiet, mind racing through millions of images in seconds, then says, 'Yes.' We quietly fist bump, then go back to work."[28] If nothing else, these questions establish *Django Unchained* as a pioneering contribution to film, but the film also provides an opportunity for conversations about racism, the legacy of American slavery, and human rights in popular media. The text or content of *Django Unchained* capably brings into relief several contemporary human rights discursive points: the complexities of relaying the "truth" of human rights violations; the necessary exploration of the nefarious potential of human nature; and the desire to temper the representation of those who suffer human rights abuses as victims with stories of resistance and heroism. The effective potential of the text of Tarantino's film for productive human rights conversations is due in large part to his aesthetic choices—directorial techniques that both imitate and depart from his familiar disjunctive use of violence, dialogue, music, and humor, all of which encourage a "not quite right" disposition in the viewer that can act as the seed for investigating the complex themes and messages of the film. As Django reminds those he encounters in the film that the "D" in his name is silent, let us be reminded that *Django Unchained* presents an occasion for thoughtful human rights talk.

Without too terribly detracting from the contributions that *Django Unchained* can make to human rights discourse, the film is troubling in several respects that run the risk of compromising its otherwise productive aspects. For example, *Django Unchained* perpetuates representations of "blackness" that are equivalent to being "dangerous" or "violent," what Gormley recognizes in *Reservoir Dogs* as exploiting the "anxieties around the violence of black masculinity in the US."[29] With his muscled and scarred back, expert gun slinging, and murderous spree, Django, too, fits this stereotype, although much of the fear of his "blackness" is assuaged because his rage and retribution is channeled toward deserving targets and for the sake of recovering his lost love. Rather than fearing Django, audiences cheer him on, but his imposing, violent blackness is on display, nonetheless. One could argue that Tarantino engages in another kind of racial stereotyping that appeals to the "commodification" of blackness in his choice of appearance of the character Stephen, who resembles the visage of Uncle Ben of the Uncle Ben's rice brand. Uncle Ben is a dark-skinned, elderly black man with white hair wearing a suit and bow tie (the dress of one who serves, such as a porter or maître d'). The racist overtones of the Uncle Ben image are analogous to Emilie Townes' argument regarding the minstrel "black mammy" archetype—a dark-skinned, rotund, black woman with red lips and a do-rag to match—that typifies the Aunt Jemima brand (note that "Uncle" and "Aunt" were common terms used in the slaveholding South to refer to aged black slaves who were not considered due the honorific address of "Mr." and "Mrs."). Both the "Uncle" and "Aunt" images are illustrations of how a racist (and in the case of Aunt Jemima, patriarchal) society gave birth to the minstrel images of blacks. These manufactured images, designed for product appeal, rarely existed in history as actual persons, yet they persist as a commodification of the identity of the black woman [and man] that was the result of the "hegemonic imagination" of romantic Southerners.[30] Whether Tarantino does so intentionally or unintentionally, by fashioning Stephen's appearance after Uncle Ben, Tarantino perpetuates this commodification of blackness by appealing to the Southern historical memory of blacks as represented by their white oppressors; he, too, exploits a representation of blackness that resonates with, rather than challenges, racist sentiments.

Another issue, one that is seated in the pleasure, and not all together unwarranted pleasure, that Django enjoys from exacting his revenge and that the audience vicariously enjoys from seeing such a historical evil as slavery so spectacularly avenged potentially obfuscates a glaring moral problem: the mimetic violence that Tarantino's films endorse. Just as Jews were marked for life with a tattoo of their inmate number, so did the Basterds indelibly mark Nazis by carving swastikas into their foreheads. Similarly, Django whips his former slaveholder with his own whip and shoots a man in the crotch just hours before that same man had a hold of his genitals. In Tarantino's redemptive histories, victims adopt the same methods of abuse as their tormentors (and may even exceed their tormentor's cruelty and carnage). This forces us to evaluate the violence of victims within a context circumscribed by their respective oppressor, putting victim and oppressor violence on par with one other when their distinction should be maintained, and glorifies the use of violence as an effective remedy to violence and as laudable heroic endeavor.

Last, *Django Unchained* takes bloody violence to cartoonish heights, and film studies is replete with scholarship on both the perils and artistic value of violence. In addition to these concerns is the concern that Tarantino's ultraviolent episodes in the film distract, or worse, diminish the brutal realities of slavery. This is especially concerning, given that many Americans already seem to be inured to the pain of slavery.[31] It is also particularly unfortunate that nearly the sum total of the exaggerated violence in the film converges in the closing 165 minutes. People often remember the last of what they hear and see, and fatigued by the running time and assaulted by the sustained carnage of the film's bookend shoot-out, it is this violence and not the unsurpassed horrors of slavery that may be most remembered. Given the commendable aspects of the film in addressing slavery, this would be a shame indeed.

Notes

1   Jordan Zakarin, "Spike Lee: 'Django Unchained' is 'Disrespectful,' I Will Not See It," http://www.hollywoodreporter.com/news/ spike-lee-django-unchained-is-406313 (accessed July 13, 2012).

2   For a compilation of truncated reviews of *Django Unchained*, see http://www.metacritic.com/movie/django-unchained/critic-reviews (accessed July 13, 2013).

3   Rex Reed, "The Chain Gang: Django Unchained," http://observer. com/2012/12/ the-chain-gang-django-unchained/ (accessed March 24, 2014).

4 Roger Ebert, "Faster Quentin! Thrill! Thrill!," http://www.rogerebert.
com/rogers-journal/faster-quentin-thrill-thrill (accessed July 13,
2013).

5 Scott Foundas, "*Django Unchained* Upends the Western," http://
www.villagevoice.com/2012-12-19/film/django-unchained-upends-
the-western/ (accessed July 13, 2013).

6 A. O. Scott, "The Black, the White, and the Angry," http://movies.
nytimes.com/2012/12/25/movies/quentin-tarantinos-django-
unchained-stars-jamie-foxx.html?pagewanted=all&_r=0 (accessed
July 13, 2013).

7 Paul Gormley, *New Brutality Film: Race and Affect in Contemporary
Hollywood Cinema* (Bristol: Intellect Ltd, 2005), 25.

8 Sonia Tacson, "Considering Human Rights Films," *Human Rights
Quarterly*, 34, 3 (2012), 879. Emphasis mine.

9 Tascon, 864–865.

10 Henry Louis Gates, Jr., "Did Dogs Really Eat Slaves, Like in
'Django'? 100 Amazing Facts About the Negro: Plus, Whether
Slaves Rode Horses or Had Mandingo Death Matches," http://www.
theroot.com/views/did-dogs-really-eat-slaves-django?page=0,0
(accessed July 9, 2013).

11 Joseph Conrad, "Henry James: An Appreciation from *Notes on
Life and Letters*," in *Heart of Darkness Norton Critical Edition*, 4th
ed. ed. Paul B. Armstrong (New York and London: W.W. Norton &
Company, 2006), 286.

12 Audie Cornish, "Tarantino on 'Django,' Violence, and
Catharsis," http://www.npr.org/templates/transcript/transcript.
php?storyId=168193823 (accessed July 9, 2013).

13 Henry Louis Gates, Jr., "Tarantino 'Unchained,' Part 2: On the
N-Word," http://www.theroot.com/views/tarantino-unchained-part-2-
n-word?wpisrc=obinsite (accessed July 9, 2013).

14 Joseph Conrad, "Heart of Darkness," in *Heart of Darkness Norton
Critical Edition*, 4th ed. ed. Paul B. Armstrong (New York and
London: W.W. Norton & Company, 2006), 17.

15 Interestingly, Jamie Foxx was surprised to learn that the mask he
wore in the film was not a medieval inspired invention of Tarantino's
imagination but a replica of the masks slaves were forced to don.
See Parker, 73.

16 Henry Louis Gates, Jr. "Did Dogs Really Eat Slaves, Like in
'Django'?" http://www.theroot.com/views/did-dogs-really-eat-
slaves-django?page=0,0 (accessed July 9, 2013).

17 Tascon, 872.

18 Tascon, 872. The "Other" was first introduced by philosopher Georg Wilhelm Friedrich Hegel and subsequently adopted and modified by other disciplines, such as cognitive psychology and sociology, to refer to the redefining and reimagining a group as fundamentally different from another group, and the result of such an imagining typically cultivates into an "us/them" mentality.

19 Jonathan Glover, *Humanity: A Moral History of the Twentieth Century* (New Haven, CT: Yale University Press, 1999), 6–7.

20 Hannah Arendt, *Eichmann in Jerusalem* (New York: Penguin Books, 2006).

21 Mahmood Mamdani, *When Victims Become Killers: Colonialism, Nativism, and the Genocide in Rwanda* (Princeton, NJ: Princeton University Press, 2001).

22 Philip Zimbardo, *The Lucifer Effect: Understanding How Good People Turn Evil* (New York: Random House Trade Paperback Edition, 2008).

23 Henry Louis Gates, Jr. "Tarantino 'Unchained,' Part 3: White Saviors." http://www.theroot.com/views/tarantino-unchained-part-3-white-saviors?page=0,4&wpisrc=obinsite (accessed July 9, 2013).

24 Patrick McGee, *Bad History and the Logics of Blockbuster Cinema: Titanic, Gangs of New York, Australia, Inglourious Basterds* (New York: Palgrave Macmillan, 2012), 190.

25 Gilles Deleuze, *Cinema 2: The Time Image.* Translated by Hugh Tomlinson and Robert Galeta. Reprint (Minneapolis, Minn: University of Minnesota, 1985). Quoted in 1994 in Kara Keeling, *The Witch's Flight: The Cinematic, the Black Femme, and the Image of Common Sense* (Durham, NC: Duke University Press, 2007), 3.

26 Audie Cornish, "Tarantino On 'Django,' Violence and Catharsis," http://www.npr.org/templates/transcript/transcript.php?storyId=168193823 (accessed July 9, 2013).

27 Parker, 93.

28 Reginald Hudlin, "Django Unchained Producer's Diary," http://www.hudlinentertainment.com/pages/goodies/hudlins-huddle.php?p=10&g=7 (accessed July 9, 2013).

29 Gormley, 26–27.

30 Emilie M. Townes, *Womanist Ethics and the Cultural Production of Evil* (New York: Palgrave Macmillan, 2006), 7–8.

31 Gates, "Tarantino 'Unchained,' Part 2: On the N-Word."

7

Hark, Hark, the (dis) Enchanted Kantian, or Tarantino's "Evil" and Its Anti-Cathartic Resonance

Dara Waldron

"Okay," he said, "listen to this." He started to pace between the drawing tables, looking down at his feet, declaiming in a sharp, barking tenor that Joe recognized from the announcers on American radio. "To, uh, to all those who, uh, toil in the bonds of slavery—"
"Bonds?"
"Yeah." Sammy's cheeks reddened, and he dropped the radio voice.
"Chains, like. Just listen. It's comics, all right.[1]"
—Michael Chabon, *The Amazing Adventures of Kavalier & Clay* (2010)

The signifying chain

Critique of *Django Unchained* begins with the title; the title as beginning: *Django Unchained*. The title uses a name. Yet using the name "Django" in *Django Unchained*, Tarantino can give to his metacinematic excursion the attributes of a double entendre. At its most literal (and perhaps most enjoyable level), the film concerns a black slave, Django (Jamie Foxx), freed by bounty hunter and erstwhile dentist Dr. "King" Schultz (Christoph Waltz) to help hunt down criminal outlaws, before helping Django to find and free his wife. Django is unchained—the film set during the antebellum period—and only when unchained can he enact—irretrievably immoral—revenge against those who have taken her. This is nothing unusual: the film is Tarantino doing what he does—mining history to buck historical norms, and doing so within the fantasy-screen space otherwise known as the cinematic. Did black slaves rise up against their masters? They did. Did they do so in the way Tarantino suggests? They may have done. But we refrain from giving a definitive answer to this question just yet.

The second meaning for the title resides in a theoretical nexus: metacinema as truncated postmodernism. The metacinematic resides in the often-overt references to the Spaghetti Western original, the first *Django* banned for its excruciating violence, exemplified by Django's hiding a machine gun used for gunning down his adversaries in a portable coffin. Yet Django is simply the first in an assembly line of almost thirty Djangos, each tweaking the plot of the last, forming a mini-industry of cheesy, often badly acted, cowboy porn, with a peculiar ability to intellectually please.[2] There is something about Django. There is indeed something cathartic about a white cowboy in brown face, lugging a coffin around, whose contempt for the masses is powerfully expressed by machine-gunning those who interrupt the justice he himself embodies.

Tarantino, however, goes a step further than simply referencing the original Django. He releases Django from his chains. On one level, then, Django, taking the form of a black slave, casting aside his sullen white man in brown face identity, is released from the considered "chain" of a series. On the other, just like the chain found by semioticians in a series of signs, the signifiers the name attaches itself to, Django, is bound by name to the Django chain (or series), his status as "unchained" suggesting rupture from both the series and the slavery of slavery.[3] While the title is emblematic of both (a reference to Tarantino's need to release Django from the slavery of history itself), it is interesting to think of Django enslaved by the semiotic or signifying chain. In a revisionist remix, the semiotic is a series referred to in the vernacular as a chain.

Tarantino's remediation of Corbucci's original title sequence adds further credence to the film as part of a chain. The title sequence for Corbucci's original begins with an out-of-focus close-up of Django pulling a coffin through a dusty sand valley, as his silhouette moves further from the camera. The title appears in a 3D bright red gothic style font. The photographic image is undermined by the black shadows over the information.[4] Luis Bacalov's baritone *Django* accompanies the image, with the lyrics questioning if Django (Franco Nero), who appears for the first time, has always been alone. Love is lost, the song attests. But, whether the universality of love or merely Django's love is lost remains crucially unresolved. In Tarantino's remix, the title sequence syncs with Bacalov's baritone, as the camera focuses on a rock formation in a sandy landscape, panning from left to right as the camera sets upon a chain gang of sundrenched slaves. Django appears in chains. But this Django is chained literally in the diegesis, while chained cinematically—that is, chained to a legacy of former Djangos, his cinematic "name" set against the landscape which embodies it.[5]

Django appears against the backdrop of sun-beaten Negro bodies, the red text of "Django" accompanied by a sharper white symmetrical font for "Unchained," clearly modernist in style (the clash of the past and the modern is of course crucial to the narrative in the film). Tarantino now cuts to a side-angle shot of Django (as singled out). Django appears in profile, alone, yet is actually in chains. If we say he is bound by the cinematic chain, the Django series itself defined by certain modes of behavior, he is also physically bound by the chains in the diegesis. The camera zooms to a side-profiled image of Django, before cutting to Django moving through the terrain as part of a gang. As a technique, cross-cutting gives particular unction to the idea this is a film about the referent—Django (a particular referent fashioned as metacinematic subject)—and the historical,

Django tied to "signifying chains which subsist as such, and which from their structure … (and) influence what appear from the outside as a symptom."[6] If the symptom is defined by the "chain," as detailed here, the fact that the chain gang has no proper judicial status, as legal group, means Tarantino, from the very outset, is problematizing the representation of groups. Django is part of a signifying and semiotic chain, Tarantino's metacinematic Django. But he is also of a gang not yet formulated as a legal group—the chains haven't been "properly" removed (Figure 7.1).

The following takes the "chain" as a critical entry point into issues of representation raised by the film, using the cinematic and historical as a point of departure. I believe that Tarantino is using a subgenre of westerns to explore the issue of representation, referencing the Django series when doing so. Released from the strictly historical—yet a period film—*Django Unchained* forms part of a chain or series. This is a chain that shows Tarantino to be working again in the textual remix of the cinematic. Yet if casting his hero in the form of black bounty hunter, Django, is questionable, this is because it has no cinematic precedence. Hence what it means to have no precedence bears on other questions, such as whether the cinematic representation of a subject bound by no legal group is a subject in the strictly moral sense? And what is a subject when part of a group? These are questions I'd like to put to *Django Unchained* as a cultural phenomenon. I see the film as an inquiry into the cinematic *qua* historic representation of groups. Slavery, and the (non)group around it, is the concern. This, I believe, is ethical, precisely because

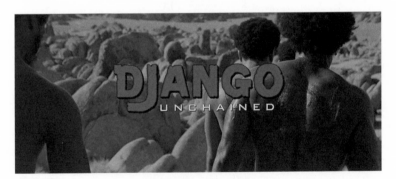

FIGURE 7.1 *The clash of the past and the modern*

representing "slavery" is of issue. I believe that the treatment of "slavery" in *Django Unchained* raises significant issues about representation per se. In one sense, there is a criticality—no less—when dealing with the status of slaves as a judicial group. In another, the group as a historical entity is of critical concern around an issue as big as representing slavery.

Lev Manovich has highlighted the turn, coined as nothing less than the postmodern, as an aesthetic sensibility. Self-referencing—in the form of the metacinematic—has become a terminable end in itself.[7] Manovich adds to Frederic Jameson's now classic critique by stating the "endless recycling and quoting of past media content, artistic styles and forms, became the new 'international style' and the new cultural logic of modern society."[8] He maintains "this new cultural condition found its perfect reflection in the emerging software of the 1980s that privileged selection from ready-made media elements over creating them from scratch."[9] Django is a ready-made form: the Spaghetti Western genre from which he emerges an already reworked, recycled variation on an already existing cultural form: the Western.

Django is, however, unchained. Breaking, yet linked to the past, Django is also singularly defined. There is a need then to understand such singularity—the unchained—when the forming, the naming, and transgressing of the signifying chain is set in motion by the film title. Having made films which flaunt filmicity—the first triumvirate—to films flaunting historicity—the second triumvirate—Tarantino turns to the trauma of history itself as a point of inquiry. *Inglourious Basterds* (2009) reworks history as cinematic fantasia, deconstructing the victim–oppressor distinction pertinent to the cinema of genre. Michael D. Richardson goes as far as to say the film can be said to circumvent "moral restrictions, undermining precisely those moral and ethical standards that are seen as distinguishing Nazi from victim."[10] If reworking "official" history as entertainment has an unethical edge, this is likely because the victim, in this case Jew, cannot remain victimized. When a similar propensity to do evil is projected onto the victim, as that normally associated with the perpetrator, the status of victim is crucially undermined. It can therefore be said that such historical reworking allows Tarantino to challenge the interpellating methods of film; methods reinforcing the status of victims as groups, confronting the "places of intellectual safety and anesthesia" he himself has been accused of inhabiting.[11] The cinema shows how certain groups behave, and film itself generates distinctions between these aforementioned groups. As David Gauntlett states, "interpellation occurs when a person connects with a media text: when we enjoy a magazine or TV show, for example, this uncritical consumption means that the text has interpellated us into a certain set of assumptions, and caused us to tacitly accept a particular approach to the world."[12]

Now, the journey from El Paso to the bowels of Mississippi takes place in *Django Unchained* against the backdrop of evil in the form of slavery, serving as a remarkably subtle inquiry into the culture of interpellation. Interpellation, identification with a particular group, finds itself undermined by the question of evil. A pertinent example of the group is the Jew in Spielberg's *Schindler's List* (1993), or alternatively, the Mexican wetback in Welles's *Touch of Evil* (1958). Each film sees a "group" in crisis, questionably "legal" in status, whose "representation" is complicated by the systematic evil that represses it. The same, I argue, is true for *Django Unchained*. But it is true in ways that are ethically challenging. Kant devised the concept of radical evil when he put forward a moral philosophy unique to the Enlightenment, specifically associated with the moral law. Radical evil evolved from consideration of volition in the will, evil corrupting a law the purpose of which is to counteract evil. Kant believed that maxims that manifest as evil could corrupt the law from the *inside*. Andrew Hewitt puts it succinctly, "radical evil is evil in which the means of overcoming evil are themselves contaminated by the evil that is to be overcome."[13]

Frequent references are made to the Enlightenment in *Django Unchained*—Schultz telling Django's chain gang they should escape to enlightened shores, the Broomhilda/Brunhilde myth—with the film taking the age-old issue of slavery as a point of deliberation (the screenplay for the film refers to Auschwitz in its description of Candyland). Just as naming the Negro avenger, Django, gives to the chain a metacinematic status, the film's status, the revenge narrative, concerned as it is with saving his wife, gives to Django (even though revenge—in a strictly Kantian sense—is considered unbridled "animality") certain ethical merit.[14] This is evoked in a subtitle signifying two things. The first, as mentioned earlier, refers to the unchained status of *this* Django. Django is unchained in a diegetic sense (while still part of the signifying chain). But the title also refers to a narrative unburdened by the chains of institutional history. In this sense, Tarantino maintains an aesthetic guard, of a certain "transtextual filmicity."[15]

The Tarantinian aesthetic may well reside in this filmicity. But the ethic can be said to lie less reflexively, in (rather than the dominant approach to his filmmaking which reverses the order here) contrasting Schultz, a German dentist–turned bounty hunter with Enlightened views of freedom, with the Negro slave Django he frees. Django's "freedom" from the group, however, remains problematic. Schultz partners up with Django, the "freedom" bestowed upon Schultz's slave an expression of their equality. He then offers support to Django when seeking to free his wife Broomhilda (Kerry Washington), who was sold to a different plantation as part of their punishment as runaways. However, the journey to where Broomhilda is enslaved—Candyland, a nirvana of Mandingo prizefighting—is a journey from the quasi-enlightened West, a terrain in which the kind of value system identified with the now disenchanted Kantian Schultz (for whom a morality is maintained against the triumph of evil) still holds, to an estate—Candyland—where "animality expresses itself in conflict … (and) 'the human being's self-will is always ready to break out in aversion to his neighbour.'"[16]

Dehumanized by a ruling ascendency, turned into animals in the brass physicality of Mandingo, radical aversion to the neighbor takes the form of a base evil. The once overextending horizon, Fordian landscape epitomized by the boundless frontier, finds its own abrupt ending in Candyland. The estate is defined by the Mandingo brutalization of one slave by his fellow. It is a point in the film which brings to mind Pier Paolo Pasolini's last film *Salò* (1975), a film interrogating the problems of Italian history. Pasolini points his arrow at the conceptual edifice of fascistic evil.[17] Set at the fall of Mussolini's government, a group of teenagers are herded to an estate by four government dignitaries, in the knowledge that the government is on its last legs. They are then forced into a series of sexual exploits.

Sadistic violence in the form of excruciating torture is explored in minutiae detail, with the teenagers as sexual objects, the purpose of which is to explore pleasure reduced to scientific truth.

Between victim and perpetrator of fascistic evil is a line clearly delineated in the opening scenes of *Salò*, when the suited fascists harangue the teenagers. The teenagers' individuality is erased as each is stripped and classified based on their physiognomy, objectified amid an estate adorned with beautiful Baroque and Modern art. The clean lines of the building, mirroring the sartorial eloquence of the suited fascist dignitaries, contrast with the singularity of nakedness to which the teenagers are reduced; the first scene in the estate is a perfect example of this. The camera remains stable in this scene, transfixed upon the dignitaries surveying the incoming teenagers, some reduced to tears, as the camera itself settles on a physiognomy, reduced—in something of a quasi-documentary style—to animal status.

This victim–victimizer distinction is gradually erased in *Salò* as the dignitaries progress from circle to circle; varying sadist techniques, culminating in a scene in which Enrizio, found sleeping with a black maid, seeks to save himself by demonstrating his allegiance to the cause. The objectification of the human body, emphasized as the sole design of fascists attempting to reduce pleasure to a base sexual "impulse," is singularly reversed; what first appears as a transgression of fascist principles—Enrizio's sexual relationship with a black maid—and a clear "up yours" to the "moral" principles outlined by the dignitaries at the beginning is revealed as remarkably different—or at least possible to read as such. Enrizio is killed for his transgressions, but it is likely, and Pasolini's tongue is firmly in cheek throughout this film,[18] that his expressed loyalty to the fascist cause—having himself engaged in the debauchery Pasolini sees as fascist—is itself more fascist than the fascism espoused by the dignitaries. For it is well known that fascist debauchery, at least that found in the camps, followed few of the rules the dignitaries espouse. Fascism is defined by a "dirty secret," one that sexually exploits before exterminating its victims. Evil, in Kantian terms, is radical, when the law serves as mask for violating the moral law.

Django and Schultz enter Candyland—itself a tongue-in-cheek reference to the kind of theme park performativity associated with Disneyland—and enter a space similar to that constructed by Pasolini, one in which the evil that corrupts presents itself in the form of law and the human form of slave a "group" unworthy of its status. It is worth recounting when Django arrives as a freeman—the roles radically unhinged from their essentially, one might say ideologically consolidated form, that is, the slave as victim, to when Django presents himself "in character" remarkably disinterested in the plight of fellow slave D'Artagnan (Ato Essandoh). "In character" may well be a pun on ideologically *qua* cinematic typologies, types of character otherwise cast as chains.

Django's first "character" is as valet to the illustrious Schultz, dressed in a blue-colored suit as he and Schultz arrive at Big Daddy's (Don Johnson) estate. He is introduced by Schultz as a freeman valet so that he will be treated differently to other black slaves. Yet Django remains sanguine when introduced to Big Daddy and his fellow plantationists, intent on fulfilling his part of the bargain to hunt down the Brittle Brothers. The flashbacks experienced by Django as he wanders through the fields of the estate, in which the beatings his wife was privy to are vividly recalled, her back laden with bloodied scars, encourage identification with his victim status. These are masterfully orchestrated scenes by a somewhat restrained Tarantino, and are, in addition, some of the most captivating in the film: the impeccably dressed Django filmed against the sparse, almost truculent landscape around which the slaves labor.

There is then, on the surface at least, a moral rationale for the bounty, the hunting down of criminals, and indeed the partnership between former slave and master. The bounty, generally regarded as a manifestation of an archaic justice, offers a robust means for countering the evil of slavery. Django remembers the torture of his wife, as he moves through the lush green pastures, his goal to find her tormentors before seeking her out and freeing her. When battling the plantationist system in all its primitive immorality, a system in which the law upholding slavery is the only means for battling it, it is comforting, at least from a purely cinematic and somewhat detached perspective, to identify with Django's identification with violence in somewhat cathartic terms. In this sense, Django's revenge helps pacify an audience whose own deeply held misgivings about the system of slavery can be correlated with the misgivings Django experiences. Django hereby represents a group.

But what if Django is not the moral crusader to be identified with, and arguably the same moral crusader Schultz, with his misgiving about revenge, wants him to be. He is rather, a deeply flawed character, himself marked by "the perversity of the human heart" Kant talks of. In some ways Schultz is a disenchanted Kantian, forced to experience what he comes to define as evil. Yet if Django is just as flawed as the stalwarts of slavery he takes revenge on, what could this say about the trauma of American slavery, to which Tarantino responds, irrespective of whether as a director he wants to or not[19]? Questions such as this find a platform of consideration in an "in character" scene, one which is ultimately crucial to the outcome of the partnership's task. Django and Schultz are traveling through the Candyland plantation and for the first time, as the entourage, made up of Candie (Leonardo Di Caprio) and his henchman, encounter the runaway Mandingo D'Artagnan hiding in a tree. Candie begins by disparaging D'Artagnan's failure to fulfill his five-fight contract, having already won three fights. Before he sets the hunting dogs on him, in what can only be felt as a clear association between the hunted animal and hunted slave, a further reminder of the slave system's reduction of human life to bare existence, Candie inquires as to whether any of the gathering dilettantes are prepared to reimburse him the 500 dollars he has paid for the five-fight contract in order to save D'Artagnan. Schultz appears to break character, before being stopped in his tracks by Django.

A low-angle shot of D'Artagnan kneeling in front of the tree distinguishing his profile from the surrounding cartel is followed by a reverse shot of Candie standing over him, the background cartel blurred somewhat by a distinct lack of focus. The court scene from Fritz Lang's *M* (1931), when child murderer Beckert (Peter Lorre) is chased into the underground chambers of the city by the criminal mob, as the baying mob contrasts his singular profile, is evoked at this point. What appears in *M* as "the almost carnivalesque inversion of a criminal court"[20] is cast in similar terms here, as the distinction between human and subhuman, specifically correlated with the Mandingo slave system, is embellished. A reason for this is that Schultz agrees to reimburse Candie, another manifestation of his enlightened approach to equality, only to be told that no such thing will happen by Django. Clearly confused as to why this is the case

Schultz, for the first time in the film, is disenchanted, uneasy about the real-life reenactment of the Siegfried myth.

"We ain't payin a penny for that pickaninny, we aint got no use for him, ain't that right Doc," Django responds, as he sits upright on his mount and looks down upon Candie. Candie then turns to Mr. Stonesipher (David Steen), who is holding the baying dogs, and requests that he send D'Artagnan "to nigger heaven."[21] Schultz is visibly shaken as D'Artagnan is attacked; Candie staring motionless into Django's gaze.

It is never explained why Django withdraws help for his "fellow" slave. Having been scolded for letting the desire for retribution get the better of his reasoned self, and the plan to reunite with Broomhilda, it is likely Django acts in the way he does to conceal his and Schultz's identity, masking an enlightened propensity to save on-the-run niggers. Indifference to the plight of the runaway Mandingo more readily convinces their enemies that he and Schultz are indeed Mandingo traders. Yet at this point, Django's association with the Negro slave "entity" (dare I say group) from which he is sprung is readily problematized, the slow deconstruction of perpetrator and victim magnified by Django's decision to put personal gain ahead of universal suffrage.

Joan Copjec's critical evaluation of the art of black artist Kara Walker is an interesting point of reference here. In the incendiary violence and sexuality of her black silhouetted paper cutouts, antebellum figures cast against the white walls of the gallery, Walker has caused outrage in the black community—akin, in many ways, to that caused by *Django Unchained*.[22] Copjec finds an engagement with the broader realm of identity in Walker's art. What, she asks, is the nature of the relationship between Walker and the historical "group" her artworks (mis)represent? The caricatured iconography, flattened two-dimensional cutouts have been interpreted as a suitably unethical exploitation of trauma, amplifying and consolidating the crude stereotypes associated with Negro identity as a group. That Walker hails from an affluent black middle-class family, is the beneficiary of institutional awards and grants, is important to note. In this light, Copjec poses a somewhat pertinent question, one which posits Walker's art as a complex engagement with stereotypes in the context of singularity and difference. Copjec asks, "ordinarily, the question is asked how one group—blacks say—differ from others; Walker asks how, given the differences among them, its members can be counted as belonging to the same group."[23]

Difference, and the fact that a group cannot form in the face of such evil, the slave system a manifestation of the radical evil Kant writes of, bears on Walker's art, and equally upon the relationship between Django and the black others to whom he is exposed in Candyland. Tarantino, in the first half of the film, carefully construes Django as a representative of the slave "group," the opening shot of Django chained to fellow slaves the most pervious example. Furthermore, working for Schultz in capturing the Brittle Brothers, whose aggression against black slaves consolidates their capture as retribution for the black people en masse, serves as a platform from which to view Django as a member of a group he seems to seek retribution for. But what if the group is itself the product of a cinematic culture which retrospectively "constructs" something that didn't realistically exist? What if there is no group to speak of? What if Django is chained *and* unchained—unchained in that he is free within the diegesis, yet chained by character types from which he cannot inordinately break? What if the very essence of Django's freedom is that it is paradoxical, and paradoxical in the precise sense that Django is bound by the chains of the metacinematic; that is, he is always "in character", part of a filmicity that precedes him and therefore defines him. In other words, cinema is a representative means used to explore the ethical trappings of cinematic representation.

The second half, when Django and Schultz enter Candyland, where all seemed stained by the irascible presence of evil, further problematizes the issues of representation. In fact, the very question of a group comprised of a set of positive features to which the various members aspire unravels as Django and Schultz enter a world epitomized by the evil tyrant Candie. Candie, like the Nazis who will come after him, espouses a crude form of science, analyzing the skulls of dead slaves as proof of their servility. But, as outlined earlier, the journey from Tennessee into Candyland coincides with a gradual splintering of any preconceived notion of group, with Django distancing himself from the slave issue, indifferent to their plight. His change, from the haute aristocrat at Big Daddy's plantation, to the leather-trousered cowboy, coincides with an increased sense of indifference to the group he apparently represents, the cowboy an embodiment of his increasingly elusive role. No longer a slave, Django lacks the skin color that would allow him to be properly integrated into the white ordinarily "free" population. This lack, and its increasingly shallow freedom, comes to fruition earlier, when Big Daddy attempts to designate Django's status. Schultz requests that Django is given a tour of the grounds, as a wry commentary on Django's "nonstatus" within the group follows in one of the darker more thought provoking moments of the film.

Schultz and Django are greeted by Big Daddy as they arrive at the plantation. Big Daddy, in a white suit, looks from his veranda onto the newly arrived party. When Schultz is invited to "parlez," he requests that Django be given a tour of the estate while being treated as an extension of Schultz's self (a kind of crude variation on Kant's categorical imperative). To accommodate this, Big Daddy says that "Django is not a slave, Django is a freeman. You can't treat him like any of the other niggas around here because Django isn't like any of the other niggas around here. You got it." His house servant Betina (Miriam F. Glover) is confused, responding "you want I should treat him like white folks," when the camera turns to the figure of Big Daddy standing on the outer steps beneath the veranda. The shot changes as the dialogue continues, with Schultz now shown nodding to the house slave's response, as if the imperative has been met. Big Daddy nonetheless interrupts the smooth functioning of his request, unable to process Django's status as subject, declaring, "that's not what I said"—reminding his guest the Enlightenment has yet to penetrate the American Deep South.

Brotherhood and equality, as espoused by the somewhat enlightened, albeit disenchanted Schultz, remain even if morally strained by Big Daddy's eschewed value system. Whether they fall apart when Schultz and Django enter Candyland bears upon whether Django, unable to experience the enlightened freedom Schultz wants for him, yet all too aware of the differences between him and the slaves he encounters in Candyland, has anything positive to identify with. The group Django appears to represent is of course not a group at all, and therefore values—such as brotherhood and equality—Schultz wants Django to maintain, cannot be maintained without a group to maintain them in. Only in a group can brotherhood, itself the positive definition of a group, thrive. And because the black community is not a community but a collection of individuals defined by being exactly what the white population is not, Mandingo a crude expression, the force used in saving Broomhilda, is one contaminated by the evil it redresses, Schultz having warned Django of this.

By the time Django has ridden away with Broomhilda, the Django–Broomhilda relationship a concerted play on the Germanic Siegfried myth, the modern, as expressed by the now dead King Schultz, has also died; and archaic revenge usurps the law and its enlightened pretension to universalism, as expressed by Schultz. If the name King Schultz evokes Germanic royalty, and a morality not unlike Kant's, testing this amid a morally intransigent Wild and Deep South, the law itself—expressed in slavery he and Django encounter in its degrees of maliciousness—espouses the type of radical evil seen by Kant as a maxim corrupting all maxims.[24] This is the corruption Django is contaminated by, the lure of retribution that which Schultz had warned him against. Django's contamination is double: first as the freed black slave who fits no judicial, that is legal category; secondly, as a cowboy on the margins of the civilized world—that of law and order—who seeks revenge as part of a self-decreed moral code.

In a most memorable Tarantino scene, Marcellus Wallace (Ving Rhames), a no-nonsense black ganglord, has been sexually assaulted by two perverts, when—by chance—he is saved by incumbent enemy Butch Coolidge (Bruce Willis). Butch and Marcellus make peace, an agreed silence around what has just occurred, before Marcellus looks into the eyes of his abusers and declares he's going to "get medieval on your ass." The idea—expressed by Marcellus— that revenge is more pleasurable in a medieval as distinct from modern form is revisited on numerous occasions—becoming the *leitmotif* of Tarantino films—and again surfaces in the exorbitant *Django Unchained*. However, while irrational and excessive revenge, beyond meaning and sense, is desirable *and* cathartic, setting a lesser against what appears to be a greater evil, using extreme violence to do so, it can also be said to generate the reverse effect. Rather than a performance of senseless excessive violence, in the knowledge the avenger is a victim subsumed by the passion that their exuberant— albeit justified—revenge takes, the excessive violence is conducted against a group whose lack of judicial recognition at the time the film is set, two years prior to the outbreak of Civil War, is significant. In making his adversary, the slave Stephen (Samuel L. Jackson), the object of his revenge, Django is morally compromised as hero to the group he seemingly represents. Under the frontier identity of the cowboy, he is also chained to the cinematics of "identity" and representation, an (less explicit) equally subservient Uncle Tom, chained to the ethnic code of the cowboy.

The cathartic reversal

When I cleanse myself, I shall kill evil.
—Kasimir Malevich

The downside to Django's nonaffiliation (the fact that the brotherhood he experiences with Schultz is not a brotherhood that can be extended to his own "people") with any diegetic group (meaning the only group he is part of is the Django chain) is that Django is indeed radically unchained, devoid of any signifying link with a group that will come to exist but doesn't as yet exist. Such nonaffiliation sees the mediaeval, archaic impulses trump those espoused by Schultz. This occurs to such an extent that the final front-off takes place not between the victim, Django, and the white population that has tyrannically ruled over him, but between Django and the one character who, within the wide trajectory of characters in the film, represents a mirror image of himself: Stephen. The archetypal Uncle Tom, Stephen's loyalty to Candie is unflinching. His death, killed at Django's hands, after the mother of all shoot-outs, appears, within the context of the victim–victimizer dichotomy, as a cathartic moment. But it is only cathartic in the sense that Django, as victim, and the heroic character identified with by an engaged audience, intervenes—in the powerful discourse we come to call history—to take revenge on those who have persecuted him.

Like Peckinpah, however, who "decisively shifted the moral parameters of commercial cinema away from a clear separation of good and evil and toward the unsettling contemplation of flawed, debased behavior viewed up close and without a secure moral reference point"[25] Tarantino's (non)heroic avenger is not immune from immoral contamination. In fact, the final gun frenzy, which would appear to act as a cleansing device, enabling the spectator to cleanse herself of unwanted association with the "badness" of slavery, is anything but. The result of the carnage is the murder of one slave—whose identification with the white master is so intense to be a point of ridicule—by another. As Django rides away with Broomhilda by his side, the apparition of triumph masks the unsavory fact that triumph itself results from a similarly eschewed process of identification. Only when cast as the "in character" persona of "cowboy," at which point the difference between Django and the other djangos within the canon of djangos collapses, can Django unchain himself from the "group" which we can now say he belongs, the chain of slaves that opens the film an image of this "group." Yet when he does this he is still chained: part of the Django series. Hence, the front-off between Django and the group which he and Stephen—paradoxically—represent, a group not actually a group and the excessive violence of the final shoot-out, expresses the terminable void pertaining to this. The real tragedy is the system of regulated radical evil slavery represents obliterates the "identity" associated with the "group" it represses. It turns history into trauma. Django cannot be the all-conquering savior to the people he appears part of, because the group materializes *ex post facto* in an historical continuum. Django is unchained, the title suggests, but because his people are chained, they cannot be *his* people.

For Richard Prince,

> Tarantino, though, is drawn in his work to violence because he knows it as a movie style, and it is one that he finds compelling. The style itself is the subject and form of his work. Accordingly, he has not moved to explore the psychological and emotional dynamics of violence that might reference life apart from the movies.[26]

The excessive overtly stylized shoot-out that ends *Django Unchained* can, of course, be looked upon as an exercise in formalism, an aesthetic and stylized ending. But it can also be looked upon as a particular riposte to Prince and like-minded critics, the meaning of which is to unpack the impact slavery has on its victims in more nuanced terms than has traditionally been the case. In this sense, Django, shorn of any positive identity attribute ends up acting out his aggression on a subject whose "identity-issues" mirrors his own, Stephen, and the nongroup of slaves he (mis)represents. "When its borders begin to be blurred" (as Giorgio Agamben said of the modern political system)—recall that *Django Unchained* is contemporaneous with the modern politic portrayed in *Lincoln* (2012)—"the bare life that frees itself in the city…becomes both subject and object." [27] In this context, Stephen, subservient to Candie, is no different to a Django subservient to Schultz; subject and object converges, the film playing out around the intransigent dead-end of victims becoming perpetrators. If there is a tragic and therefore cathartic ending to all of this, purging guilt associated with slavery, it is, invariably, countered by the comedic reuniting of Django and Broomhilda. Here the justice which appears to prevail with the death of Stephen has an intrinsically comedic retort, aided by the stylized ketchup violence of the finale. The happiness and triumph invoked by the comedic unification of Django and Broomhilda is purged, only when the bigger issue of slavery and the bare life on which it rests, buoyed by its momentary fantastical explosion, remains the ultimate tragedy.

Notes

1 Michael Chabon, *The Amazing Adventures of Kavalier & Clay* (London: 4th Estate, 2010), 121.

2 Those who complain that *Django* is poorly acted, using cheesy sets and set pieces miss the point. *Django* attracts precisely for these reasons. Its seriousness is too much, Django's inwardness and angst too extreme. It theatricalizes experience in the sense outlined by Susan Sontag in her now classic essay *Notes on Camp*, so that the anguish is experienced as a "glorification of character" (see Susan Sontag, "Notes on Camp"). This emphasis on "character" and being "in character" takes on a much more prescient role in *Django Unchained*.

3 It's interesting to think of the "chain" or series that genre films such as *Django* engender. Would it be wrong to think of generic characterization as itself a kind of slavery, bound by certain kinds of behavior, certain moral principles, and so on?

4 The immediacy of the photograph depends on depth of field, perspectival linearity, and transparency. Bolter and Grusin argue that the "photograph offered its own route to immediacy: the photograph was transparent and followed the rules of linear perspective; it achieved transparency through automatic reproduction; and it apparently removed the artist as mediating agent between the viewer and the reality of the image" (J. D. Bolster and R. Gursin, "Remediation," in *Configurations*, 4, 3 (1996), 31). The asymmetrical type, as if painted on screen, emphasizes the mediation process.

5   Jim Croce's *I Got a Name* (in the soundtrack) singularizes Django against his predecessors, elegantly commenting on his newfound status as a freeman. The song plays when Django, having accepted to spend the winter in partnership with Schultz, sets off across the landscape in his newly acquired cowboy attire. We then see him bathing in a lake up to his neck, fantasizing about Broomhilda. The cinematography, which captures the sublime frontier, echoes the lyrical contestation that naming is in itself a sublime act of freedom; Django has, at this point, "got a name." The song itself takes on a more comic resonance later, when Django and Schultz, having arrived in Mississippi, rendezvous with Candie at his club. Django sits at the bar when a stranger, played by original Django Franco Nero, asks him his name. Django, in a curt response, illustrates the metacinematic bind, the intractable semiotic chain, as smoke is blown outwards and Nero is told that Django's name is Django, with a silent D.

6   Lacan, "Seminar V: The Formations of the Unconscious (Unpublished)," http://www.lacanonline.com/index/quotes/ (accessed June 14, 2013). Is there a certain analytical prerogative to Tarantino's use of slavery, both in the sense of how it's represented cinematically and how it's consequentially dealt with historically?

7   Lev Manovich, *The Language of New Media* (Cambridge: MIT Press, 2001).

8   Manovich, 131.

9   Manovich, 131.

10 Michael D. Richardson "Vengeful Violence: *Inglourious Basterds*, Allohistory, and the Inversion of Victims and Perpetrators," in *Quentin Tarantino's Inglourious Basterds: A Manipulation of Metacinema*, ed. Robert Von Dassanowsky (New York: Continuum, 2012), 95.

11 Pat Dowell's critique of Tarantino takes a now common route. Dowell, perhaps unfavorably, compares Tarantino to his cinematic hero Jean-Luc Godard. He claims that Godard's borrowing, what can be received here as metacinema, is decidedly intellectual while

Tarantino's, borne of the arcade, the unethical opposite (see Dowell, "Pulp Friction: Two Shots at Quentin Tarantino's Pulp Fiction," *Cineaste*, 21,3 (1995), 4–5).

12 David Gauntlett, *Media, Gender, Identity* (London: Routledge, 2002), 27.

13 Andrew Hewitt, "The Bad Seed: 'Auschwitz' and the Physiology of Evil," in *Radical Evil*, ed. Joan Copjec (New York: Verso, 1996), 81.

14 John Kerrigan has written a most instructive text on the legacy of revenge narratives, in both popular culture and classical literature (see Kerrigan's, *Revenge Tragedy: Aeschylus to Armageddon* (Oxford: Clarendon, 1996)).

15 Asbjørn Grønstad devised this term for intertextuality and the ethics around this in Tarantino's oeuvre, most specifically in *Reservoir Dogs* (1992). For a more prescient instruction on how this concept is used, see Grønstad's, *Transfigurations: Violence, Death and Masculinity in American Cinema* (Amsterdam: Amsterdam University Press, 2008).

16 Séan Molloy, "The Instruction of Suffering: Kant's Theological Anthropology for a Prodigal Species" (Unpublished Manuscript, University of Edinburgh, 2013), 16.

17 Both subordinate "moral law" to "laws of self-interest," delivering protagonists to "animal interests and to the principles of predation that govern them"—Joan Copjec, *Imagine There's No Woman* (Cambridge: MIT Press), 146. See here for a more concerted analysis of the Kantian strain in *Salò*.

18 For a more developed discussion of the black humor employed by Pasolini, see Gary Indiana's splendid BFI classic, *Salò or the 120 Days of Sodom* (London: BFI, 2000).

19 Is it reductive to say that Tarantino films are about evil? *Pulp Fiction* (1995) is a film which, like Kant (sic), takes the Biblical understanding of evil as a point of departure. It is worth repeating Jules' (Samuel L. Jackson) infamous final monologue, if only because the idea of man as invariably stained by evil is a suitable premise from which to engage Tarantino's ouevre. Having quoted Ezekiel 25:17 verbatim, Jules offers a reading "I been sayin' that shit for years. And if you ever heard it, it meant your ass. I just thought it was cold-blooded shit to say to a motherfucker before I popped a cap in his ass. I saw some shit this mornin' made me think twice. See now I'm thinkin,' maybe it means you're the evil man. And I'm righteous man. And Mr. 9 millimeter here, he's the shepherd protecting my righteous ass in the valley of darkness. Or it could mean you're the righteous man and I'm shepherd and it's the world that's evil and selfish. Now I'd like that. But that shit ain't the truth. The truth is you're the weak. And I'm the tyranny of evil men. But I'm tryin,' Ringo. I'm trying real hard to be the shepherd."

20 Tom Gunning, *The Films of Fitz Lang: Allegories of Vision and Modernity* (London: BFI Press, 2001), 194.

21 This is probably a reference to "Nigger Heaven," the famous novel by Carl Van Vechten (1926).

22 I'm referring specifically here to Spike Lee's contentious dismissal of a film he hadn't actually seen. While his response amplified the contentiousness of the film as a film about slavery, Lee's own misgivings about a film he hadn't seen personified the very issues Tarantino was addressing: the policing of black characterization in cinema.

23 Copjec, *Imagine There's No Woman*, 83.

24 Immanuel Kant, *Religion Within the Limits of Reason Alone* (New York: Harper Torchbooks, 1960).

25 Richard Prince, *Sam Peckinpah and the Rise of Ultraviolent Movies* (London: The Athlone Press), xi.

26 Prince, 241.

27 Giorgio Agamben, *Homo Sacer: Sovereign Power and Bare Life* (California: Stanford University Press, 1998).

8

Value and Violence in *Django Unchained*

William Brown

*D*jango Unchained tells the story of Dr. "King" Schultz (Christoph Waltz), who liberates a slave, Django (Jamie Foxx), from the Speck Brothers (James Remar and James Russo) so that he can then use Django's familiarity with the Brittle Brothers (M. C. Gainey, Cooper Huckabee, Doc Duhame) to kill and win bounty for them. Having achieved this, and having won bounty on various other outlaws, Django and Schultz decide to find and to liberate Django's wife, Broomhilda (Kerry Washington), from Southern slave owner Calvin Candie (Leonardo DiCaprio). Believing that Candie will not accept a straight offer for Broomhilda, Schultz persuades Django that they should adopt the personae of slavers looking for Mandingo wrestlers, which are one of Candie's passions. Having convinced Candie of their plan, Schultz and Django accompany Candie back to his plantation, Candyland, to find Broomhilda. Candie's perspicacious house slave Stephen (Samuel L. Jackson) realizes that Broomhilda and Django know each other, and as a result figures out that the interest in Mandingo wrestlers is just a ploy. When Stephen tells him as much, Candie then angrily sells Broomhilda to Schultz and Django for the sum of US$ 12,000. However, when Candie insists that Schultz shake his hand to seal the deal, the latter, appalled by Candie's treatment of his slaves, shoots Candie dead. A gunfight breaks out;

Schultz is murdered, while Django kills many people before Stephen uses Broomhilda as collateral for Django to give himself up. Sold back into slavery, Django escapes once again, returns to Candyland, kills all remaining white people and Stephen, and then rides off with Broomhilda, having recovered the papers confirming her freedom from Schultz's dead body.

Although the above synopsis of the film indicates that *Django Unchained* does feature a few twists and turns, the film's story is relatively simple. In fact, one might even say that a bit of twisting toward the end notwithstanding, the film is very straightforward: Schultz finds Django at the film's outset and his original quest— to collect bounty on the Brittle Brothers—is accomplished not 40 minutes into the film. Finding Broomhilda is not difficult, nor is convincing Candie that they are interested in Mandingo wrestlers. They even buy Broomhilda in spite of Stephen's intervention on Candie's behalf. Schultz's refusal to shake Candie's hand then sets into motion the film's violent ending, but basically Django turns up, kills nearly everyone, gets sold back into slavery, tricks his way out of slavery, comes back to Candyland, kills those he left behind, and rides off with Broomhilda. What is more, the characters in the film are relatively simplistic or schematic: Schultz is a bounty hunter who dislikes slavery and slavers; Django loves Broomhilda and wants to save her; Candie is a racist slaver; and the various criminals in the film are, well, criminals—practically all of whom get killed as the film progresses. In other words, *Django Unchained* is a surprisingly simple film—and yet to watch it feels like an intense and engaging experience, as personal experience alone testifies.

If *Django Unchained* is not really a film that involves a complex plot, nor a film that has complex characters, then what is it about the film that does make it so engaging? In this chapter, I shall argue that what makes *Django Unchained* such an engaging experience are the ideas that it suggests regarding a number of things that have at their center the historical fact of slavery. These include the relationship between the body and value—or how it is that we put a price on the human body. This relationship is central to capitalism, which as a result also becomes a core concern for the film, even if it is not named by any of the film's characters. The film also reflects quite consciously at times on the act of seeing and what it means to see, suggesting, as I shall argue, that the concept of disembodied vision is central to capitalism, which in turn sees bodies obtain value, which in turn is at the root of slavery. However, while *Django Unchained* is a film and therefore itself something that we see (meaning that the film might be understood as "capitalist"), it is also a film that encourages us to *feel*—not simply in accordance with any particular character, but to feel (the effects of) slavery itself. In this way, the film uses cinematic techniques, especially sound, in order to become a film that rejects the disembodied regime of vision and visuality that is central to capitalism, and instead to propose that we feel slavery, a sensation that makes slavery—and by extension capitalism— intolerable. As such, *Django Unchained* critiques the way in which slavery and exploitation are—and in mutated form perhaps continue to be—at the heart of capitalism, and how feeling instead of seeing from a distance might help us to become less exploitative, maybe even "better" human beings.

Bodies and value

Django Unchained is unambiguous in depicting the relationship between the human body and value. Repeatedly in the film, we see prices placed on the heads of humans, both dead and alive. Schultz "buys" Django from the Speck Brothers at the film's beginning (for US$ 125), before then killing and collecting bounty (US$ 200) on Willard Peck (Don Stroud), who had been masquerading as Sheriff Bill Sharp in the town of Daughtry, Texas. In their pursuit of the Brittle Brothers, Schultz and Django initially claim to be on the farm of "Big Daddy" Spencer Bennett (Don Johnson) to buy a black woman for US$ 5,000, although they then kill the Brittle Brothers instead. Django and Schultz find and shoot down Smitty Bacall (Michael Bacall) for a bounty of US$ 7,000, as well as members of both the Bacall and the Wilson-Lyle gangs—also for bounty. Schultz then offers US$ 500 to Candie to reimburse him for the loss of D'Artagnan (Ato Essandoh), a wrestler who escapes Candyland because he no longer wants to fight to the death. Django stops Schultz from making this payment and D'Artagnan is instead ripped apart by dogs belonging to the

Stonesiphers, a white family living in/near Candyland and working for Calvin Candie. Finally, Django and Schultz offer US$ 12,000 for an unseen Mandingo wrestler named Eskimo Joe, a sum that eventually they pay for Broomhilda. In other words, it is very clear in *Django Unchained* that bodies can have a price.

It is important to distinguish here between value and price. For, as the figures above suggest, *Django Unchained* follows a logic of increasing the price paid for human bodies—from US$ 125 to US$ 12,000—as the film progresses—with the exception of D'Artagnan, who seems to have been a bargain fighter at US$ 500 if others are worth several thousand dollars. However, while price involves naming a specific figure for a body, value is the name that we can give to the system of pricing as a whole. In other words, it is not that bodies are given "high" or "low" prices that is the concern of *Django Unchained*; indeed, it seems odd that Django is "worth" nearly ten times less than Broomhilda—but the specific figures are perhaps not important except to convey a sense of growing tension in the film (the figures rise as the tension rises). What is of concern in *Django Unchained* is that one puts a price on a human body at all—and the system of pricing is what we (after Karl Marx) are calling value.

It is not a particular price on a human head that is at issue in *Django Unchained*. That is, the film does not say that Django is "cheap" and that Broomhilda is "expensive"—even if, based on the sums exchanged in the film, we can draw this conclusion if we wanted to (though I think we would be wrong to do so). It is the whole system of value that is at issue. For, once a system of value is in place, then it only stands to reason that human bodies become dehumanized (humans are seen as prices rather than as humans) and competition for better and better prices ensues. In other words, we move away from the commonly accepted epithet that no sum of money is worth a human life to the historical reality that human lives have been—and still are—measured economically. And if value produces competition as traders in flesh want to get better prices for the human goods that they are selling, then it logically follows that one begins to treat humans not as "priceless," but rather as ciphers for sums of money: Candie sees D'Artagnan not as a human being, but as an investment of US$ 500. It is only a short step from seeing humans as a sum of money to seeing humans, then, as entertainment (Candie making Mandingo wrestlers fight each other) and as no more than animals.

Now, animals do play a big role in *Django Unchained*, and while it is a common feature of Quentin Tarantino's scripts to give a name to all of his characters—even if we do not hear that name spoken during the film—in *Django Unchained* he seems also to have given names to some of the animals, including the horses Fritz and Tony. We also see goats (in Daughtry), dogs (on the outskirts of Candyland), and buffalo and antelope as Django and Schultz ride together through the winter wilderness of the American South. But while Tarantino—and Schultz and Django—might name their horses, most of the other characters do not. Instead we hear slaves referred to as "black creatures" by Big Daddy—as if the "good" characters in the film treated their animals like humans, while the "bad" characters treat humans like animals—even though, ironically, Candie's chief henchman is a man by the name of Mr Pooch (James Remar in a second role). This dichotomy is not perfect, because when preparing the Mandingo wrestling cover to rescue Broomhilda from Candie, even Schultz starts off by making an analogy between Django's desire to obtain Broomhilda and a man who wants to buy a horse—as if Broomhilda were a horse, a piece of property that one simply buys and sells. However, with regard to Schultz, we shall explore later on his ambivalence as a character (he is ambivalent even if he is not particularly deep or complex, since we know little about him except that he hails from Düsseldorf in Germany, that he has been in the United States some four years, and that he used to be a dentist before turning bounty hunter).

Before returning to the problematic nature of Schultz as a character (and potentially of *Django Unchained* as a whole), however, we should look in more detail at the capitalist system that has at its core the system of value that in turn puts prices on bodies and thus results in slavery.

Capitalism: Slavery

I mentioned the name of Karl Marx earlier. Some readers might be wary that they have before their eyes a communist tract, and/or that I am about to offer up a Marxist reading of the film that is more about (my own?) Marxism than about the film itself. With regard to the former fear, I can only say that while communism has for a long time had a bad press (in the West), as has Marx, too, there has of late been afforded to Marx greater credit as a perceptive analyst of the workings of capital, regardless of whether his prediction with Engels that capitalism become communism has thus far proven wrong. This is not just a case of preexisting Marxists, such as Terry Eagleton and David Harvey, publishing works on and/or that draw heavily on Marx. This is also a case of leading economists, with Paul Krugman most prominent among them, finding prescience and relevance in Marx to help us understand the workings of capitalism today. Within film studies, Marx has also taken on renewed relevance in some quarters, with an edited collection and a monograph by Ewa Mazierska being perhaps the most notable among them.[1] Nonetheless, even if Marx is understood as still relevant today, I do not want to make of *Django Unchained* an unduly Marxist film. Even though it features a prominent German character, the film makes no reference to Marx or Marxism. However, *Django Unchained* is a film about slavery; it is also a film that, as we shall see, inspects the conditions that allow slavery to exist; it is, as a result of this, also a film that is at least in part about capitalism; and therefore, having over the course of several thousand pages examined the workings of capitalism, Marx might be useful in helping us to understand the film.

Marx can be dry, and my intention here is not to hammer readers around the head—as Calvin Candie might do—with lengthy quotations from Marx and brittle analysis of slavery (though I personally am not against such things; exhaustive analysis of slavery—and how it is perhaps the bedrock of all contemporary wealth—is, I suspect, more fruitful than simplistic homilies saying slavery is bad). However, I shall quote Marx once—in order to show how he viewed slavery as forming an integral part of the capitalist system. In a letter to Pavel Vasilyevich Annenko from 1846, Marx writes,

Direct slavery is just as much the pivot of bourgeois industry as machinery, credits, etc. Without slavery you have no cotton; without cotton you have no modern industry. It is slavery that has given the colonies their value; it is the colonies that have created world trade, and it is world trade that is the precondition of large-scale industry. Thus slavery is an economic category of the greatest importance. Without slavery North America, the roost progressive of countries, would be transformed into a patriarchal country. Wipe out North America from the map of the world, and you will have anarchy—the complete decay of modern commerce and civilisation. Cause slavery to disappear and you will have wiped America off the map of nations. Thus slavery, because it is an economic category, has always existed among the institutions of the peoples. Modern nations have been able only to disguise slavery in their own countries, but they have imposed it without disguise upon the New World.[2]

As noted by Ken Lawrence, who also cites this passage, Marx's views on slavery did develop over time, and my desire is not to ignore as much.[3] However, the above quotation does indicate the way in which Marx viewed slavery as being integral to bourgeois industry—not just in North America, but globally. Colonialism might have involved colonizing countries extracting material resources from colonized countries, thereby making the colonizing countries richer; but it is the extraction of human bodies ("human resources") from the colonies that Marx singles out as "giving the colonies their value": when a human is bought and sold, but never to be paid for the labor that they give to their owner, then the owner extracts something close to pure profit from that person, meaning that the owner's path to riches is accelerated enormously when compared with instituting what we might today call legitimate working conditions and acknowledging workers' and human rights. In short, then, slavery was part of a worldwide "get rich quick" scheme; and it was the bourgeoisie that got rich, by no means the slaves.

As mentioned, *Django Unchained* does not refer directly to Marx and the film is not obviously one about global capital. It seems, instead, to refer more specifically, or better exclusively, to slavery in the United States—not the United States as part of a global economy. However, there are perhaps signs of globalization in the film: as mentioned, Schultz is a German, while Candie has an affectation for all things French. Meanwhile, Django frees himself at the end of the film from a group of Australian and American slave drivers (Tarantino himself plays an Australian, with a somewhat questionable accent). In other words, *Django Unchained* arguably does allude to globalization, and perhaps the global nature of the slave trade, through the film's references to non-American places and its non-American characters (which also include an Italian played by Franco Nero, to be discussed below). While the "global" aspects of *Django Unchained* are not particularly pronounced, they are nonetheless there.

Furthermore, much more pronounced in the film is the way in which slavery is key to *bourgeois* society, which translates here into white American society. During the film, we see Candie enjoying seeing slaves fight each other; but perhaps more telling is that while the prices of human lives are continually negotiated, it is always white people bartering over black people. At the film's outset, Schultz haggles for Django with Dicky Speck; he initially barters with Big Daddy for a female slave before finding the Brittle Brothers; and of course he tries to convince Candie that he is after a Mandingo wrestler rather than Broomhilda. The latter case is important: Candie is furious when he finds out that Schultz is after Broomhilda, not a Mandingo wrestler, and yet his reaction—and the need for the film to develop the Mandingo wrestler subterfuge as a whole—is problematic.

Some viewers might ask themselves: why not just ask Candie up-front for Broomhilda? Since he does finally sell her, Schultz and Django might have saved themselves a lot of trouble—and Schultz would have saved his own life—if they'd *not* developed the Mandingo wrestling ruse, and had instead just tried to buy Broomhilda outright. Sure, they may not have got a good price for her—but as it turns out they pay a sum described as "ridiculous" for her anyway, and lots of people die in the process. It's not that Schultz and Django should be beyond making mistakes; they misjudge how things will go at Candyland and while the consequences are disastrous, to err is only human. Important is the fact that they want to get Broomhilda for a good price. And Candie's anger seems to stem as much from the fact that he was close to selling Broomhilda for less than she is worth in the eyes of Schultz and Django than from the fact that the Mandingo wrestler cover was, precisely, a cover. In other words, Candie is riled for not getting maximum profit out of Broomhilda; otherwise he appears to care little for her and could happily see her come and go if it were not that Schultz and Django specifically want her.

Let us be as clear as possible. Candie's anger might also be motivated by racism: he does not want to be conned by a black man, Django; nor does he want to see a black man walk away with a black woman from his slave plantation. Similarly, what partially drives Candie might also be straight disappointment that he is not going to sell a Mandingo wrestler to Schultz. But mainly it seems that Candie's motivation is to maximize profit and to get as much money as possible out of Broomhilda, about whom he otherwise seems to care little and on whom he thus might otherwise place little value. In other words, slavery here is a tool for *bourgeois* (and white) enrichment, with slaves as playthings whose price may rise and fall, and who are really just an excuse for white folks to do business with each other—with business here being a euphemism for going into competition with each other, the competition being who can make the most amount of profit from a human body.

Furthermore, the links between slavery and industry more generally are demonstrated in *Django Unchained* by the way in which Django is sold back into slavery to the LeQuint Dickey Mining Company. Over the course of the film, we do see some slaves picking cotton in the fields—in particular at Big Daddy's plantation. But the majority of slaves in the film are house slaves owned by individuals. The reference to the LeQuint Dickey Mining Company reminds us, then, of the *corporate* nature of slavery; slavery does not simply involve a history of house servants, but also a history, described by Stephen to Django, of people turning big rocks into little rocks. As anyone who has seen *Harlan County USA* (Barbara Kopple, USA, 1976) will know, mining has long since involved exploited workers without slavery (what Marx might characterize as "disguised slavery"), even though mining produces the raw materials needed to construct or provide energy for our whole society. In other words, slavery is not confined to the home, but is key to industry as a whole; it is an integral part of capitalism. Furthermore, *Django Unchained* opens with shots of the Speck Brothers driving a chain gang of slaves through the desert. We see shots of Django himself set against the rocks of the desert—with one shot in particular featuring the focus being pulled from rock to Django and back again. We might be tempted to read the image as suggesting Django to be some "force of nature", but in the context of the LeQuint Dickey Mining Company, it also seems as though Django is a reminder of how the creation of capitalist society's entire infrastructure—predicated upon turning those big rocks into little rocks—historically is rooted in actual and disguised slavery.

The act of seeing

There is a strong emphasis in *Django Unchained* on vision and seeing. This comes through most prominently in a couple of places. First, there is an amusing scene in which some proto-Ku Klux Klan members argue about how they cannot see through the bags that they wear on their heads. Not only does this sequence convey something along the lines of *racists are blind, or blinkered, people*, but it also suggests two other things: that vision is embodied, and that capitalism relies on denying this. Vision is markedly embodied for these characters precisely because the bags prevent them from seeing; they cannot distance their eyes from their bodies in such a way that they see from a detached perspective; instead that their eyes are attached to their heads, which are also on their shoulders is palpable to them. Nonetheless, one of the intended upshots of wearing bags with eyeholes is to create anonymity while also preserving vision—to become eyes without bodies that look upon and judge those whom these would-be Klan members deem to condemn. In other words, the Klan gives itself authority by appealing not to an embodied vision, but to an "objective" or detached vision that sees "accurately" the world and which therefore is justified in its racism.

The link between would-be disembodied vision and capital in *Django Unchained* is made even clearer when one of the Stonesipher trackers, played by Zoë Bell, is pictured looking at a stereoscope. The mysterious female wears a bandana around her face, meaning that she, like the bagheads, gives the impression of being a pair of disembodied eyes. That she looks at a stereoscope reinforces her role as detached observer. What is more, the stereoscopic image that she observes is reminiscent of the early stereoscopic images that artist Ken Jacobs has recently reworked in his experimental 3D film, *Capitalism: Slavery* (USA, 2006). *Capitalism: Slavery* uses early 3D images of slaves and slavers to demonstrate the way in which capitalism makes spectacles of human bodies, turning them into an attraction to be consumed, and thus depriving them of their humanity. It is thought that the stereoscopic image is of the Poseidon Temple at Paestum in Italy;[4] however, the image appears so briefly in the film that it is hard not to imagine seeing the two figures before the temple as slaves, as we see in the Jacobs film. Indeed, blogger Mstrmnd makes exactly this mistake—albeit without reference to Jacobs.[5] Given that the female tracker is a slaver, her use of the stereoscope thus suggests how spectacle (bodies as attractions that one looks at in a supposedly detached manner) is key to capitalism and slavery, since when one sees bodies as merely means for entertainment, one no longer sees bodies as human beings. In other words, one is already a step closer to seeing bodies as commodities that one buys and sells. *Django Unchained*, then, offers an implicit critique of the regime of vision and visuality that allows capitalism and slavery to take place.

The bagheads and the masked woman suggest disembodied vision, and how the perpetuation of its possibility helps to spread capitalism and its concomitant emphasis on bodies as objects, or as slaves. This we can compare to Django himself, who uses a spyglass to spot Ellis Brittle as he flees Big Daddy's plantation after the death of his brothers Big John and Lil Raj. Django observes through the glass, but he also uses this as a tool to interact with, rather than detachedly to observe, the world: Ellis is not to be looked at, but to be shot. This perhaps accounts for the use of rifle sights in the film as a whole: Django and Schultz can both see, but they do not just look, they also change (by shooting).

Since *Django Unchained* is a film, one might say that it, too, partakes of a system of looking, since the film viewer sits in the movie theater and observes spectacular bodies-as-attractions that are somehow dehumanized, objects for entertainment rather than real people. However, this is not really the case, since *Django Unchained* is a film that invites not a disembodied, but precisely an embodied viewing position on the part of the spectator. Let us look at how this is so, and how we can read the film's Spaghetti Western aesthetics in a political/politicized manner.

Feeling the Spaghetti Western

Django Unchained contains numerous rapid zooms in and zooms out, with zooms in marking particular moments when a character's attention is grabbed: Schultz's arrival in the dead of night to the Specks' chain gang, seeing a black man on a horse in Daughtry, drawing attention to Candie when we first meet him. The technique of the zoom works well, since we see (and, via "whooshing" on the soundtrack, hear) movement as part of vision: the rushed blur of image as the camera reframes suggests the physical nature of the image and the camera, thereby lending to the image a metaphorical "body" that in turn suggests not a detached film viewer, but an embodied viewer who does not simply observe, but who also in various respects *feels* the film.

There are other ways in which *Django Unchained* is less a film that one simply watches and more a film that one also feels—with the film's sound design being integral to this. To take one small example, when Schultz and Broomhilda meet in Schultz's guestroom at Candyland, she takes a glass of water. We hear the gentle sound of fingers on glass as Broomhilda stands before Schultz. Almost certainly this was not sound captured on set, but rather sound added to the image in postproduction; a tiny detail—the musical echo of fingers touching glass—transports us from detached observers of the scene to viewers who think about and recall what it feels like to have a glass in hand. It is not necessarily that we can feel all that Broomhilda is feeling (nervousness, perhaps anticipation, as she sizes up this German man before her), but we certainly are given a greater sense of the physical dimension of this moment.

When it comes to the graphic violence for which Tarantino is of course famous, then, this haptic/feeling dimension of his filmmaking is only more clear: deep thuds, horrific squelches of blood, and the crushing of bone all make of violence not something that we can watch for amusement, as does Candie with the Mandingo wrestling slaves, but something that we feel. By *feeling* the cruelty of slavery, we are in a much better position as viewers to understand more fully the effects of slavery, and thereby we might be in a position not to replicate or perpetuate slavery today. What is more, rather than being a film that is complicit with the very system of detached observation that enables slavery in the first place (seeing people as objects/attractions/spectacles, not as human beings) means we commodify them, with the commodification of bodies being at the core of overt and disguised slavery, both of which are logical extensions of capitalism, as per Marx (Figure 8.1).

FIGURE 8.1 *The two Djangos*

During the scene where Candie watches his slave Big Fred (Escalante Lundy) beat the slave (Clay Donahue Fontenot) of Amerigo Vessepi, it is perhaps important that we see Franco Nero as Vessepi, since Nero played the title character in Sergio Corbucci's *Django* (Italy/Spain, 1966). This is not simply a case of Nero being Italian and thus suggesting globalization. Instead, it is about how Nero embodies the Spaghetti Western genre as a whole. David Martin-Jones writes about how *Django* (among other Spaghetti Westerns) involves action-packed situation after action-packed situation, thereby becoming structurally episodic, as opposed to linear and causal, while also reflecting the way in which modern capital besets those who live under it with an endless/relentless set of obstacles to overcome.[6] The long duration of *Django Unchained*, its lack of interest in detailed character development and/or plot complexity, together with the film's equally episodic structure similarly suggest the relentless nature of capitalism—but here with a fantasy happy ending rather than with the more muted ending of Corbucci's original film (Django survives, but with crushed hands, while his love interest, María (Loredana Nusciak), gets shot, even if she also survives). In other words, not only does *Django Unchained* strive to be a film that is to be felt as much as it is to be seen, which means that its form works alongside its content in critiquing capitalism and slavery, but it also belongs to a genre that has been read historically as a genre that is critical of contemporary global capital.

Issues with the film

For all of the above "politically correct" criticism that *Django Unchained* offers up, however, the film is more ambiguous than I have so far suggested. Schultz is a bounty hunter and his killing humans for money is not dissimilar to slavers also using and killing humans for money—a parallel that he himself draws. In other words, the prices put on the heads of criminals is simply another part of the capitalist world that has the placing of material value on human life at its core; indeed, it demonstrates that the law is complicit with placing value on human life, and thus perhaps encouraging of slavery. Perhaps it is for this reason that Django must operate outside of the law by the film's end if he is to escape slavery with Broomhilda and to become a freeman—since the law in fact offers him no protection. Nonetheless, while we side with Schultz and Django, both are also killers—Schultz, for example, kills the Speck Brothers, various bagheads, and Calvin Candie even though there is no bounty on their heads. Furthermore, Schultz buys Django at first; he is happy to comply with slavery when it suits him, it seems.

We could potentially excuse Schultz for his bad traits, because he learns to hate slavery, and it is Candie's treatment of D'Artagnan that disgusts him so much that he refuses to shake hands with him (thereby compromising his own, Django and Broomhilda's lives, ironically enough, because of his refusal to touch Candie). However, the perceived flimsiness of *Django Unchained*'s plot is also problematic: even though we are encouraged to *feel* the violent moments in the film, they nonetheless seem gratuitously staged rather than embedded into a film in which the violence seems inevitable. Perhaps this conveys the gratuitous nature of historical violence toward slaves; nonetheless, Tarantino still walks a fine line between critiquing and repeating the very same structures that he critiques. And while *Django Unchained* does not repeat the common cinematic trick of implying that slavery's end was uniquely the work of white men, as is perhaps suggested in both *Amistad* (Steven Spielberg, 1997) and *Lincoln* (Steven Spielberg, 2012), nevertheless we do see repeated scenes in which white characters teach black characters how to act or speak, or the meaning of words (e.g. Django not understanding what "positive" means)—meaning that even when free, Django will not be accepted into the world until he effectively becomes "white" (arguably a fact reasserted by the film's spectacularly violent end—Django in the end simply kills everyone, with savagery his only option for success—before performing circus tricks/becoming a spectacle/attraction on his horse).

However, while these issues remain unresolved here, I conclude by suggesting the relevance of *Django Unchained* to today. Slavery is today outlawed in most/many parts of the world, even though there are as many if not more people in slavery today as there have been at any other period in history.[7] However, as per the Marx quotation earlier in this chapter, overt slavery in the United States and other parts of the world was simply the flipside of "disguised slavery"— which is the exploitative workings of capitalism more generally. "Disguised slavery" is, broadly speaking, the implementation of a society in which humans are treated as commodities, and who are underpaid and who must work all the hours God gives them simply in order to keep afloat, if possible. As slavery was, for Marx, the phenomenon that in fact held together capitalism worldwide, so is capitalism today (even if overlooking slavery as it continues to exist) held together by the exploitation of the working classes. For this reason, *Django Unchained* still speaks of inequality and exploitation today, not least because the regime of vision criticized in *Django Unchained* is still very much in power (perhaps it is no coincidence that 3D and spectacle are once again central to contemporary visual culture). *Django Unchained* may present a fantastic escape from this world—thereby ultimately offering a spectacle that does not quite help us to think around or rethink the issues of social inequality that face us today. But in helping us to feel slavery, and to feel the suffering brought about by the whip and the rope, perhaps we will be in a better position not to look at our fellow humans as spectacular attractions offered up for our consumption/entertainment, but as, precisely, our fellows, whom we treat as we would expect others to treat us.

Notes

1 Ewa Mazierska, *From Self-Fulfilment to Survival of the Fittest: The Representation of Work in European Cinema from the 1960s to the Present Day* (Oxford: Berghahn, Forthcoming). See also her edited collection *Work in Cinema: Labour and the Human Condition* (London: Palgrave Macmillan, 2013).

2 Karl Marx, *The Poverty of Philosophy: A Reply to M Proudhon's Philosophy of Poverty* (New York: International Publishers, n.d.), 94–95.

3 See Ken Lawrence, "Karl Marx on American Slavery," *Freedom Information Service* 1976, http://www.sojournertruth.net/marxslavery.pdf (accessed July 8, 2013).

4 See Jeff Hathaway, "*Django Unchained* Stereoscopic Photo," *What the...*, January 14, 2013, http://jahathaway.wordpress.com/2013/01/14/django-unchained-stereoscopic-photo/ (accessed July 8, 2013).

5 See Mstrmnd, "The Last Auteur: *Django Unchained*," *Mstrmnd*, http://www.mstrmnd.com/log/2390 (n.d.) (accessed July 8, 2013).

6 David Martin-Jones, "Schizoanalysis, Cinema and the Spaghetti Western," in *Deleuze and the Schizoanalysis of Cinema*, ed. Ian Buchanan and Patricia MacCormack (London: Continuum, 2008), 75–88.

7 See William Brown, Dina Iordanova, and Leshu Torchin, *Moving People, Moving Images: Cinema and Trafficking in the New Europe* (St Andrews: St Andrews Film Studies, 2010).

PART THREE

Questions of Race and Representation: What Is a "Black Film"?

9

Thirteen Ways of Looking at a Black Film: What Does It Mean to Be a Black Film in Twenty-First Century America?

Heather Ashley Hayes and Gilbert B. Rodman

I.

We can agree that the notion of a unitary black man is as imaginary (and as real) as Wallace Stevens's blackbirds are; and yet to be a black man in twentieth-century America is to be heir to a set of anxieties: beginning with what it means to be a black man. All of the protagonists of this book confront the "burden of representation," the homely notion that you represent your race, thus that your actions can betray your race or honor it.... Each, in his own way, rages against the dread requirement to represent; against the demands of "authenticity."[1]

—Henry Louis Gates, Jr, *Thirteen Ways of Looking at a Black Man* (1997)

*D*jango Unchained was heir to a particular set of racial anxieties from its inception, carrying a "burden of representation" on its shoulders that no single film could possibly bear. In contrast to the black men who populate Gates' book, however, *Django*'s burden was taken on knowingly and willingly. The people who made *Django* knew they were making a risky film. They also knew that "dangers are not places you run away from but places that you go towards."[2] Making a film about chattel slavery in the United States is an inherently dangerous undertaking that is guaranteed to upset a lot of people. *Django* isn't an important film, however, simply because it pushes people's buttons: it is an important film because it tells a story about race and racism that desperately needs to be told.

II.

Django is a black film. More than that, it is an exemplary black film. We would even go so far as to say that it is one of the most important black films of the century...which is where some of you will interrupt us to point out that Quentin Tarantino, the film's director and screenwriter, is white, making it impossible for *Django* to be a black film.

So we begin again, in order to clear up some misconceptions about "black film" that stand in the way of the argument we want to make about *Django*. Typically, the term is used to refer to films that are made by (actual) black people, offer depictions of (authentic) black experience, and/or are primarily intended for (real) black audiences. Taken at face value, *Django* falls short on at least two of those counts—but taking things at "face value" is precisely the sort of uncritical interpretive stance that we want to avoid. Embedded in the claim that white directors cannot make black films are two problematic assumptions: one about essentialism, and the other about auteurism.

The essentialist assumption is that there is a direct relationship between people's racial identities (on the one hand) and the aesthetic, cultural, and/or political characteristics of whatever art they make (on the other). Only black people, the argument goes, have enough firsthand knowledge of "the black experience" to represent that experience properly in art. Because white people lack such knowledge, their efforts to tell black stories and/or work within black aesthetics are inevitably inferior and/or politically problematic (e.g. *Mississippi Burning*, Alan Parker, 1988).

Meanwhile, the auteurist assumption is the widespread belief that we can reasonably attribute cinematic authorship to lone individuals. Typically, this distinction is reserved for directors, though occasionally producers may be granted such honors. So Alfred Hitchcock (rather than screenwriter Ernest Lehman) is widely understood as the main creative force behind *North by Northwest* (1959), Stanley Kubrick (rather than Stephen King) gets credit for *The Shining* (1980), Orson Welles (rather than Herman Mankiewicz) is celebrated for *Citizen Kane* (1941), and so on.

In the case at hand, auteurism tells us that Tarantino—and only Tarantino—deserves credit (or blame) for *Django*. Meanwhile, essentialism tells us that Tarantino's whiteness prevents him from understanding black culture well enough to capture its essence on film. Taken together, these philosophies tell us that *Django* can't possibly be a black film, because only directors matter when it comes to cinematic authorship, and because white directors cannot make black films. Neither of these seemingly straightforward claims, however, manages to reflect the realities of authorship or identity very well.

If auteurist visions of the singular genius artist work at all, it is only for the small number of aesthetic practices that are feasible as solo efforts: for example, novel writing, poetry, painting. Most art forms, however, simply do not function this way. As the most collaborative of all major art forms, however, film is especially ill-suited to this particular understanding of authorship. Even the most low-budget feature film requires creative input from hundreds of different people. To be sure, a film's cast and crew are not an egalitarian commune in which artistic decisions are made through a democratic process, and directors exert far more creative control over "their" films than, for example, key grips or lighting technicians. But directors never make films alone. Whatever creative genius Tarantino brought to the making of *Django* (and there was certainly plenty of this), it would not be such an aesthetically rich, politically savvy film without significant creative labor from its principal actors (Jamie Foxx, Samuel L.

Jackson, Christoph Waltz, Leonardo DiCaprio, and Kerry Washington), its cinematographer (Robert Richardson), its editor (Fred Raskin), and its production designer (J. Michael Riva).

Moreover, even if one believes that Tarantino really is the principal creative force behind "his" films, his most striking auteurish contributions come from his liberal borrowing of shots, scenes, costuming, and characters from Blaxploitation films, martial arts films, Spaghetti Westerns, and the like. Significantly, most of those genres depend heavily on non-Western, non-white, and/or hybrid aesthetic styles. To be sure, Tarantino blends these genres in ways that give "his" films a recognizable feel of their own, but the resulting style is much closer to a remix or mash-up aesthetic than it is to traditional notions of a unique auteurish vision.[3]

Essentialism is no more helpful than auteurism when it comes to understanding the relationship between artists and their creations. The apparent clarity of a categorical label (such as "black") hides a messy, thorny tangle (dare we call it a briar patch?) of context-dependent significations: enough so that, when one examines it closely, the essentialist equation—for example, that only "real" black people have access to "authentic" black experience—implodes.

The identity side of the equation depends on the notion that "race" is a natural phenomenon that can be used to accurately place the peoples of the world into discrete, nonoverlapping categories. In actual practice, however, such categories vary significantly over time and across space—which makes them cultural and historical fictions, rather than universal, scientific facts. Moreover, as the growing population of self-identified multiracial people[4] should remind us, those categories overlap a great deal. Racial identity is more of a finely granulated spectrum than a simple binary choice, which, in turn, makes it impossible to anchor the identity end of the essentialism equation with any precision.

Meanwhile, at the other end of that equation, the abstract quality that is "blackness" is even harder to pin down. Debates over the politics of putatively black cultural texts routinely flounder over the question of what counts as "authentic" blackness in the first place. *The Cosby Show*, for example, was *both* celebrated for its realistic portrayal of "mainstream" (i.e. bourgeois) black life *and* critiqued for its failure to represent the struggles (cultural, social, economic, political) that "real" black people face in their everyday lives—with much of the debate hinging on the question of whether upper-middle-class blacks or working-class blacks count as the "true" face of black America.[5] What such divergent analyses reveal is that "blackness" is far too variable to be understood as a homogeneous phenomenon. There is no singular "black experience," and no individual black person has access to the full range (or even the majority) of different "black experiences" that one might name.

III.

In spite of all their unavoidable messiness, racial labels perform significant (albeit not always positive) work in the world. The imprecision of such terms doesn't render them meaningless or useless, but it suggests that we need to think about them in more nuanced ways than essentialism allows. With respect to "black film," we want to suggest two related possibilities: one descriptive, the other prescriptive.

On the descriptive side of things, we would argue that "black film" doesn't refer to a set of natural, essentialist truths as much as it does a range of culturally specific *articulations*.[6] Writing about this issue as it relates to rap, Gil Rodman has argued that,

> insofar as they help to shape the musical terrain in significant fashion, these racialized ways of categorizing music are very real— and very powerful—but they are not simply natural facts. Rather, they are culturally constructed articulations: processes by which otherwise unrelated cultural phenomena—practices, beliefs, texts, social groups, and so on—come to be linked together in a meaningful and *seemingly* natural way.[7]

We can—and should—understand "black film" in a similar capacity, especially insofar as many films that fit the category quite "naturally" (e.g. Blaxploitation classics such as *Coffy* by Jack Hill, 1973, and *Foxy Brown* by Jack Hill, 1974) were actually made by white directors and thus fail the essentialism/auterism test. By the same token, this understanding of the term frees us from having to squeeze *all* films made by black people into the category by default.[8]

More prescriptively, we want to suggest that the modifier "black" should be understood as a marker of progressive, anti-racist politics, rather than as a "simple" statement about a filmmaker's racial identity. Addressing a much broader version of the essentialism question (i.e. "Black Like Who?"), *Village Voice* columnist Joe Wood makes the following argument:

> We need a clearly articulated theory of coalition—political, economic, and cultural coalition across biological, and class, and cultural lines—towards the liberation of African and other marginal peoples. Such a theory would be a new "black" objectivism, a grand theory that would include an expansive and progressive definition of "blackness," one to describe African folk who choose "blackness," as well as any fellow travelers …. Next go-round we'll drop Clarence Thomas quickly, and with theoretical confidence. And we won't confuse questions about Michael Jackson's African authenticity with the nuts and bolts concerns—his political loyalty, his "blackness." … If "black" the term is to be of any use, it ought to mean something, and not any old African thing.[9]

To understand "black film" in *this* context is to insist that any film worthy of the label do significant work toward identifying, condemning, and dismantling systemic and institutional racism. It also necessarily opens the door for "fellow travelers"—political allies who are not black—to make "black film."

This is not to advance some sort of simple "colorblind" claim in which racial identity is wholly irrelevant to someone's capacity for making black film. Undoubtedly, it is much harder for white filmmakers (be they directors or not) to make "black film" than it is for black filmmakers to do so, since most white people have never had to face the harsh realities of systemic racism in the way that people of color (filmmakers or not) are forced to every day. Because the meaningful relationship here, however, is about articulation, rather than identity, it is still possible (even if it is rare) for white people to make black films. We would not claim that all (or even most) of Tarantino's directorial efforts meet the criteria we describe here—but *Django* most certainly does.

IV.

One of the most troubling aspects of the auteurist bias in the public discourse around *Django* is the way that commentators have routinely overlooked the agency of the film's black actors. For example, a *Moviemaniacs* roundtable interview with Tarantino and the film's major cast members begins with a question for Tarantino about *his* "sense of responsibility … in terms of making a movie that brings slavery out front and center like this," but the actors are not addressed as if they, too, had made important creative contributions to the film. Instead, they are asked for their thoughts on Tarantino's artistic vision: for example, "When you read the script, what were your first impressions?"[10] Similarly, in an ABC News *Nightline* interview with Tarantino, Foxx, and DiCaprio, Cynthia McFadden spends several minutes focusing on the risks that Tarantino took by using "the n-word" so liberally, and the risks that DiCaprio took by choosing to play a character of "pure evil" in a supporting role—but she has nothing to say that recognizes the choices (risky or otherwise) that Foxx made with respect to *Django*. Even Henry Louis Gates, Jr., (who really should know better) spends the majority of a three-part interview with Tarantino about the film[11] asking questions that frame the film as the exclusive by-product of Tarantino's creative vision.

Perhaps the most ironic version of this erasure of black agency, however, comes from Dexter Gabriel. In an otherwise convincing essay about the history of Hollywood's (largely abysmal) efforts to depict slavery, he derides *Django* as nothing more than a white fantasy about black acquiescence:

> While Django (Jamie Foxx) takes his cues from Blaxploitation, his fellow slaves seem throwbacks to the old plantation epics. Dazed and voiceless, they stand around as backdrops to Django's heroics. The one standout role, the sinister Stephen (Samuel Jackson), recycles "Lost Cause" caricatures of the faithful Tom stitched together with contemporary African-American folklore on so-called house versus field slaves. In this post-racial revision of American history, mythical Uncle Toms and sadistic whites collude to maintain slavery—a clever moral escape-hatch to negate white guilt and guarantee crossover appeal.[12]

Gabriel may have a point about the silent docility of most of the slaves in *Django* (though, even here, he ignores the fact that film extras are *supposed* to be voiceless backdrops), but his larger argument only works if the film's black actors are too "dazed and voiceless" to contest (what he takes to be) Tarantino's racist fantasies—or, worse, if those actors are modern-day Uncle Toms who are all too eager to do a white man's bidding. Either way, Gabriel winds up transforming Foxx, Jackson, and company into the very same caricatures that he dismisses as "mythical."

V.

Time and time again, *Django*'s black actors have to interrupt their interviewers and/or reframe the questions being asked of them in order to be seen as anything more than Tarantino's hired help. Significantly, when those actors get to talk about what *they* find important about *Django*, they consistently demonstrate a deep concern for the representational burden the film carries, and offer nuanced thoughts on the film's anti-racist politics. For instance, Foxx has to forcibly insert himself into the *Nightline* conversation mentioned earlier in order to establish that he, too, had significant choices to make with respect to the making of *Django*. Eventually, he manages to tell a story about filming the scene in which Broomhilda is whipped:

> Everybody, people on trucks, people in catering, stood still ... I asked for a certain piece of music, Fred Hammond, "No Weapons." So as Kerry's being strapped up, we played that song.... I looked over and saw a girl who had never been on a set before and she was one of the extras and her hands went up like this, she started testifying. And as everybody had tears in their eyes, you felt the ancestors, you felt the significance of why we're doing this film and showing it this way.[13]

Here, Foxx doesn't just push back against critiques of the film's "disrespectful" representation of slavery (specifically Spike Lee's claim that the film is an insult to his ancestors): he makes a powerful argument about the historical and political significance of the project to the black cast (stars and extras alike) who worked on it.

Similarly, during the *Moviemaniacs* roundtable, Washington explicitly points out that the film is about "the *institution* of slavery" (emphasis added), and claims that she chose to make this film precisely because it offers an exceptionally positive vision of black empowerment:

> So many of the narratives that we've told in film and television about slavery are about powerlessness, and this is not a film about that.... I was very moved by the love story, particularly in a time in our American history when black people were not allowed to fall in love and get married because that kind of connection got in the way of the selling of human beings.... I said to Quentin in our first meeting, I feel like I want to do this movie for my father because my father grew up in a world where there were no black superheroes, and that's what this movie is.[14]

In that same roundtable, Jackson has to remind the interviewer that he (Jackson) isn't just a voiceless body ("You don't want to know how I felt about all this? ... I have intelligent things to say about this shit."). When the interviewer presses on, trying to get Jackson to discuss the "psychology" of Stephen and the "small power" he has in the story, Jackson responds, "Small power? I'm the power behind the throne. What are you talking about? I'm like the spook Cheney of Candyland. I'm all up in that."[15]

Jackson's point about Stephen's backstage power also describes the roles that he, Foxx, and Washington played in shaping the film. They are the power behind Tarantino's throne. They not only have intelligent things to say about *Django*: they had intelligent things to contribute to making it the articulate condemnation of structural racism that it is.

VI.

Without a doubt, the most controversial character in *Django* is Stephen: the cunningly cruel "head house nigger" of Candyland.

Why, some critics have wondered, did Tarantino make the nastiest villain in the film an over-the-top Uncle Tom? Where is the racial justice in a narrative that asks audiences to see Stephen, rather than Calvin Candie, as Django's ultimate nemesis? Why does a film that invites audiences to cheer for a black man who gets paid for killing white men (and who openly enjoys that aspect of his job) end with us rooting for that black man to kill another black man?[16]

Implicit in such questions is a problematic desire for a simplistic morality play, in which heroes and villains obey a predictable set of color-coded rules. In classic Hollywood westerns, the heroes wore white and the villains wore black. For some of *Django*'s more skeptical viewers, this code apparently should have been flipped and then applied to skin tone, so that all the heroes were black and all the villains were white. Stephen clearly violates this typology, and he does so without a single sympathetic on-screen moment that might allow viewers to understand him as an erstwhile hero who has simply lost his way.

Of course, the absolute purity of Stephen's villainy makes him an easy character for audiences to hate—and, in many ways, this is precisely what makes so many critics uncomfortable with him. The idea that audiences—especially white audiences—might openly yearn for the violent death of a fictional black man is, after all, awfully close to the very real disdain that so many white Americans have for real black people. We can't entirely blame some critics for finding Stephen to be distasteful. Yet we can't quite share this reading of his character. Partially, this is because a weak, ineffectual Stephen would have been just as problematic in terms of representational politics. It's hard to imagine any of the critics who disliked Stephen as a villainous race traitor being any happier with him as a shuffling, ignorant pawn for Candie to push around. Partially, this is because we see a great deal of political value in a film that places *two* exceptionally strong black characters at the center of the action— even if they happen to be on opposite sides of the narrative struggle— especially since it's still rare for a mainstream Hollywood film to give audiences even one such character. And partially, this is because, in the context of the film's action, it's almost impossible to actively root for Stephen's righteous comeuppance without simultaneously rooting for Django to deliver the *coup de grâce*. If *Django*'s white viewers are going to cheer for the death of a black villain, they also have to cheer for the triumph of a black hero.

Mostly, though, we have a difficult time condemning Stephen as a character because, short of making the entire movie about him (and probably not even then), there is no feasible way to portray the "head house nigger" of one of the largest and most notorious plantations in the South as a sympathetic or politically progressive character. The problem with Stephen, after all, isn't in how Tarantino scripted the character: it's that he exists at all. Critics who want something else from Stephen seem to believe that there's some politically acceptable way to depict a black slave whose primary role in life is to keep his wealthy white owner's household running smoothly: a role which, in turn, requires him to actively participate in maintaining the brutal hierarchy of racial oppression that lies at the core of the plantation system.

VII.

Django's real villain is not Stephen or Candie. It's not even a person at all. It is racism. And not racism as a scattered problem produced by isolated, individual bigots, but racism as a pervasive, unrelenting *structural* phenomenon—and this is a large part of what makes *Django* such an unusual and important film. There is nothing romantic about *Django*'s depiction of life in the antebellum South. From top to bottom, this is a world built out of brutal oppression and cruel racial hierarchy. If there's a physical embodiment of racism in the world of Django, it's Candyland: the notorious "big house" that every slave knows about (and fears being sold to), and that—significantly—Django blows to smithereens at the end of the film.

There is, of course, a very long history of "big houses"—from English manors to Dixieland plantations—in mainstream film and television: glorious mansions, populated by chivalrous gentlemen and virtuous ladies who, in turn, are waited on hand and foot by a sizable retinue of happy, loyal, docile servants/slaves. What makes Candyland so different from a century of fictional big houses before it, though, isn't the treachery of Stephen. If anything, Stephen's role is no different than that of any semi-privileged house slave in classic Hollywood depictions of antebellum plantations. To the degree that such characters were ever presented to viewers as more than just silent props, they showed fawning, unswerving devotion to their masters and mistresses: they were always already race traitors.[17] The difference here is that *Django* doesn't take the house's side. Stephen can only be a villainous character in the context of a film that gives us "the big house" as the fundamental structural evil that needs to be destroyed.

Within the world of the film, there was no need for Django to do anything about the "big house" at all. Except for Stephen, he had killed everyone who stood between him and freedom for himself and Broomhilda—and Stephen was no longer a threat. Django could have killed Stephen—or even just walked away from him—without touching the house at all. Django doesn't blow up Candyland because *he* needs to do so: he blows it up because *we* need him to do so. By this point in the story, *Django* has spent nearly three hours painting a picture of a society permeated, top to bottom, by a deep and abiding racism. If Django is going to triumph against *that* villain, he can't just kill off Candie and Stephen and then ride off into the night with Hildy: he needs to kill "the big house" too. Stephen's final speech underscores this point emphatically:

> You ain't gonna get away wit' this, Django. They gonna catch yo' black ass. You gonna be on the wanted posters now, nigger. Them bounty hunters gonna be lookin' for you. You can run, nigger, but they gonna find yo' ass. And when they do, oh I love what they gonna do to yo' ass. They ain't gonna just kill you, nigger. You done fucked up. This Candyland, nigger! You can't destroy Candyland! We been here—they's always gonna be a Candyland! ... Can't no nigger gunfighter kill all the white folks in the world! They gonna find yo' black ass!

Stephen knows—and the inclusion of this speech in the film is an attempt to make sure that *we* know—that Django's destruction of Candyland is supposed to symbolize something bigger than just the end of a quest for personal revenge. But Stephen also knows that

Django's victory is only a symbolic one: that you can't kill systemic racism with nothing but bullets and dynamite. It will survive this setback. And it will come after Django with a furious vengeance.

VIII.

Discussing *My Beautiful Laundrette*, and the debates that it sparked in Britain in the 1980s about the politics of racial representation, Stuart Hall writes,

> Films are not necessarily good because black people make them. They are not necessarily "right-on" by virtue of the fact that they deal with the black experience. Once you enter the politics of the end of the essential black subject you are plunged headlong into the maelstrom of a continuously contingent, unguaranteed, political argument and debate: a critical politics, a politics of criticism. You can no longer conduct black politics through the strategy of a simple set of reversals, putting in the place of the bad old essentialist white subject, the new essentially good black subject.[18]

Ironically, the major U.S. filmmaker whose work embodies this philosophy most fully is Spike Lee. Part of what makes Lee's films powerful and refreshing is that they routinely portray blackness as a variable, multifaceted, heterogeneous phenomenon. *Do the Right Thing*, *Bamboozled*, *School Daze*, *Jungle Fever* (etc.) all contain an incredibly broad range of black characters. Some are sweet, some are mean; some are good, some are evil; some are smart, some are dumb; some are kind, some are cruel. We are invited to root for some of them to succeed and for others to get a truly righteous comeuppance. There is no singular blackness in Lee's cinematic worlds: an extraordinarily rare thing in Hollywood's depictions of black America.

Nonetheless, Lee has done a curious two-step around *Django*. On the one hand, he wants to avoid talking about it publicly. On the other hand, he's made very public statements claiming that film is "disrespectful to [his] ancestors."[19] It's likely that part of Lee's disdain for *Django* is tied up with his long-running public feud with Tarantino over the latter's heavy use of the word "nigger" in "his" films.[20] We can respect Lee's point that "nigger" signifies in *much* different ways when it's used by white people than when it is by black people. White artists, after all, have a long, ugly history of "blackening" up in ways that read more as theft than as love.[21] At the same time, however, we respect Tarantino's artistic right to create characters who say and do all sorts of "bad" things. And given the physical brutality that Tarantino's characters routinely inflict on one another, it's hardly surprising that they speak to each other using coarse, impolitic language. Moreover, a film that focuses on slavery in the antebellum South is almost obligated to use "nigger" on a regular basis. In this sense, *Django* is a lot like *Huck Finn*: if you are going to tell this story with anything that pretends to have a semblance of historical accuracy, then you *have* to use the word—and use it a lot.

More problematically, Lee has said that he has no intention of seeing *Django*. And it's disheartening to see him so thoroughly condemn a film he hasn't seen—not the least because Lee has been subject to plenty of that sort of blind, reactionary condemnation himself. Lee has also wandered into some exceptionally murky waters with respect to ugly representations of black people on the big screen. For example, *Bamboozled*, while a brilliant piece of work, produced its own fair share of audience discomfort with its depictions of contemporary blackface minstrelsy. Perhaps more than any other working director, Lee should be aware that smart, politically progressive films about racism will necessarily take their audiences places where they will be uncomfortable. Discomfort for discomfort's sake, of course, is not desirable in and of itself—but Lee should at least see the film before he declares that its representational politics are unacceptable.

IX.

As filmmakers, Lee and Tarantino are actually very much alike: they are both opinionated, cantankerous, provocative directors and screenwriters, each of whom has risked alienating the established powers in Hollywood by pursuing controversial projects that suit their respective artistic and/or political visions. One of the main places where their careers have differed, however, is that Lee has had to struggle far harder than Tarantino in order to get his films financed and completed— Exhibit A: *Malcolm X* (Spike Lee, 1993); Exhibit B: Lee crowdfunding his most recent film, *Oldboy* (Spike Lee, 2013). That Tarantino could get "green-lighted" to make a film like *Django*—a violent revenge fantasy in which a black man rides roughshod over antebellum white America—must be a bitter pill for Lee to swallow.

In this light, though, the proper target for Lee's righteous anger isn't *Django*, or even Tarantino. It's the larger set of institutional forces related to how Hollywood makes films about black culture, history, and politics. To this end, we would pose the following questions:

- Why have Hollywood films featuring black action heroes enacting revenge fantasies largely, if not entirely, been confined to the "campy," marginalized genre of Blaxploitation? Where is the black version of *Rambo*? Or *Die Hard*?

- Why is it that the few Hollywood films that focus on slavery and the antebellum South inevitably do so from the perspective of white characters? Why hasn't there been a major motion picture made about Nat Turner, Harriet Tubman, or Frederick Douglass?

- Why is it that black directors and producers trying to make politically charged films about contemporary versions of "the black experience" can only seem to find major financial backing to do so if they focus on ghettos, gangsta rap, and/or modern-day minstrelsy?

- Why is it that major "message" films about U.S. racism are either historical narratives (*The Butler*, *The Help*) that allow viewers to believe that racism is entirely a thing of the past, or they're "sensitive," "balanced" stories (*Crash*) that pretend that racism is nothing more than individual bigotry (and to be "fair," remind us that people of color can be bigots too)?

Ultimately, though, the amount of attention given to the ongoing Lee–Tarantino "feud" arguably does more to reproduce Hollywood's racism than it does to address that problem. What truly matters here, after all, isn't the public sniping between two "bad boy" film directors—even if that may provide gossip blogs with useful material—since that "story" merely reduces the issue to a clash of individual personalities, and it directs our attention away from the broader structural problems that help to fuel that feud in the first place.

X.

Apparently, the film about slavery that America *really* wanted in 2012 wasn't *Django*: it was *Lincoln*. Directed by Steven Spielberg, with a masterful performance by Daniel Day Lewis in the title role, the film tells the story of Lincoln's embattled month surrounding the passage of the Thirteenth Amendment. Both films were written and directed by white men, but—tellingly—all seven of the principal actors in *Lincoln* are white, while three of *Django*'s five principal actors are black. *Lincoln* also somehow manages to erase Frederick Douglass from the historical debates that led to the passage of the Thirteenth Amendment, opting instead to focus on white abolitionist and congressman Thaddeus Stevens. The only black characters in *Lincoln* come to us as nameless soldiers, slaves, or—most troublingly— Stevens' lover, whose only appearance in the film comes after the Thirteenth Amendment's passage. She's so grateful that she falls right into bed with Stevens.[22]

The sharp differences in the ways that *Django* and *Lincoln* were (or were not) celebrated also tell us something significant about the sad state of contemporary U.S. racial politics. Perhaps the most obvious example of this differential treatment comes from Oprah Winfrey. In her latest television series, *Oprah's Next Chapter*, Winfrey dedicated an entire episode to *Lincoln*, which she prefaces by telling her audience:

> If you haven't seen Lincoln yet, I encourage you to do so. There really is nothing like it.... The entire film will reach into the

marrow of your soul…. I can't remember when I've experienced anything like it…. [It] is a masterpiece.[23]

Two weeks later, Winfrey aired a two-part episode on Jamie Foxx, in which *Django* went unmentioned until the second hour of conversation. Tellingly, when Winfrey finally broaches the subject, she does so in clearly disapproving tones: "Everybody had read the script, a lot of people felt that this movie shouldn't have been made…. How are you going to react when people say 'what'd you do that for?'" Foxx responds with conviction: "I don't feel that I'm dumb…and I don't feel that Samuel Jackson is dumb, and I don't feel Quentin Tarantino or Kerry Washington—we're not dumb guys in this business…. I didn't worry one iota of is it gonna be ridiculed" (Oprah Winfrey Network, 2013). Even after this eloquent defense of the film, however, Winfrey still seems unwilling to take the film anywhere near as seriously as she does *Lincoln*. All she can manage is the vague and awkward statement: "You can't imagine the conversations we're having today after seeing it."

Meanwhile, *Lincoln* was widely praised, not just as a major cinematic achievement, but as a significant political intervention. *New York Magazine* published a lengthy list of laudatory comments on the film from a bipartisan range of politicians (Rich, 2013). *Washington Post* columnist Ruth Marcus seemed to think that *Lincoln* could somehow fix everything that is broken about the U.S. government:

> President Obama hosted a screening of Steven Spielberg's Lincoln at the White House the other day. He should do it again— and again and again. For the subsequent showings, though, the president ought to invite every member of Congress. *Lincoln* is exquisitely crafted and even more exquisitely timed…. It presents useful lessons in the subtle arts of presidential leadership and the practice of politics, at once grimy and sublime.[24]

In this "Oprahfication" of *Lincoln*, the racial significance of the historical events that (supposedly) lie at the core of the narrative— the end of chattel slavery—is pushed to the side, in favor of a less threatening set of lessons: how powerful white men can protect the nation (and their own power) while keeping the culture's major racial hierarchies firmly in place. By contrast, *Django*'s far more pointed lessons about the horrors of institutional racism have largely been ignored, and the film itself pushed to the margins of the "national conversation" on race (the one that we never *quite* seem to have) because the film is (allegedly) too controversial to take seriously—as art or as politics.

XI.

Django begins with an astonishingly huge historical gaffe: a factual error so blatant, obvious, and easy to correct that it almost *has* to be deliberate. After the opening credits finish, a title appears indicating that the year is 1858—"Two years before the Civil War." And, of course, the Civil War didn't begin until April 1861. It is possible that somehow *no one* connected with the film's production knew their U.S. history well enough to have caught this basic mistake. Or, perhaps, that no one cared enough to fix it.

More plausible, however, is the notion that Tarantino knew that the opening title was historically inaccurate in ways that millions of filmgoers would spot, and that he *chose* to keep the mistake in place deliberately. From the very start, he is signaling that he's more interested in telling a good story than he is in showing rigid fealty to historical facts. There is historical precision to be found here, but it revolves more around Tarantino demonstrating how thoroughly he knows cinematic history than it does around capturing the realities of mid–nineteenth century Southern life.

In part, *Django* demonstrates the depth of Tarantino's knowledge of, and love for, the B-movie genres from which he borrows so heavily. But the film is also a lesson about the problematic history of mainstream cinematic representations of blacks, slavery, and the (antebellum) South.[25] What *Django* underscores—brutally so, at times—is the degree to which Hollywood has spent the past century producing outrageously dishonest visions of Dixie. *Django* doesn't do this, however, by presenting us with a painstakingly researched quasi-documentary account of what southern life in the 1850s was really like. Instead, it takes those old stereotypes, places them on the screen before us, and systematically shows us the social and political horrors that hide beneath their surfaces. Glamorous scenes of happy slaves enjoying the pastoral beauty of the land are merely Django's feverish fantasies of being reunited with his wife. A lush shot of a sumptuous cotton field is sullied by a violent splattering of blood from off-screen. The perfectly mannered, aristocratic southern gentleman first appears in a private club where he is watching two slaves try to beat each other to death with their bare hands. The genteel southern belle turns out to be little more than a glorified sex trafficker. And so on.

Very few mainstream Hollywood films have attempted this sort of frontal assault on Hollywood's history of racially problematic representations. Probably the best known (and, more sadly, probably the most recent) of such efforts is the 1974 comedic send-up of Hollywood westerns, *Blazing Saddles*. Most of the film's humor revolves around the appointment of a black man as the new sheriff of the all-white town of Rock Ridge: a setup that allows for ninety-five minutes of nonstop satirical jabs at bigotry and racial stereotypes. The film fared so well upon its initial release that it was re-released six months later to help boost a sluggish summer at the box office for Warner Brothers. In 2006, the Library of Congress deemed it worthy enough to preserve in the National Film Registry. Tellingly, though, *Saddles* was almost never released, because Warner Brothers' executives were scared that the film's racial politics were too controversial, and that the film's use of "the n-word" would make it box office poison. As director Mel Brooks tells the story, what ultimately saved the film was a wildly successful in-house screening of a rough cut for studio underlings, and the fact that Brooks' contract gave him control over the film's final cut.[26]

Arguably, part of what allowed *Saddles* to succeed—and still be heralded decades later as a classic—is that it used comedy as its primary weapon against "racism." Also, it framed the problem as one rooted in individual bigotry, rather than as a structural, institutional force that shapes the entire culture. We don't want to downplay the degree to which *Saddles*, like *Django*, was a politically dangerous film to make. But if a film that skewers racism as *gently* as *Saddles* does was almost too risky to release, then it's not surprising—though it *is* disappointing—that it took nearly forty years before another mainstream Hollywood film would dare to tackle the subject so directly again.

XII.

Many observers have criticized *Django* for what it *doesn't* do in terms of portraying racial solidarity between blacks, or in terms of gesturing, even minimally, toward collective rebellion. And there's some truth to be found in such critiques. Django is not a selfless martyr, choosing certain death over personal freedom because he cannot bear to leave his brothers and sisters behind in chains. Nor is he a remade Nat Turner, leading armies of slaves into open rebellion against white supremacy. His mission is purely personal (though not entirely selfish), and he is never distracted from it by even a moment of sympathetic solidarity for the obvious suffering of other black folk around him.

And that's okay by us. At least for now. *Django* gives us a vision of racism as a cancer that permeates the entirety of U.S. society, top to bottom—and that is an extraordinarily rare thing for Hollywood. We can live with Django, the fictional man, getting to live out his personal revenge fantasy and ride off into the night with his one true love, because *Django*, the movie, doesn't let audiences pretend that slavery was really just some sort of pleasant *Gone-With-the-Wind*-style costume drama after all.

More importantly, there's a cruel, racialized double standard to the complaints that *Django* "fails" to present a sufficiently revolutionary narrative of black liberation. Hollywood hasn't exactly demonstrated much desire, after all, to make feature films that portray *anyone's* collective rebellion against systematic, institutional oppression. Sergei Eisenstein might have been able to make that sort of thing work in the heyday of Soviet silent film (*Battleship Potemkin*, *Strike*, *October*), but Hollywood invariably transforms collective political struggles into purely personal battles between individuals. Class struggle gets reduced to the heroic efforts of lone individuals to win a symbolic fight against a singularly evil boss (*Norma Rae*). Feminism gets reduced to the heroic efforts of lone individuals to win a symbolic fight against a singularly evil man (*9 to 5*). Anti-racism gets reduced to the heroic efforts of lone individuals to win a symbolic fight against a singularly evil bigot (*Driving Miss Daisy*). So why is it that people of color—both in real life and in fiction—are routinely expected to sacrifice their personal desires and ambitions for the sake of the collective? White people who work hard and overcome obstacles to rise out of poverty are never expected to "give back" to the impoverished communities they left behind—much less be publicly excoriated for "failing" to do such a thing in the ways that people of color are.[27]

Similarly, one of Hollywood's oldest and most popular tropes is the man (or, occasionally, a woman) who sacrifices *everything*—family, friends, career, home, etc.—for the sake of his one true love, because "love conquers all"…though, significantly, this trope only really gets applied to white love. Hollywood, after all, rarely gives us love stories about people of color at all, and it certainly doesn't give us any such tales where the love in question is *celebrated* for being selfish and all-consuming in the way that white love routinely is. How many Hollywood films are there about white men who have somehow lost their one true loves, and where the driving force behind those narratives is a purely personal quest to rescue/reclaim those lost women, rather than a political mission to repair/destroy the broken criminal justice system, military-industrial complex, capitalist economy, or whatever systemic inequity it is that has separated the happy couple? Dozens? Hundreds? Thousands? *Casablanca* may be the last major Hollywood movie where a white hero willingly sacrifices his chance to be reunited with his one true love for the sake of a larger, more noble cause—and that is arguably because, for all its charms, the film functions more as a form of historical war propaganda than as a love story.

This begs the question: if Django were a *white* action hero, would we be having this debate at all? When Hollywood starts routinely giving us mainstream films dedicated to collective political agendas, then—and only then—can we start worrying about why more black heroes aren't positioned as the leaders of such efforts. In the meantime, however, expecting Django to (deep breath here) rise up out of slavery, learn to shoot better than anyone else in the South, scour the countryside for his lost wife, free her from bondage, organize and lead a massive slave revolt, destroy the plantation system, and bring about an end to white supremacy across the land (you can exhale now) is an unfair burden to place on any hero—or any film.

XIII.

We recognize that this advice flies in the face of what is usually regarded as sound, practical sense.... The conventional wisdom teaches that the way to achieve social change is to strive to express the desires of an existing constituency. That is perhaps why most social reform is so useless. We are calling for the opposite: a minority willing to undertake outrageous acts of provocation, aware that they will incur the opposition of many who might agree with them if they adopted a more moderate approach. How many will it take? No one can say for sure. It is a bit like the problem of currency: how much counterfeit money has to circulate in order to destroy the value of the official currency? The answer is, nowhere near a majority—just enough to undermine public confidence in the official stuff.[28]

There are people (e.g. Kaplan, 2012) who want to open up a long overdue conversation about slavery in the United States, but who insist that the proper way to do so is with sober, serious ruminations on the historical realities of slavery and its aftermath: not with foul-mouthed, blood-soaked bits of commercial entertainment. We've got nothing against sober, serious debates about racial politics—the nation could stand to have more of those—but we cannot fully accept this particular line of argument.

For starters, we reject the assumption that popular culture is an inappropriate ground on which to wage serious political struggles. "The popular," after all, is one of the major sites where such battles have been waged for decades: far too long now to pretend that it doesn't matter in this regard.[29] It's true that "the popular" isn't the only place where such debates need to occur, and that many (though by no means all) of the necessary solutions to the problem of systemic racism need to be implemented in other spheres. But if anti-racist critics refuse to fight on this turf, then they—we—are effectively ceding it to the other side, which, in turn, almost certainly means that we will lose those struggles. "The popular," after all, is often the site where people's hearts (rather than their minds) are won or lost. And we will not win the fight against racism simply by appealing to people's intellects.

We also reject the assumption that this conversation can only take place in polite, bourgeois language and contexts.[30] We're not interested in chaotic free-for-alls, where everyone shouts as loudly as they can, nobody listens, and nothing is ever resolved. But the topic at hand is ugly, brutal, and painful. It *demands* a sense of outrage and anger—especially if we're still struggling with the topic 150 years after the formal end of slavery—and to pretend otherwise is to diminish the scope and the importance of the problem.

Django is not a perfect film, nor is it a perfect representation of either the horrors of U.S. slavery or the realities of black resistance. But then again, no such perfect representation exists. Or could. For all of its faults, *Django* puts a much stronger, much more forceful condemnation of institutional and structural racism in the public eye than anything that, say, Barack Obama has managed to accomplish from the White House. We don't believe that *Django* can fully resolve the political problems at stake here—that's an impossible burden to place on any single film—but we do believe that it pushes the conversation along in valuable and productive ways.

Notes

1 Gates, 1997: xvii.

2 Hall, 1992: 285.

3 See Lessig (2008). We have nothing against either remix or mash-up aesthetics, nor are we claiming that they are somehow less creative than more traditional forms of art. We draw this distinction simply to note that Tarantino's "signature style" of filmmaking doesn't fit traditional models of auteurism well in the first place.

4 To be clear, there's nothing new about people with multiracial heritages. There is, however, a growing tendency for multiracial people to self-identify as such, rather than to claim single, normative racial identities for themselves.

5 See here Michael Eric Dyson, *Reflecting Black: African-American Cultural Criticism* (Minneapolis: University of Minnesota Press, 1993), 78–87; Herman Gray, *Watching Race: Television and the Struggle for "Blackness"* (Minneapolis: University of Minnesota Press, 1995), 79–84; Sut Jhally and Justin Lewis, *Enlightened Racism: The Cosby Show, Audiences, and the Myth of the American Dream* (Boulder, CO: Westview, 1992).

6 Stuart Hall, "On Postmodernism and Articulation: An Interview with Stuart Hall," *Journal of Communication Inquiry*, 10, 2 (1986), 45–60.

7 Gilbert B. Rodman, "Race ... and Other Four Letter Words: Eminem and the Cultural Politics of Authenticity," *Popular Communication*, 4, 2 (2006), 107.

8 For example, despite the presence of John Singleton (*Boyz n the Hood*, *Rosewood*, *Shaft*) in the director's chair, we are not convinced that *2 Fast 2 Furious* (sequel to the Vin Diesel vehicle, *The Fast and the Furious*) counts as a "black film."

9 Joe Wood, "Niggers, Negroes, Blacks, Niggaz, and Africans," *Village Voice* (September 17, 1991), 39. See Stuart Hall, "Old and New Identities, Old and New Ethnicities," in *Culture, Globalization, and the World-System*, ed. Anthony King (London: Macmillan, 1991), 41–68, for a discussion of a comparable rearticulation of blackness, used to help forge anti-racist political alliances in Britain in the 1970s.

10 Moviemaniacs. "Django Unchained: Meet the Press" (2013), http://youtu.be/-1QpScB-HJg (accessed September 6, 2013).

11 Henry Louis Gates, Jr., "Tarantino 'Unchained,' part 1: 'Django' Trilogy?," *The Root* (2012), http://www.theroot.com/views/tarantino-unchained-part-1-django-trilogy (accessed August 29, 2013); "Tarantino 'Unchained,' part 2: On the n-word," *The Root* (2012), http://www.theroot.com/views/tarantino-unchained-part-2-n-word (accessed August 29, 2013); "Tarantino 'Unchained,' part 3: White Saviors," *The Root* (2012), http://www.theroot.com/views/tarantino-unchained-part-3-white-saviors (accessed August 29, 2013).

12 Dexter Gabriel, "Hollywood's Slavery Films Tell Us More about the Present than the Past," *Colorlines* (2013), http://colorlines.com/archives/2013/01/slavery_in_film.html (accessed August 29, 2013).

13 ABC News, "'Django Unchained': Tarantino, DiCaprio, Foxx Answer Critics," (2013) http://youtu.be/JMUhaCXPyg8 (accessed September 6, 2013).

14 Moviemaniacs.

15 Moviemaniacs.

16 See Jelani Cobb, "Tarantino Unchained," *The New Yorker* (2013), http://www.newyorker.com/online/blogs/culture/2013/01/how-accurate-is-quentin-tarantinos-portrayal-of-slavery-in-django-unchained.html (accessed August 30, 2013); Gabriel; Charles Reece, "Snowball's Chance in Hell: *Django Unchained*," *The Hooded Utilitarian* (2013), http://www.hoodedutilitarian.com/2013/01/snowballs-chance-in-hell-django-unchained/ (accessed August 30, 2013); Ishmael Reed, "Black Audiences, White Stars, and 'Django Unchained,'" *The Wall Street Journal* (2012), http://blogs.wsj.com/speakeasy/2012/12/28/black-audiences-white-stars-and-django-unchained/ (accessed August 30, 2013); Armond White, "Still Not a Brother." *CityArts: New York's Review of Culture* (2012) http://cityarts.info/2012/12/28/still-not-a-brother/ (accessed August 30, 2013).

17 Gates, "Were There Slaves Like Stephen in 'Django'?," *The Root* (2013) http://www.theroot.com/views/were-there-slaves-stephen-django (accessed August 30, 2013), offers a helpful discussion of the historical facts and myths connected to the "house slave vs. field slave" debate.

18 Stuart Hall, "New Ethnicities," in *Stuart Hall: Critical Dialogues in Cultural Studies*, ed. David Morley and Kuan-Hsing Chen (New York: Routledge, 1996), 443–444.

19 VibeTV, "Spike Lee Talks 'Django Unchained,'" (2012) http://youtu.be/LJTIWe_71mw (accessed September 6, 2013).

20 The feud itself dates back to 1997, when *Jackie Brown* was released, though Tarantino certainly wasn't shy about using the "n-word" in *Reservoir Dogs* (1992) or *Pulp Fiction* (1994).

21 Eric Lott, *Love and Theft: Blackface Minstrelsy and the American Working Class* (New York: Oxford University Press, 1993).

22 For more on the dicey representational politics of black women whose only function in a film is to serve as mistresses to white men, see Melissa Harris-Perry, *Sister Citizen: Shame, Stereotypes, and Black Women in America* (New Haven, CT: Yale University Press, 2011); and bell hooks, *Black Looks: Race and Representation* (Cambridge, MA: South End Press, 1992).

23 Oprah Winfrey Network, "Oprah, Spielberg, Daniel Day-Lewis talk about 'Lincoln,'" *The Huffington Post* (2012), http://www.huffingtonpost.com/2012/11/29/oprah-spielberg-daniel-day-lewis-lincoln_n_2207277.html (accessed September 6, 2013).

24 Ruth Marcus, "A Cliffhanger in the White House," *The Washington Post* (2012), http://articles.washingtonpost.com/2012-11-20/

opinions/35510873_1_fiscal-cliff-mary-lincoln-13th-amendment
(accessed September 2, 2013).

25 Amanda Marcotte, "*Django Unchained*: A Movie about Other
    Movies about the 19th Century," *Raw Story* (2013), http://www.
    rawstory.com/rs/2013/01/03/django-unchained-a-movie-about-other-
    movies-about-the-19th-century/ (accessed September 2, 2013).

26 Cindy Davis, "Mindhole Blowers: 20 Facts about *Blazing Saddles*
    that Might Leave Your Mind Aglow with Whirling, Transient Nodes
    of Thought Careening through a Cosmic Vapor of Invention," *Pajiba*
    (2012), http://www.pajiba.com/seriously_random_lists/mindhole-
    blowers-20-facts-about-blazing-saddles-that-might-leave-your-mind-
    aglow-with-whirling-transient-nodes-of-thought-careening-through-a-
    cosmic-vapor-of-invention-.php (accessed September 2, 2013).

27 Todd Boyd, *The New H.N.I.C.: The Death of Civil Rights and the
    Reign of Hip Hop* (New York: New York University Press, 2003);
    Gates, *Thirteen Ways of Looking at a Black Man*.

28 Noel Ignatiev and John Garvey, eds. *Race Traitor* (New York:
    Routledge, 1996), 36–37.

29 See Lauren Berlant, "The Face of America and the State of
    Emergency," in *Disciplinarity and Dissent in Cultural Studies*, ed.
    Cary Nelson and Dilip Parameshwar Gaonkar (New York: Routledge,
    1996), 397–439, Lawrence Grossberg, *We Gotta Get Out of This
    Place: Popular Conservatism and Postmodern Culture* (New York:
    Routledge, 1992); Stuart Hall, "Notes on Deconstructing 'the
    Popular,'" in *People's History and Socialist Theory*, ed. Raphael
    Samuel (London: Routledge and Kegan Paul, 1981), 227–240; Laura
    Kipnis, "(Male) Desire and (Female) Disgust: Reading *Hustler*,"
    in *Cultural Studies*, ed. Lawrence Grossberg, Cary Nelson, Paula
    A. Treichler, Linda Baughman, and J. Macgregor Wise (New York:
    Routledge, 1992), 373–391; Constance Penley, *NASA/TREK: Popular
    Science and Sex in America* (New York: Verso, 1997); Janice A.
    Radway, *A Feeling for Books: The Book-of-the-Month Club, Literary
    Taste, and Middle-Class Desire* (Chapel Hill: University of North
    Carolina Press, 1997); Gilbert B. Rodman, *Elvis after Elvis: The
    Posthumous Career of a Living Legend* (New York: Routledge, 1996).

30 For more on the merits of "impolite" political interventions, see
    Michael Awkward, *Burying Don Imus* (Minneapolis: University
    of Minnesota Press, 2009); Boyd, *The New H.N.I.C.*; bell hooks,
    Where We Stand: Class Matters (New York: Routledge, 2000);
    Kipnis, "(Male) Desire and (Female) Disgust;" and Rodman, "Race."

10

Chained to It:
The Recurrence of the
Frontier Hero in the Films
of Quentin Tarantino

Samuel P. Perry

A short list of well-known Quentin Tarantino trademarks might include the following: (1) genre mash-ups, (2) provocative dialogue, (3) garish representations of violence, (4) racially incendiary themes and language, and (5) copious references to other films and his own films. This list is not exhaustive, but it offers a starting point to critique Tarantino's *Django Unchained*, as this film offers all five of these things. The fusion of Spaghetti Westerns and Blaxploitation films replete with references to films in both genres, a steady chorus of witty dialogue to build tension and offer laughs, exploding squibs and gushing blood, and perhaps, as much or more than any of his other films, racially charged scenes featuring violence both realistic and fantastic. Not everyone enjoys such things. Before the film was even released, Spike Lee vowed not to see it and claimed that Tarantino

---

An earlier version of this chapter was presented at the ALTA Conference on Argumentation and is set to be published in the Selected Papers volume for the conference under the title: "Django Unchained and the Undisturbed Frontier Hero Archetype."

was being insensitive with regard to black history. Lee posted on Twitter regarding the film, "American Slavery Was Not a Sergio Leone Spaghetti Western. It Was a Holocaust."[1] Others chimed in to voice their displeasure with Tarantino for various reasons, but the film was largely successful with a worldwide box office gross of $425 million.[2]

Additionally, the film received robust critical acclaim. It was nominated for the Best Picture at both the Academy Awards and The Golden Globe Awards. Tarantino won the Oscar for Screenwriting and Christoph Waltz picked up the award for best supporting actor, his second time to do so for a turn in a Tarantino film.[3] Scholarly assessments of the film have been mixed, but many have been positive including a good number of the chapters in this book. Many of the positive assessments of the film feature praise in one form or another regarding the things on the short list above. My own enjoyment of the film as an entertaining "shoot 'em up" addition to the Tarantino oeuvre has to do with these elements. However, my critical and philosophical objections to the film increasingly feature an amalgam of the items on the list to the extent that Tarantino's provocations and garishness concerning violence forgo critical reflection necessary to carry the weight of the historical events referenced and the subject matter incorporated in his films. In other words, those of us who have no prior history of public feuding with Tarantino and did not refuse to see the film as Spike Lee did might need to evaluate it in the terms that Lee put forth because, quite frankly after multiple viewings of *Django Unchained*, I am not convinced that slavery should be the focus of a Tarantino-style Spaghetti Western.

This reading of the film is contrarian in many ways. *Django Unchained* is not without interesting provocations. The very idea of a freed slave slaughtering a plantation full of white people and complicit slaves as a Christmas Day release blockbuster is exciting in the same way that A. Susan Owen, Sarah R. Stein, and Leah R. Vande Berg note their excitement at seeing strong female characters in movies, despite said films not achieving all they intended in terms of female empowerment. They answer in the affirmative, when asked if the films are pleasurable explaining, "Yes, even for us because it is still so rare in *any* narrative context to see female bodies driving the narrative forward."[4] Yet, as Owen and company note, there is something bittersweet about such a victory. *Django* leaves something of the same bittersweet taste, because it stops short of breaking the predictable narrative the frontier hero archetype provides, just as it stops short of changing the blockbuster formula to which Tarantino steadfastly adheres. Tarantino, however, claims that the movie is causing conversations regarding race that have not taken place in decades.[5]

Tarantino's posturing and grandiose claims about *Django* make it seem that he intended to create something new and different. In fact, Tarantino claimed of the film that it successfully "deconstructed *Birth of a Nation*,"[6] and that his charge was to create a new "folkloric" black hero.[7] Tarantino did not deconstruct *Birth of a Nation*, nor did he create a new black hero. The film rehashes much of the work already completed by Tarantino. These works spin Spaghetti Western style yarns predicated on the completion of revenge fantasies. The stories feature unconventional embodiments of protagonists engaging in highly conventionalized forms of action movie violence. In a fashion similar to other Tarantino frontier hero protagonists in the *Kill Bill* films and *Inglourious Basterds*, *Django Unchained* returns much of the agency available to its hero back to hegemonic notions of what a hero ought to be. In order for *Django* to successfully carry off what Tarantino claims he intended for the film and what some critiques of the film claim it accomplishes with regard to creating a liberating black hero, it would have to meaningfully appropriate the frontier hero archetype. Additionally, Tarantino's recurrence to the frontier hero and recurrence to genre fusion that places the frontier hero in an atypical frontier setting makes the work of appropriation all the more unlikely to succeed. Appropriation is necessary within *Django*, because the atypical frontier setting of the slaveholding South is a difficult historical subject and the lingering material effects of that history pervade the social contexts within which the film is viewed.

Failure to properly appropriate the frontier hero archetype and provide agency to Django that exceeds the oppressive paradigmatic functions of the scene and the archetype itself simply returns agency back to the hegemonic structures traditionally propagated by the scene and the myth in which the archetype is located. In other words, Tarantino features and makes salient oppressive scenes and narrative arcs, and in order to overcome those salient features the hero must be able to subversively alter both. *Django* plays with them at a remove. Elsewhere, I argue that *Django* engages in what Jean Baudrillard refers to as "operational whitewash."[8] Baudrillard argues in *The Transparency of Evil* that the condition of late capitalism exposes its denizens to

> a complete aseptic whiteness. Violence is whitewashed, history is whitewashed, all as part of a vast enterprise of cosmetic surgery at whose completion nothing will be left but a society for which, and individuals for whom, all violence, all negativity, are strictly forbidden. In these circumstances everything which is unable to relinquish its own identity is inevitably plunged into a realm of radical uncertainty and endless simulation.[9]

Tarantino's whitewashing of violence and history in *Django* performs cosmetic surgery on the already existing frontier hero archetype and the negativity of slavery loses historical contextualization in favor of aesthetic choices made through the frame of the Spaghetti Western revenge fantasy. Tarantino's inability to let Django deviate from the frontier hero archetype creates uncertainty regarding the possibility of creating a new black hero and his fascination with the revenge fantasy aesthetic, wrought through the quest of the frontier hero, drives the movie into an endless cycle of repetition, which recalls his previous films—most notably *Kill Bill, Vols. 1 & 2* and *Inglourious Basterds*—and his persistent referencing of other films.

The burden of appropriation on the frontier

First, the appropriation of the frontier myth is possible. My contention is not that the myth is off-limits or that it acts as some sort of impenetrable shibboleth. However, the appropriation of a myth so embedded in the American consciousness does not come easily. Helene A. Shugart argues that the Western motif and hero archetype are successfully appropriated in the film *Shame*, a play on the classic Western film *Shane*.[10] According to Shugart, successful appropriation "articulates a clear challenge to an oppressive paradigm," which forwards alternative readings of power constructions and rigid identity categories otherwise stifled by the oppressive paradigm.[11] While not every aspect of disproportionate power structures disappears in the appropriation, enough subversion takes place that new processes of identity formation and previously prohibited actions become possible as a result of appropriation.

The critique of *Django Unchained* in this chapter takes this definition of appropriation, then extends the concept to argue that characters or stories which successfully appropriate archetypes and mythic structures gain agency not usually available to characters in such stories. Here, agency follows the Burkean notion of the term. That is, agency is defined as the means by which the agents, characters in this case, accomplish the actions that ultimately drive the dramatic elements of a situation.[12] In appropriation, new forms of agency empower characters in such a way that their newly granted access to tools and means of acting allow them to do so without surrendering pieces of their individual identity. These same identities were, in many cases, the basis for denying the character agency in the first place. A woman character successfully appropriating an archetype unusually available to her should not cede aspects of her femininity. Black characters successfully appropriating an archetype unusually available to them should not cede aspects of their racial identity in order to embody the character appropriated.

This is difficult, because even when new possibilities open up on the frontier, old machinations return to the fore. Janice Hocker Rushing noted this phenomenon in the films *Alien* and *Aliens*. Rushing argues of the movies, the feminine hero, Ellen Ripley played by Sigourney Weaver, succumbs to the hero archetype in such a way that she loses her femininity in the new frontier of space. Rushing claims of the frontier hero archetype, "The old heroic myth, once essential and glorious, has run its course. In the new context of interdependence suggested by the infinite special scene, its continuation is dangerous and, as we have seen, it cannot accommodate the feminine consciousness without corrupting it."[13] In other words, the agency for counterhegemonic character identities is returned to the very system which denied agency in the first place. Ripley cannot express her femininity in the role of frontier hero without surrendering the very essence of her femininity back to the narrative that traditionally has and continues to suppress the expression of feminine traits. Owen et al. note that Ripley's expressions of femininity in *Alien* rely on objectification and sexualizing her character in a way which reminds the audience that "the female body arguably represents extreme vulnerability for a range of viewers."[14] For every expectation broken through the empowerment of the female body, the narrative structure takes back the power and returns it to expected places.

Rushing explains the tendency of the frontier myth to do this anytime the hero is placed in a setting incommensurate with the typified frontier setting. This is true for male and female characters. She notes the disjuncture in the film *Urban Cowboy* and in the accompanying trend that followed the movie.[15] The common recurrence of the disjuncture of scene and the frontier hero's ability to adapt to it is featured in films such as *Midnight Cowboy* (1969), where Jon Voight's attempt to play to cowboy in an urban setting leads to his tragic stint as a homeless gigolo on the streets of New York. *The Man Who Shot Liberty Valance* (1962) and its comedic children's update *Rango* (2011) also feature the journey of characters molded by the frontier in ways that cause them to forgo their earlier, weaker tendencies toward city living. In both the original and the remake of *True Grit* (1969 and 2010), the female protagonist, Mattie Ross, gains acceptance by being meaner and tougher than the hard-living frontier cowboy Rooster Cogburn. In each instance, the characters assume the frontier hero persona in favor of a previous persona or they forgo the frontier persona altogether. This list is not exhaustive, but is representative of the difficulty of changing the features of the frontier hero to suit a new character.

For Rushing, the frontier myth relies heavily on the scene in order to derive agency for its hero archetype.[16] Changing the relationship of the hero to the scene or changing the scene altogether produces possibilities for a change in the archetype, but because of the deep structure of archetypes change is quite difficult. Additionally, the myth itself offers its own constraints because "its vague and various meanings perpetuate[d] triumphalist fantasies and trapped western history in a sexist and ethnocentric straitjacket."[17] If we return to Shugart for a moment, the structure of the myth propagates its own oppressive paradigm. Oppressive paradigms such as the frontier myth return any surplus value or new value added to the sign of the hero back to the system from which it came. Much of the acclaim surrounding *Django Unchained* argues that, or operates under the assumption that, the film successfully avoids returning power to the frontier myth or that it successfully alters the paradigm in a way that is productive of agency for Django's character. The following section discusses Tarantino's attempts to appropriate the frontier hero archetype and the pitfalls of following his formula for doing so.

Tarantino's recourse to formula

While favorable readings of *Django Unchained* mentioned earlier offer valuable insights about the film and representations of race in contemporary film, they sometimes forgo the effects of Tarantino's particular brand of genre fusion. In *Django Unchained*, Tarantino tends toward faithful caricature rather than subversive reclamation, so even new wrinkles in the frontier hero mythology resulting from its fusion with Blaxploitation films propagate the continuation and survival of the less desirable pieces of the old myth. This is in part because Tarantino has fallen into a pattern of filmmaking that takes the frontier myth as its backbone. Recourse to the myth as the fundamental structure homogenizes the actions available to characters even when the scene of the frontier changes, as it does in *Django Unchained*. The frontier myth often does this. Richard Slatta suggests of the frontier myth, "Even as new scholarship defuses old myths, new ones spring hydra-like from novelists, painters, politicians, film-makers, game-makers, and other creative souls."[18] This is symptomatic of Tarantino's work more generally. *Django*, as well as Tarantino's previous three films, follow the same plot arc and mythic pattern and vary only in so far as Tarantino takes up different B genres of film to fuse with the Spaghetti Western—a particular iteration of the frontier mythology. The common point that allows for genre fusion is violence, a point to which I return at the end of this chapter. The pattern of the four films expressed as a formula reads something like this:

x (Spaghetti Western) + y (B movie genre) + z (unconventional embodiment of hero)

That such a pattern is readily identifiable presents problems for appropriation. Generally, informed criticism eschews the idea that the liberation of particular identities from hegemonic structures is a one-size-fits-all process. Inserting a traditionally oppressed body type into a genre fusion sequence does not necessarily grant agency to the person or character occupying that particular body type. I offer a quick explanation of the ways in which the formula described offers only glimpses of agency to traditionally oppressed characters and returns that agency back to the frontier myth via the motif of revenge.

Since the constant in each of these films is the Spaghetti Western arc and the establishment of the heroic qualities of the protagonist through the frontier construction and aesthetic of the film, zero sum and constant recourse to violence becomes the overriding resolution to any problem encountered.[19] Ronald Carpenter, remembering Rushing's qualifications for the frontier hero in his remembrance of her, explains the character traits that lead to this never-ending zero-sum game: (a) "A hero is not of truly mythic proportions unless his struggle is difficult and his success is wrought from sacrifice"; (b) a Western hero refuses "to give in to temptations associated with community" and leaves "his normal state of indolence only when the villain threatened the town"; (c) but "with no truly difficult challenge to face in environment or enemy," potential Western heroes are "tamed and become dormant"; and (d) ultimately, to avoid that insignificance, after "avoiding violence for as long as possible," the Western hero concludes that "a man's gotta do what a man's gotta do" and rids "the town" [or contemporary city if not a nation] of evil personae with "consummate gunmanship."[20]

This progression through a readily identifiable set of steps that leads inevitably to violence homogenizes what can qualify as agency. It presupposes that adroit gun play resolves the problems the hero encounters. Each of the next pieces of the formula is decidedly simpler. The last two pieces operating as variables in the formula work in this way, y is the next film genre that Tarantino fuses with the Spaghetti Western theme. In the final piece of the equation, Tarantino picks a seemingly unconventional hero to embody the elements of x. In the *Kill Bill* films, y is Kung Fu movies and z is a female character. In *Inglourious Basterds*, y is World War II films and television shows and *z* is, again, a female character. In *Django*, *y* is Blaxploitation films and *z* is a black character.

Tarantino set on this path with the *Kill Bill* films (2003 and 2004). In *Kill Bill, Vols. 1 & 2*, Beatrix Kiddo, played by Uma Thurman, fights to get revenge on David Carradine's Bill character in order to restore a familial relationship with her daughter. She travels to Southeast Asia to relearn the hero trade, acquire the hero's weapons, and to move to the fringe of society long enough to collect the resolve and strength to confront the bad guy face-to-face. *Kill Bill* fuses Kung Fu movies with the Spaghetti Western pattern, which is not necessarily a new fusion given the TV show *Kung Fu* in which Tarantino's title character Bill was played by David Carradine. Tarantino's fascination with the show has been evident since Samuel L. Jackson's character in *Pulp Fiction* proclaimed that in his retirement from plying his wares as a hit man he would, "Wander the earth like Kane." Tarantino's infatuation with and homage to Kung Fu movies arguably engages in what Edward Said referred to as orientalism,[21] and the setting of Southeast Asia is one fraught with problems for a frontier hero.[22] Additionally, the movie plays with Kiddo's character in ways that make the empowering role of female Kung Fu expert less empowering. While Tarantino has fetishized violence since he first came on the scene with the script of *True Romance* (also the first display of his fascination with the n-word) and his flirtation with torture porn in *Reservoir Dogs*, he eroticizes violence in *Kill Bill* through the character of Kiddo. Owen et al. remark, " … *Kill Bill* is Quentin Tarantino's fantasy of eroticized violence. The bitch fight at the end of *Kill Bill II* is a quintessential comic book sexual fantasy."[23] One might also note that the entire revenge fantasy is predicated on a woman scorned returning to kill the offending lover and reclaim her child. The eroticized violence is coupled with "female homicidal rage,"[24] which does not necessarily equal empowerment or agency. When read in this light, it looks more like a profane version of Sarah Palin's "Mama Grizzly" narrative, which as Katie L. Gibson and Amy L. Heyse note is not without its own problems regarding its relationship to feminism and empowerment.[25] Tarantino maintains this female homicide rage mode of agency on the frontier in *Inglourious Basterds*.

In *Inglourious Basterds*, the Western/frontier connection is aesthetic and referential. Tarantino takes the aesthetic and plot structure of a Western movie and applies it to the 1970s B-movie, *The Inglorious Bastards* and World War II movies. The heroine, Shosanna, follows the revenge quest in order to avenge slain family members. While the setting of Nazi Germany might not immediately evoke the frontier, the first scene of the movie is Tarantino's tribute to *Once Upon a Time in the West*, hence the scene placard "Once Upon a Time in Nazi Germany." The cinematography of the film borrows liberally from the films of Sergio Leone and in particular the film *Once Upon a Time in the West*. The opening scene also references Western classics, *The Unforgiven* and *The Searchers*.[26] The aesthetic of the frontier in large open camera shots during the beginning of the film establishes Shosanna as a frontier hero set apart, and after the death of her family, she too sets out on the quest for revenge. In this regard, the plot of the film takes on the features of Westerns like Sam Raimi's *The Quick and the Dead* (1995), in which Sharon Stone avenges the death of her father with the help of various male gun slingers, who assist intentionally and unintentionally, just as the Basterds unwittingly assist Shosanna in their shared efforts to massacre Nazi leadership inside the movie theater. Shosanna's rage leads to the deaths of her enemies, but also seals her own fate. Her laughing ghost taunts the dying Nazis trapped in the theater.

Basterds is a bit more complicated than the *Kill Bill* movies, however. The discussion of agency is complicated to a larger degree because of the scene, a complication which recurs in *Django Unchained*. Tarantino stages his frontier epic in a Nazi occupied area during World War II. The indeterminate vast swaths of desert topography featured in *Kill Bill* do not evoke such particular notions of historical vitriol, though the extermination of Native Americans across this terrain might rightfully elicit that reaction from audiences. Beatrix Kiddo is not a Native American slaying white encroachers. However, Shosanna is a Jewish woman slaughtering Nazis. The Basterds are Jewish guerillas murdering and disfiguring Nazis; their connection to the frontier, as their leader Aldo Raine articulates it, is commissioning Apache style raids that feature scalping Nazis. The violence is base and excessive. Eli Roth, who played Donnie Donnowitz in the film, referred to the film as "kosher porn."[27]

Making occupied Europe the site of the frontier, where the frontier hero proves herself as such, carries with it implications. In aggregating a number of negative reviews from bloggers, film directors, and film scholars, Andrew O'Hehir collects a succinct explanation of the implications and the problems that come with them. O'Hehir quotes Jeffrey Goldberg's excitement regarding, "emotionally uncomplicated, physically threatening, non-morally-anguished Jews dealing out spaghetti-Western justice to their would-be exterminators," but goes on to note Goldberg's reservations upon further reflection and posits that the film "conventionalizes Jews, puts them in the same revenge motif as everyone else."[28] Goldberg recognizes that the Spaghetti Western style violence doled out to Nazi's homogenizes not only the revenge narrative, but also the Jewish experience of the Holocaust and strips away the moral and emotional turmoil that comes with the righteous confrontation of one's oppressors. The agency is in the mythic construction and commissioning of frontier justice, not something uniquely attributed the character carrying out that justice. Put another way, the myth retains agency rather than the character gaining agency specific to their particular identity.

Oppression is not uniform and took place in different ways on the frontier, the plantation, and during the Nazi occupation. As a result, reactions to varied forms of oppression manifested themselves in different ways among the different people groups faced with pain, suffering, torture, and death. Homogenizing the individual reactions to oppression reduces the agency of those reactions. The patterns of ceding agency back to the myth here recall the warnings of Baudrillard with regard to the loss of referents in communication. Baudrillard raises the question, "[What] If communication were concerned not with messages but instead with the promotion of communication itself *qua* myth?"[29] The questioned turned toward the work of Tarantino takes up whether Tarantino forwards a message specific to the scenes and characters he employs or communicates through myth for the sake of repeating the myth for his audiences.

If Tarantino makes these movies more for the sake of paying homage to the frontier myth and Spaghetti Westerns than for the sake of developing individual characters, then it makes sense to say that Tarantino makes movies about movies. Tarantino makes movies about movies for the sake of movies sounds tautological, but it may shed light on the problems with both *Basterds* and *Django* and their treatment of historical tragedies. O'Hehir rebukes *Basterds* saying,

…Quentin Tarantino has no serious opinions or convictions whatever regarding Nazis or Jews or the Holocaust. Beneath all his B-movie genre-worship, Tarantino remains a pomo disciple of Jean-Luc Godard, playing an elaborate game of bait-and-switch with his audience and seeking to disarrange the conventional stories—or stories about stories—we've got in our heads. More simply, he's just fucking with us.[30]

To be fair, if Tarantino is just "fucking with us" as O'Hehir claims, there is nothing inherently wrong with that. Movies are fun and movies about movies are fun, but when they begin to play with themes and historical events that are not funny or fond remembrances, some adjustment of expectations is necessary. Looking for a deeper meaning that posits great critical work has taken place in such films may create its own set of problems. Just as *Basterds* really does not deconstruct the films of Leni Riefenstahl or Joseph Goebbels, though it makes reference to them, *Django* does not deconstruct *Birth of Nation* though Tarantino had those films in mind when he made his own. Rather than creating a new hero, Tarantino tries out the same hero in new places. He did not create a new black hero, he instead created a black hero who fits into his own movies. He happens to make that hero a composite of Blaxploitation heroes in appearance and style, but in narrative arc he remains almost entirely faithful to the frontier hero archetype. The rest of this chapter takes up these claims through a reading of *Django* that takes to task the ways in which the frontier hero archetype retains its agency to the detriment of Django's individual agency.

The growth of the frontier, the growth of the desert, and *Django Unchained*

One must be conscious that, no matter how the analysis proceeds, it proceeds toward the freezing over of meaning, it assists in the precession of simulacra and of indifferent forms. The desert grows.[31]
—Jean Baudrillard

Baudrillard, of course, refers to the precession of the simulacrum and the dying vestiges of the real. *Django* begins the desert. From the outset of the film, the desert grows. The film opens with the Western ballad "Django," playing over the images of slave traders atop horses leading slaves on foot through desert terrain into wooded areas of Texas. The Rocky Roberts song, featured in the opening of the 1966 Sergio Corbucci film *Django*, and the topography foreshadow the coming transition of the title character Django from chattel slave to gun-slinging frontier hero. From the outset, Tarantino's penchant for reference at the cost of sense making is clear. Slave traders walking slaves hundreds of miles out of the way into the desert terrain of West Texas makes little sense, other than as a foreshadowing plot device. In this sense, the desert literally grows into the scene of the film in order for Tarantino to place his protagonist on the typically imagined frontier. The aesthetic trumps the reasonable explication and progression of the plot of a movie involving the slave trade. That is because the slave trade is not the subject of the movie. The movie is more or less about Django's transition into "the fastest gun in the South," as King Schultz will call him later in the movie.

In the early stages of Django's transition into the character of the frontier hero, King Schultz explains to Django the importance of cultivating and maintaining his newly crafted persona and the dangers of breaking character. Schultz explains to Django that he will be playing the part of his valet when entering a Tennessee plantation under false pretenses in order to collect a bounty, but the conversation might be thought of as more of a guide to the entire movie. Schultz explains, "When we gain access to these plantations, we'll be putting on an act…During the act, you can never break character. Do you understand?" Django replies that he will not. At this point in the film, Django's character has not evolved fully into the frontier hero, as he chooses a silly silk outfit for his role and is not yet well versed in the strategies and tactics of the frontier hero. The point, however, is well received. Once Django understands his character fully, he never breaks from it. Baudrillard argues, "A hyperreal henceforth sheltered from the imaginary, and from any distinction between the real and the imaginary, leaving room only for the orbital recurrence of models and for the simulated generation of differences."[32] Django's model is the hired gun on the frontier and he readily embraces the model. When Django remarks to King Schultz of his new profession of bounty hunting, "Kill white people and get paid for it. What's not to like?" Django's sadism and nihilism serve as the vehicle for an aesthetic violence only loosely tied to race. Race makes for easily identifiable targets. Django's job is to shoot those targets and look good doing it.

Of course, the movie even forgoes its own complication of such a Manichean distinction between black and white in this moment, as Django relies on King Schultz to gain access to plantations and find his wife. It also ignores that Django seems to have little connection to black people in the movie beyond the connection to his wife. Django kills less because people are white, but because white people have his wife. He kills black characters that stand in his way, too. Django's maintenance of the basic imperative to not break character and his singular focus on rescuing his wife deny him connection to or empathy with other slaves. Salamisha Tillet describes Django's aloofness thus, "And yet his exceptionality comes at a price: Unlike '*Amistad*'s' Cinque or '*Beloved*'s' Sethe, he [Django] seems to exist in a vacuum. Most of the slave characters he meets are not his equals ... they barely dent racial stereotypes."[33] Django is a frontier hero. He is less interested in the systematic means of oppression that deny every other black character in the movie agency than he is fulfilling his role as a frontier hero. *Django Unchained* repeatedly forwards the claim that the title character is 1 in 10,000 among his race. What makes him exceptional is his ability to adhere to a hero archetype, to not break character, within the constructs of a mythical pattern often deployed in the service of subjugation of the very groups for which Django would presumably stand as a hero. The appropriation of the myth remains difficult because frontier heroes need frontiers and, "in order for there to be open frontiers it has been the case that some groups of people will be displaced, assimilated, or annihilated."[34] While Django contributes his own fair share of annihilation within the frontier construct in killing a number of bad white men and at least one really bad black man, included in the collateral damage seems to be the untouched mechanisms that allow for the paradigmatic oppression of an entire race—the very reason Django and Broomhilda are thrown into the tragic situation that motivates Django to revenge (Figure 10.1).

FIGURE 10.1 *One in ten thousand*

Django's revenge has to do with slavery in so far as it separates him from Broomhilda. His fight is personal. Django certainly has personal experiences of slavery that feature in the movie, but the institution of slavery seems more a means by which Tarantino can further indulge the sensibilities of his own violent aesthetic. The pornographic excess of the violence addresses slavery, but is also Tarantino's point of comparison for something that he imagines would be similarly violent. Tarantino posits the violence on the frontier and the violence of slavery as exchangeable. When asked about the scene in *Django Unchained* where D'Artagnan, one of Candie's slaves, is eaten by dogs as Candie, Schultz, Django, and others watch idly by, Tarantino explains his thinking when crafting the violence in the film, "And with that in mind, this violent, pitiless [Sergio] Corbucci West: What would be the American equivalent of that—that really would be real—that would be an American story? It was being a slave in the antebellum South."[35] The explanation is telling. Tarantino sees pieces of the real as interchangeable and exchangeable with a cinematic aesthetic he wants to copy. The chains of reference and the uninterrupted circuit connecting the referents of slavery and the actual Western frontier to entirely fictional modes of representation contribute to the growth of the desert of the real just as the beginning of the film grew its scene to incorporate the desert landscape.

The growth of the desert is spectacular in Tarantino films. The spectacle is troublesome with regard to agency. In discussing Baudrillard's work, longtime friend and confidant Sylvère Lotringer posits, "Simulation is spectacle without agency."[36] In *Django Unchained*, Django fights an absurd number of Candie's men before being captured, threatened with castration and a lifetime of work in the mines, and returning to the Candie plantation in order to finish the job with dynamite and bullets, an ending reminiscent of the climax in *Basterds*. In each case, the violence reaches fantastic and sweeping levels unfettered by realism or any tie to the previous violence experienced in the films.

The aesthetic of violence supersedes the agency violence might offer. Further exacerbating whether or not the aesthetic of violence actually provides agency, Tarantino chooses to enact very realistic violence on the black characters in the movie like D'Artagnan, the other men in the movie forced into slave fighting, and the graphic scenes portraying the lashing of both Broomhilda and Django. In stark contrast, the violence committed by Django during his revenge, his supposed agency, white characters suffer mostly fantastic harm. They are pulled off screen when hit with bullets, bullet wounds explode and gush geyser-like amounts of blood, and henchmen are basically cut into pieces when Django shoots them. Black people experience real harm and white people experience entirely unrealistic harm. White people suffer little, and the audience is tempted to laugh at the ridiculousness of the violence visited on them.

Tarantino offers an explanation for the vacillation between realistic and fantastic nature of the violence presented in the climax of the movie as an aesthetic choice. Tarantino explains,

> ... on one hand I'm telling a historical story, and when it comes to nuts and bolts of the slave trade, I had to be real and had to tell it the right way. But when it comes to more thematic things and operatic view, I could actually have fun with stylization—because it is taking parts from a spaghetti Western. And I am taking the story of a slave narrative and blowing it up ... to operatic proportions ...[37]

Tarantino is willing to foreground the genre's aesthetic of violence to the detriment of contextualizing the violence of the film visited on whites within the same realistic modes of representation he uses to represent the slave trade—a move that would have provided all the dramatic material Tarantino needed. *Django Unchained*, like *Basterds* before it, takes a historically finite situation as its frontier. Both historically finite situations remain scenes of the greatest denials of agency to particular groups of people in human history. Rather than reckon with that history, deriving agency from it, and imparting it to characters in his stories, Tarantino employs them as places to stage simulation. That is spectacle without agency. The characters have no choices to make. They have targets to shoot and explosives to detonate. Even if we put aside the question of whether or not violence constitutes agency, we can acknowledge that agency, even if violent, would be expressed differently across different contexts. To deny the difference in expression is to surrender the agency violence might provide back to the myth that prescriptively called the violence forth. So in this way, Spike Lee was probably right that "slavery is not a Sergio Leone movie."

Conclusion: Still chained

Media representations of the frontier myth serve as an example of the precession of the simulacrum and the frontier operationalizes in the hyperreal. Without appropriation, the film strikes less a subversive chord, but more an acquiescent note of transparent complicity regarding the cosmetic alterations of the frontier myth. More simply, the movie needs to provide an interpretation of the frontier hero archetype that allows Django to engage his own blackness in meaningful ways, rather than being a frontier hero that happens to be black. Baudrillard argues, "No matter how marginal, or banal, or even obscene it may be, everything is subject to aestheticization, culturalization, museumification. Everything is said, everything is exposed, everything acquires the force, or the manner, of a sign. The system runs less on the surplus-value of the commodity than on the aesthetic surplus value of the sign."[38] In this case, slavery receives Tarantino's aestheticization and creates a movie where Django's blackness carries the aesthetic surplus value of the sign. His dandyism and frontier hero garb dictate the story. Even in the direst of circumstances, Django dares not show his connection to black humanity. While Mandingo fights featuring eye gouging and skull crushing take place, while a black man is torn to shreds and eaten by dogs, and while slaves face degradation at the hands of slave owners, Django stands apart or sits perched on a horse aloof. His only well-developed personal connection to another black character in the entire movie is with his wife, Broomhilda. Django must storm the plantation and take her back.

While no delusion should exist that *Django Unchained*, or any other Tarantino films for that matter, set out to with something other than making money as their primary pursuit, there are inherent problems in creating agency within this blockbuster format. In regard to frontier hero movies, Rushing explains of *Alien* and *Aliens*, "In these films, the characters' purpose, even before they board the first spaceship, is commercial exploitation; thus anything that gets in the way must be eliminated. It is the perfect situation for an ego hero; *patriarchal* purpose, that is, calls for a *masculinized* agent…the purpose of the story will have to be different from the beginning."[39] The idea of Django negotiating the merits of improved race relations or the pitfalls of phrenology with Candie is farcical, just as Rushing notes the farcical notion of Ripley trying to communicate her way through the alien infested morass of space would have been.[40] However, setting out to tell this story over and over again knowing that the hyper masculine trappings of the frontier hero put people in seats suggests less thought for the characters or revising history than it does for the profit margin. Tarantino tells us this much in the same interview with Krishnan Guru-Murthy where after he proclaimed to, "want to give black American males a Western hero," he became incensed when asked about the relationship between on-screen violence and actual violence, he repeated, "this is a commercial, I am here to sell my movie."[41] The problem here is that Tarantino wants the indulgent parts of revenge without having to deal with the complicated scenes that motivate that revenge in meaningful ways.

In both *Inglourious Basterds* and *Django Unchained*, Tarantino pushes the envelope by exacting the operatic violence of his revenge fantasies in well-known historically situated contexts. The tension between agency and spectacle comes to the fore as a result. The audience can indulge the fantasy of Shosanna killing Hitler and Goebbels. The audience can indulge the fantasy of Django murdering and destroying the entirety of a downriver slave plantation. The audience can indulge in a historical revision predicated on taking revenge on the most evil characters in the historical imagination, just as they indulge in the oversized bucket of popcorn and jumbo soda. They allow themselves the indulgence as a trapping of the theater. The audience indulges the impulse to leave the tragedy of slavery, genocide, and hegemonic suppression of agency behind in a cloud of smoke and rubble. I am not sure such indulgence constitutes agency for parties other than Tarantino, the Weinstein Brothers, and Sony International.

Notes

1 "Spike Lee Call 'Django Unchained' 'Disrespectful'," *Rolling Stone*, December 27, 2012. http://www.rollingstone.com/music/news/spike-lee-calls-django-unchained-disrespectful-20121227.

2 "Django Unchained," http://www.boxofficemojo.com/movies/?id=djangounchained.htm

3 "Django Unchained: Awards," http://www.imdb.com/title/tt1853728/awards?ref_=tt_awd

4 A. Susan Owen, Sarah R. Stein, and Leah R. Vande Berg, *Bad Girls: Cultural Politics and Media Representations of Transgressive Women* (New York, NY: Peter Lang Publishing) 240.

5 Quentin Tarantino, Interview by Krishnan Guru-Murthy, "Tarantino Uncut: When Quentin Met Krishnan," January 10, 2013. http://www.channel4.com/news/tarantino-uncut-when-quentin-met-krishnan-transcript.

6 Quentin Tarantino, Interview by Henry Louis Gates: Henry Louis Gates Jr., "Tarantino 'Unchained,' Part 1: 'Django' Trilogy?," *The Root* (2012), http://www.theroot.com/views/tarantino-unchained-part-1-django-trilogy (accessed August 29, 2013); "Tarantino 'Unchained,' Part 2: On the n-word," *The Root* (2012), http://www.theroot.com/views/tarantino-unchained-part-2-n-word (accessed August 29, 2013); "Tarantino 'Unchained,' Part 3: White Saviors," *The Root* (2012), http://www.theroot.com/views/tarantino-unchained-part-3-white-saviors (accessed August 29, 2013).

7 Quentin Tarantino and Krishnan Guru-Murthy, "Tarantino Uncut: When Quentin Met Krishnan," http://www.channel4.com/news/tarantino-uncut-when-quentin-met-krishnan-transcript (January 10, 2013).

8 Samuel Perry, "Django Unchained and the Undisturbed Frontier Hero Archetype" in *Disturbing Argument: Selected Works from the 18th NCA/AFA Alta Conference on Argumentation*, ed. Catherine Palczewski (New York: Routledge, 2014).

9 Jean Baudrillard, *The Transparency of Evil: Essays on Extreme Phenomenon*, trans. James Benedict (New York, NY: Verso Publishing, 1993), 45.

10 Helene A. Shugart, "Counterhegemonic Acts: Appropriation as a Feminist Rhetorical Strategy," *Quarterly Journal of Speech*, 83, 2 (1997), 210–229.

11 Shugart, 217.

12 Kenneth Burke, *A Grammar of Motives* (Berkeley, CA: University of California Press, 1969), 228.

13 Janice Hocker Rushing, " Evolution of 'The New Frontier' in *Alien* and *Aliens*: Patriarchal Co-optation of the Feminine Archetype," *Quarterly Journal of Speech*, 75, 1 (1989), 21.

14 Owen et al., 34.

15 Janice Hocker Rushing, "The Rhetoric of the American Western Myth," *Communication Monographs*, 50, 1 (1983), 27–30.

16 Janice Hocker Rushing, "Mythic Evolution of the 'New Frontier' in Mass Mediated Rhetoric," *Critical Studies in Mass Communication*, 3, 3 (1986), 266.

17 Stephen Arron, "What's Next, What's West," *OAH Magazine of History*, November 2005, 22–25; Here 23.

18 Richard Slatta, "Making and Unmaking the Frontier Myth," *European Journal of American Culture*, 29, 2 (2010), 88.

19 Richard Slotkin, *Regeneration through Violence: The Mythology of the American Frontier* (Norman, OK: University of Oklahoma Press, 1973), 5.

20 Ronald Carpenter, "Revisiting Janice Rushing about 'The Western Myth' (More Important Now than Ever Before)," *Southern Journal of Communication*, 71, 2 (2006), 179–182; Samuel P. Perry, "Douglas MacArthur as Frontier Hero: Converting Frontiers in MacArthur's Farewell to Congress," *Southern Communication Journal*, 77, 4 (2012), 268.

21 Diane Long Hoeveller and Jeffrey Cass, "Mapping Orientalism: Representations and Pedagogies." in *Interrogating Orientalism: Contextual Approaches and Pedagogical Practices*, ed. Diane Hoeveller and Jeffrey Cass (Columbus, OH: Ohio State University Press, 2006), 18.

22 Perry, "Douglas … " 263–286.

23 Owen et al., *Bad Girls*, 240.

24 Owen et al., *Bad Girls*, 240.

25 Katie L. Gibson and Amy L. Heyse, "Depoliticizing Feminism: Frontier Mythology and Sarah Palin's 'The Rise of The Mama Grizzlies,'" *Western Journal of Communication*, 78, 1 (2014), 97–117.

26 "Inglourious Basterds: References" http://www.imdb.com/title/tt0361748/trivia?tab=mc&ref_=tt_trv_cnn#references (retrieved November 26, 2013).

27 Andrew O'Hehir, "Is Tarantino Good for the Jews?," *Salon*, August 13, 2009.

28 O'Hehir, "Is Tarantino Good for the Jews?"

29 Baudrillard, *Transparency*, 50.

30 O'Hehir, "Is Tarantino Good for the Jews?"

31 Jean Baudrillard, *Simulation and Simulacrum*, trans. Sheila Faria Glaser (Ann Arbor, MI: University of Michigan Press), 161.

32 Baudrillard, *Simulation and Simulacrum*, 3.

33 Salamisha Tillet, "Quentin Tarantino Creates an Exceptional Slave," December 25, 2012. http://inamerica.blogs.cnn.com/2012/12/25/opinion-quentin-tarantino-creates-an-exceptional-slave/

34 Perry, "Douglas ...," 280.

35 Quentin Tarantino, interview by Henry Louis Gates.

36 Sylvère Lotringer, "Domination and Servitude" introduction to Jean Baudrillard, *The Agony of Power*, trans. Ames Hodges (Los Angeles, CA: Semiotext(e), 2010): 10.

37 Quentin Tarantino, interview by Henry Louis Gates.

38 Baudrillard, *Transparency ...*, 16.

39 Rushing, *Alien ...*, 21.

40 Rushing, *Alien ...*, 21.

41 Quentin Tarantino, interview with Krishnan Guru-Murthy.

11

"Crowdsourcing" "The Bad-Ass Slave": A Critique of Quentin Tarantino's *Django Unchained*

Reynaldo Anderson, D. L. Stephenson, and Chante Anderson

The philosophy of Franz Fanon articulated in his books *The Wretched of the Earth* (1963), the bible of the Black Revolution, and *Black Skin, White Masks* (1967) reached its apogee during the turbulent decade of the 1960s. Fanon theorized that revolutionary violence could transform the personality of the oppressed colonized subject and allow the emergence of a more humanistic man. This humanist transformation of an oppressed personality would reflect the best ideas of the enlightenment and create a new type of male subject. It is within this understanding that this chapter seeks to utilize a critical framework to examine the social significance of the film *Django Unchained* and critiques the appropriation by director Quentin Tarantino of the black image in order to reconstruct the historical memory of slavery. This chapter examines the ways the intersections of race, gender, class, sexuality, and violence complicate this process. Finally, drawing upon the work of Frantz Fanon, Patricia Hill Collins, and Stuart Hall's concept of the public sphere and male and female subject, we argue that *Django Unchained*, in its current form, cannot create an opportunity for a dialogical aesthetic to facilitate and engage a transformation to a more cosmopolitan media ethic.

Django Unchained, directed by Quentin Tarantino, has provoked considerable discussion about the commodification of black bodies in cinema. Commodified African American imagery was an important component in the global spread and influence of American sports and entertainment throughout the twentieth century. Representing the first generation of the post-Civil Rights generation, contemporary black athletes and entertainers showcased their athletic prowess, musical tastes, aesthetic styles, acting talents, and idiomatic expressions all over the world through an array of American multinational media networks and channels. We seek to specifically examine Quentin Tarantino's appropriation of a particular people and cultural experience that is identified as African American or black American and black. According to Coleman, contemporary stereotypical representations of African American ethnicity and what can be referred to as "blackness" are primarily products of corporate media and are influenced by a politics of race, class, sexuality, and gender unique to the United States.[1] Despite claims of genius associated with Tarantino's Oscar win, Tarantino's latest cinematic critique of race and racism in *Django Unchained* is neither as philosophically substantial as Mark Twain's *Huckleberry Finn* nor as sophisticated as Carl Van Vechten's *Nigger Heaven*. Rather, Tarantino's film is a shallow echo of William Styron's depiction of psychosexual desire in the book *Nat Turner*. Tarantino eroticizes black bodies in a way that never does more than evoke the possibility of an actual black male sexual agency. Tarantino's films are overwhelmingly celebrations of fetishistic violence, sex, and film pastiche, laden with aesthetic flourishes from the early and mid-1970s—nothing more and nothing less. However, as part of that celebration of violence and pastiche is Tarantino's obvious interest in black characters as evidenced in the films *Jackie Brown* (1997) and *Pulp Fiction* (1994), two of his most commercially popular and successful films. The purpose of this study is threefold: (1) to illuminate how the film director Quentin Tarantino appropriates race in relation to the production of contemporary cinema, (2) to understand how and why *Django Unchained*, despite

Tarantino's claims, adopts an apolitical political perspective, and (3) to illustrate how corporate media markets commodify black American male and female cultural identity in a globalized context.

In the following section, we present a review of literature on the historical formation of African American entertainers and the corporate appropriation of black cultural motifs that have been featured in the global diffusion of cultural commodities. Finally, the chapter's findings are presented in order to highlight the implications for the social construction of African American culture in relation to commodification and globalization.

Historical background: Black Americans in American entertainment

Blackface minstrelsy was first performed in the 1830s United States and was popular through the remainder of the nineteenth century.[2] Irish immigrants portrayed the first blackface minstrels, and the most famous stock character was referred to as "Jim Crow."[3] These productions became representative of actual black life and culture and became representative of what many consumers of these images would come to believe to be truthful and accurate. According to feminist theorist Patricia Hill Collins, "Mass media's tendency to blur the lines between fact and fiction has important consequences for perceptions of Black culture and Black people."[4] The globalization of the blackface minstrel was made possible by the Wild West Show of Bill Cody that performed across Europe in the late nineteenth century.[5] The early globalization of American popular performances featured stereotypes of black people that were assumed to be true. In 1914, *Uncle Tom's Cabin* was the first film produced by whites to include an actual African American.[6] Following the Civil War, the routine portrayal of black people in stage entertainment and later cinema featured white actors wearing burnt cork, which started the blackface tradition.[7] For most of the twentieth century, African American actors were excluded from mainstream entertainment created by whites. When they were included, black people were relegated to playing the sidekicks of white actors.[8] During the 1940s, films produced by

too simplified

whites began to feature black musicians and singers such as Cab Calloway, Lena Horn, Duke Ellington, Louis Armstrong, and Hazel Scott who "would provide a dazzling interlude and then fade from the scene, leaving the plot to continue without [them]."[9] By the 1950s, blacks in white productions seemed to be allowed more range and bigger roles, though entrenched racial stereotypes bound them to predictable and acceptable performances.[10] The past and current film and entertainment business is characterized by themes and messages that reinforce the American status quo of white superiority. American films, typically, are neoliberal and neoconservative ideological constructs that focus on individuals' problems and solutions, while ignoring the social structures that contribute to and exacerbate those problems.[11] For example, an entertainment product such as *Django Unchained*, we argue, can characterize *individual* blacks as morally superior to *individual* whites, while leaving undisturbed notions of an ideal, albeit slaveholding, society. Though few today would argue that the 1800s slaveholding South was an ideal society, *Django Unchained* represents slavery as an evil that existed within a society that need only end slavery and racism and acknowledge Django and other slaves as fully enfranchised human beings. What is missing in Tarantino's narrative is any consideration of the ways in which slavery and racism toward black people were only obvious elements of a larger structural reality: American society was never intended to enfranchise and accept all people as equals, and especially people identified as black.

Due to the success of the Civil Rights trailblazers of the early 1970s, many overt images of black buffoonery and docility had been supplanted with much more subtle representations. However, due to the commercial success of Melvin Van Peebles independently produced *Sweet Sweetback's Badasss Song* in 1971, Hollywood became aware of the moneymaking potential in the black urban community and the era of Hollywood Blaxploitation was born.[12] *Sweet Sweetback*, though problematic in its depiction of black women as prostitutes and little else, demonstrated the radical potential to entertain and instill in black audiences a political consciousness of sorts. The film also demonstrated the ability for black films to generate revenue independently. Films of this sort came to be known as "Blaxploitation" and constituted a genre that some people believed undermined the ethos of the Civil Rights and Black Power phenomena. Rhines explains,

> These films were released during the height of the Civil Rights and Black Liberation movements, yet their subject matter of sex, violence, and super cool individualism was the antithesis of what contemporary political organizations like the Student Non-violent Coordinating Committee, the NAACP, or the Southern Christian Leadership Council represented; hence, the name Blaxploitation, a term coined by *Variety* magazine, [was created].[13]

Moreover, it was during this era that Tarantino was introduced to Blaxploitation, a genre he would later co-opt as part of his directorial repertoire. Therefore, instead of the heroic and arguably political character of *Sweet Sweetback*, audiences were influenced by apolitical movies featuring characters like the tough law enforcement officer Shaft in the film *Shaft* (1971), and the smooth, controlled pimp Priest in the film *Superfly* (1972). Blaxploitation did not cease at the end of the 1970s. Rather, the ideological practices of 1970s Blaxploitation simply laid the foundation for things to come. The most successful tropes of Blaxploitation and narrative practices continued into the 1980s, gained strength, and became pervasive nationally and globally. Furthermore, Blaxploitation was not only relegated to film, but also metastasized into other forms of entertainment. We argue that this expansion of the genre gave rise to a slightly different, yet similar period of neo-Blaxploitation in film and entertainment as a whole in the decades following the Civil Rights and Black Liberation movements. Indeed, Tarantino merely appropriated Blaxploitation in ways that mimicked the general film style of the early and mid-1970s, while simultaneously dispensing with any of the genre's actual political ideology.

The political ascendance of the conservative movement and Ronald Reagan to the presidency following the defeat of Jimmy Carter in 1980 signaled the rise to power of the political right in American politics. Following his election, Reagan moved to dismantle federal anti-poverty, job training, and affirmative action programs and appointed conservative officials to agencies charged with protecting the interests of some of the country's most vulnerable citizens. At the same time, there was an exodus of black middle-class professionals out of inner-city communities, exacerbating the economic disparities in inner cities across the country. Black unemployment rose to 13.2 percent by 1985, and the number of incarcerated African Americans increased from 58,000 in 1980 to 87,000 by 1985.[14] With that exodus came a significant cultural shift among many African American youths that many people, both black and white, found problematic. Because of the widely disapproved aesthetic forms that this shift took, certain African American performers (e.g. Bill Cosby) began promoting an apolitical agenda of individual and social respectability that resonated with the new conservative rhetoric of personal uplift, hard work, and moral decency. Further, the increasing push to promote black entertainers who could "cross-over" (Michael Jackson, Whitney Houston, Morgan Freeman, Danny Glover, Samuel Jackson, etc.) caught the attention of powerful producers who saw an opportunity to exploit these entertainers' talent for commercial gain. Quinton Tarantino, we contend, continues this neoconservative and neoliberal trend to exploit black American history, culture, talent, and style for his own personal and commercial gain in the global marketplace.

Cultural studies as a heuristic framework

A cultural studies approach is most appropriate for understanding the potential ramifications of the commodification of black images in a global context. Cultural studies focuses on the cultural struggle for meaning through the analysis of various cultural practices that construct, reinforce, constrain, and discredit certain interpretations of popular culture texts. These cultural practices are influenced by ideological structures that construct meaning and perpetuate ideologies.

Popular culture is a field upon which dominant classes or groups attempt to gain and organize consent and obtain specific types of social control.[15] According to Raymond Williams, a culture has two aspects: (1) the known meanings that it reinforces and (2) the new observations and meanings with which members of the culture are presented.[16] Williams argues that culture needs to be interpreted in relation to the underlying structures of production and that the cultures we participate in are influenced by economic forces,[17] culture is a whole way of life and is "ordinary."[18] Thus, it is the goal of cultural studies to examine how these "cultural" positions are constructed, whose interests are served, and for what purpose(s). Moreover, contemporary media artifacts are derived from the sociopolitical and economic system of imperialism.[19] Media cultural imperialism is a component of an advanced economic system that operates symbiotically with existing financial, industrial, and political paradigms.[20] However, within advanced Western economies such as the United States, media entities serve consumer society. According to Schiller, this relationship "is an extension and creation of consumer society."[21] Thus, culture can be said to operate within the context of a political economy, thus serving the interests of existing sociopolitical economic realities.[22]

One of the cultural structures that maintain the status quo is the media.[23] The media, either knowingly or unknowingly, indoctrinate members of the society who consume and give credence to media messages. Cultural studies are interested in how the mass media define social relations and political problems while seeming to function as transparent bearers of meanings in society.[24] Therefore the implication is that members of a "free society" shape and are shaped by meanings communicated by the media.[25]

Second, meaning is determined by cultural context.[26] Inhabitants of a culture are influenced differently by messages propagated in the culture. For that reason, cultural studies assumes that meaning comes from the culture and culture is comprised of competing ideologies and competing discourses.[27] A cultural studies' perspective also attempts to expose power relations and explores the often overlooked politics inherent in media texts. All these aims of cultural studies enhance the scholar's ability to describe, interpret, evaluate, and judge media texts. Concerning texts, Fiske explains that a text is defined by the dominant group's social experience.[28] Textual analysis from a cultural studies perspective makes explicit how media productions overwhelmingly operate in the interests of more powerful groups even when appearing to do the opposite. The construction of texts reflects particular ideological viewpoints and hegemonic influences.[29]

A cultural studies critique explores texts for the sake of clarity in two areas, (1) political commitment, and (2) to make explicit the ideological influences and existing power relations that inform texts.

Analysis

Quentin Tarantino's films are noted for their appropriation and exploration of race and gender themes. They are also recognized for their themes of revenge and Tarantino's mixing of genres. Despite his claims of racial authenticity or being "more [B]lack" than African American film director Spike Lee and his expressed desire to use his films as social commentary, Tarantino's work does not interrogate existing social relations or the ones that existed in his period piece *Django Unchained*. Rather, his works reinforce existing structures of cultural and material ideology and hegemony for a global audience. More specifically, Tarantino's production of *Django Unchained* continues the cinematic tradition of promoting cultural stereotypes, ahistorical circumstances, and appropriating cultural narratives and the collective histories of marginalized groups in the interests of profits. First and foremost, Tarantino expertly exploits both stereotypes and highly charged idioms in the *Django Unchained*.

Tarantino's elocutionary practice(s)

According to Denby, *Django Unchained* is a "crap masterpiece" that takes liberties with historical facts and reinforces stereotypes that Tarantino appropriated and co-opted.[30] For example, Tarantino has the white, German bounty hunter character "Schultz," played by Austrian actor Christoph Waltz, speak in an idiom of "elaborate rhetoric." The Schultz character has been traveling around Texas for several years prior to the beginning of the Civil War, posing as a dentist who speaks perfect English. Schultz's dialogue and "elocution" are juxtaposed with the Southern drawl of "ignorant southern Americans." In the film's opening scene, he states, "Among your company, I'm led to believe, there is a specimen I hope to acquire." And after shooting one of the (white) men, who cries out in pain, Schultz states, "If you could keep your caterwauling down to a minimum, I would like to speak to young Django."[31] The elocutionary approach is a trope used in previous Tarantino films such as *Reservoir Dogs* (1992) and *Pulp Fiction* (1994) where word play, witty repartee, rhetorical decorum, and murder are combined for comedic effect.[32] In *Django Unchained*, violence is rendered elegant and sophisticated when it is meted out by the cultured Schultz.

Elocution has historically worked in Hollywood cinema by reinforcing American culture and the global brand that is "America." Elocution also marks or signals cultural elitism by helping in the construction of American national identity as a brand. Elocution also helps further brand American national identity as equal and democratic. However, the South in *Django Unchained* must be marked as different from the rest of the nation in order to preserve and further the idea that the United States is, despite the South, a democratic nation based on equality. For example, the film tradition of Hollywood has long represented the American South as a region apart from the rest of the United States and especially the North. The South has been characterized as violent, poverty-ridden, uneducated, xenophobic, and intolerant.[33] This signification of regional difference or geographic "Othering" provides a discursive space that serves as "the receptacle for the country's shadow" in contrast to the promotion of the United States as prosperous, self-reliant, and cosmopolitan.[34] Because the South is the repository in *Django Unchained* of all that is debased, the frequent use of the word "nigger" by primarily white characters seems fitting. However, the liberal sprinkling of the word in this and all of Tarantino's films in which black characters are discussed or represented seems gratuitous despite Tarantino's defense of the word's use.

Crowdsourcing "the nigger"

Tarantino's gratuitous use of the word "nigger" in the film is justified as a means to reduce its didactic value "as a sign of racism." Tarantino's aim is to treat the word "nigger" as nothing more than a historical appellation once in common usage. However, asserting the historicity of its use as nothing more than a simple anachronism or as "a form of spatial misbehavior with respect to time" ignores the rhetorical power of language and labels.[35] The word's use is problematic in light of the utilization of other rhetorical devices such as hip-hop artist Rick Ross' song "100 Black Coffins." The use of contemporary music increases the entertainment value for modern audiences and reinforces the theme of Django's individual agency and power, but it ultimately undermines any notion that the word "nigger" may simply be used for historical accuracy. Engagement with the past through modern aesthetics such as music allows history to be reinterpreted, disrupting historical stability and making history "updatable."[36] Therefore, Tarantino's production functions to shape historical memory for audiences who have little or no knowledge of the actual cultural and social realities of the slave South in the 1800s. For those familiar with Tarantino's *Pulp Fiction* (1994) and *Jackie Brown* (1997), it can be inferred that Tarantino is continuing in *Django Unchained* with his infatuation with the word "nigger."

Django Unchained: The antebellum "remix"

Tarantino's interweaving of the western with Blaxploitation and the antebellum South slave film demonstrates his ability to brilliantly combine genres. *Django Unchained* contributed to a renewed interest in Western films and reinvigorated the Italian subgenre of Spaghetti Westerns, a label applied by twentieth-century American film critics.[37] Previously, Italian Spaghetti Westerns directed by Sergio Leone, such as *A Fistful of Dollars* (1964), were influenced by Japanese samurai films such as *Yojimbo* (1961), directed by Akira Kurosawa.[38] In similar kitsch-like fashion, Tarantino's previous films *Kill Bill, Vol. 1* (2003) and *Vol. 2* (2004) each borrow elements of mass culture attributed to Spaghetti Westerns, Japanese Samurai films, female revenge movies, and adventure and horror films.[39]

Yet, *Django Unchained*, despite its depiction of revenge and its ability to inspire moral vindication for the acts of brutality against blacks that the film features, reinforces the act of black resistance as nothing more than a fantasy. In contrast, following the Civil Rights movement, during the era of Blaxploitation, "black films offer[ed] escape from gloom, roaches, and [the] social confusion of center-city colonies. This image ... offer[ed] a means of reviewing life, exaggerated or absurd as it may be, and direct[ed] the audience with the coolest route out."[40] However, the key element that black actors have brought to the trash or kitsch of Hollywood cinema stereotypes is their own interpretations of those stereotypical features within the script, often with the result of elevating the art form.[41]

Violence and revenge

Tarantino's mixture of revenge, aggression, and violence is a consistent theme in his films. Similar to the Italian or Spaghetti Westerns, Tarantino's films embody the Manichean opposition between good and evil and transcend historicity.[42] Moreover, Tarantino created a new genre of western that combined elements of samurai films and Blaxploitation films such as *Mandingo* (1975) and *Goodbye Uncle Tom* (1971) with the antebellum South as a backdrop.[43] Furthermore, Tarantino's use of violence for shock value, parodying the Ku Klux Klan, and featuring the so-called "black racism" of the character Stephen provide the key elements of his version of the Southern Gothic Western genre.[44] Tarantino's depiction of the Ku Klux Klan as comedic bunglers subverts the reality of the police state that emerged to contain black resistance to subjugation *after* slavery ended. Furthermore, the film's Mandingo fight scene ignores the actual socioeconomic interest of slave owners in relation to their property. Moreover, the dehumanizing fight scene emerges as a human cockfight, which bears no historical relationship to the actual socioeconomic practice of chattel slavery.[45] Tarantino's *Django Unchained*, while appealing successfully to the aesthetically coarser, baser elements of his audiences' cultural voyeurism, fails as a political text. However, the film does succeed as a commodified artistic nexus of hegemonic race, gender, and sexuality.

"Killing Whitey," loving capital

Django Unchained revealed much about each major black character's subject position, slavery's deadening labor practices, and the master–slave dialectic that Tarantino, by his own admissions, sought to subvert while also glorifying it. Franz Fanon's *Black Skin, White Masks* asserts to break the master–slave dialectic and resolve its contradictions noting: "Violence can thus be understood to be the perfect mediation," and "[t]he colonized man liberates himself in and through violence."[46] Initially, Django exists in a zombie-like state prior to being purchased by the bounty hunter Schultz. However, Django slowly undergoes a psychological transformation as he trains to hunt and kill the Brittle Brothers, slavers who once oversaw both Django and Broomhilda. Although Tarantino subverts the process of Django's growth by portraying the bounty hunter Schultz as the "white benefactor," ultimately Django comes to understand that freedom must be taken by force. Nonetheless, the Eurocentric paternalism of Schultz complicates Django's revolutionary agency. By contrast, the character Stephen exemplifies the desire for the status of "whiteness" through complete subservience to Calvin Candie and as the informal manager of the Candie plantation. Moreover, Stephen takes pleasure in the sadism that punishes Broomhilda for attempting to run away. Broomhilda, virtually senseless, her body drenched with water, dehydrated, beaten, and naked is unceremoniously loaded onto a cart after she is freed from a box in the ground used for punishing slaves at Candyland. Broomhilda's nudity, like the naked bodies of most women in American films, functions to both titillate and inspire indignation. Nonetheless, Broomhilda's agency devolves in ways that undermine any sense of radical independence on Broomhilda's part. Broomhilda's ability to act independently (e.g. running away) is undermined by reducing her relationship to Django to the typical patriarchal Hollywood dialectic of rescuing male hero and rescued female victim. Kerry Washington's clearly "cultured" character Broomhilda defies stereotypes of black women as unsophisticated and common. The casting of the slight, petite, long-haired Washington coincides with Hollywood's casting of black women in the lead who adhere to white aesthetics of female beauty. Further, the female lead must be worthy of Django's love and his risking his life. A black woman in the lead role would have to be exceptional, not only in terms of her physical appearance, but also in terms of her attitudes, behavior, and abilities. Broomhilda speaks German, which associates her with Schultz's urbane European, sophistication and elevates her above the other slaves in the narrative. In fact, Broomhilda, to be worthy of rescue at all costs, must be a paragon of true womanhood. Black women have historically been depicted as "bitches," "ugly," or "masculine" in cinema. Black women, culturally, occupy a social location at the bottom of the female, sexual hierarchy. For those reasons, the Broomhilda character must be *made* worthy of love and rescue.[47] However, white female lead characters are held to no such standard (e.g. Julia Roberts' portrayal of a prostitute in *Pretty Woman* [1990]). Nonetheless, Broomhilda aside, Sheba, played by Nicole Galicia, and Cora, played by Dana Gourrier, deliver the stereotypical performances that have haunted black female actors since Hattie McDaniel's portrayal of a servant in *Gone with the Wind* (1939). But far more problematic is the film's complete erasure of collective action on the part of black men and women. Tarantino's film ignores the reality that black men and women could not mimic the clear division of masculine and feminine roles that upper-class whites created if black people were to have any chance of resisting a slave system.

Holding the skull of a dead slave in Django's presence, Calvin Candie, in a nod to *Hamlet*, muses, "Why don't they kill us?" But Candie knows why. Only an organized, well-armed, collective violent action could overthrow Candie and his overseers. However, the Manichean state created and maintained by Candie and Stephen is reversed violently in a night of violence when a "new freeman" emerges from the ashes of Candyland. Though compelling, the image of Django single-handedly defeating his enemies against impossible odds is pure Hollywood fantasy. Historically, all slave revolts or rebellions— successful or not—occurred with cooperation with others—including black women. Django ignores all other slaves throughout the film, even allowing one earlier in the action to be mauled to death by dogs. Critic Ishmael Reed notes, "Tarantino, despite the history of black resistance, apparently believes that progress for blacks has been guided by a White, educated, sympathetic elite, a belief that doesn't explain the hundreds of revolts throughout this hemisphere which weren't guided by German bounty hunters, nor Abraham Lincoln, nor a talented tenth Negro."[48] _Django Unchained_, despite its entertainment value, cannot function as a liberating text in any meaningful way. It can only entertain the global masses through fiction and fraud.

Notes

1 Robin Means Coleman, _Say It Loud! African-American Audiences, Media, and Identity_ (New York: Routledge, 2002).

2 John Blair, _First Steps Toward Globalization: Nineteenth Century Exports of American Entertainment Forms_. Quoted in R. Wagneither and E. May, _Here, There and Everywhere: The Foreign Politics of American Popular Culture_ (Hanover, NH: University Press of New England, 2000).

3 Wagneither and May, _Here, There and Everywhere_.

4 Patricia Hill Collins, _Black Sexual Politics: African Americans, Gender, and the New Racism_ (New York: Routledge, 2005), 151.

5 _First Steps Toward Globalization_.

6 Stephanie Larson, _Media and Minorities: The Politics of Race and in News and Entertainment_ (Lanham, MD: Rowan & Littlefield, 2006).

7 Larson, _Media and Minorities_.

8 Larson, _Media and Minorities_.

9 Donald Bogle, _Toms, Coons, Mulattoes, Mammies, and Bucks: An Interpretive History of Blacks in American Films_. 3rd ed (New York: Continuum Publishing Company, 1999), 121.

10 Bogle, _Toms, Coons, Mulattoes, Mammies, and Bucks_.

11 _Media and Minorities_.

12 Jesse Rhines, _Black Film, White Money_ (New Brunswick, NJ: Rutgers University Press, 1996).

13 Rhines, _Black Film, White Money_, 46

14 Rhines, _Black Film, White Money_, 46.

15 Stuart Hall, _Representation: Cultural Representations and Signifying Practices_ (London: Sage, 1997).

16 Raymond Williams, *Culture and Society 1780–1950* (London: Chatto and Windus; Harmondsworth: Penguin Books, 1958).

17 Williams, *Culture and Society 1780–1950*.

18 Williams, *Culture and Society 1780–1950*.

19 Herbert Schiller, "Not Yet the Posts-Imperialism Era," *Critical Studies in Mass Communication* 8(1) (1991), 13–21.

20 Schiller, "Not Yet the Posts-Imperialism Era."

21 Schiller, "Not Yet the Posts-Imperialism Era."

22 Schiller, "Not Yet the Posts-Imperialism Era."

23 Farrel Corcoran, "Cultural Studies: From Old World to New World." *Communication Yearbook* (1989), 602.

24 Corcoran, "Cultural Studies."

25 Tanni Haas, *The Pursuit of Public Journalism: Theory, Practice, and Criticism* (New York: Routledge, 2007).

26 *Cultural Representations and Signifying Practices*.

27 *Cultural Representations and Signifying Practices*.

28 John Fiske, *British Cultural Studies and Television* (New York, NY: St. Martin's Press Inc, 1996), quoted in J. Storey, *What is Cultural Studies? A Reader* (New York: St. Martin's Press Inc, 1996), 115–147.

29 John Storey, *An Introductory Guide to Cultural Theory and Popular Culture* (Athens, GA: University of Georgia Press, 1993).

30 Jacob Denby, "'Django Unchained.' Put-On, Revenge, and the Aesthetics of Trash." *New Yorker*, January 22, 2013, http://www.newyorker.com/online/blogs/culture/2013/01/django-unchained-reviewed-tarantinos-crap-masterpiece.html

31 Denby, "'Django Unchained.' Put-On, Revenge, and the Aesthetics of Trash."

32 Denby, "'Django Unchained.' Put-On, Revenge, and the Aesthetics of Trash."

33 David R. Jansson, "A Geography of Racism: Internal Orientalism and the Construction of American National Identity in the Film Mississippi Burning," *National Identities*, 7(3) (2005), 265–285.

34 Jansson, "A Geography of Racism."

35 Wai Chee Dimock, "Crowdsourcing History: Ishmael Reed, Tony Kushner, and Steven Spielberg Update the Civil War," *American Literary History*, 25(4) (2013), 896–914.

36 Dimock, "Crowdsourcing History," 898.

37 Arianna Mancini, "The New Spaghetti Western: The Southern," Iperstoria. Testi letterature linguaggi (www.iperstoria.it). Rivista semestrale. Numero 2, ottobre 2013. http://www.iperstoria.it/joomla/numeri/15-saggi/80-mancini-prova-2 (accessed November 28, 2013).

38 Mancini, "The New Spaghetti Western."

39 Mancini, "The New Spaghetti Western."

40 Brandon Wander, "Black Dreams: The Fantasy and Ritual of Black Films." *Film Quarterly*, 1 (1975), 2–11.

41 *Toms, Coons, Mulattoes, Mammies.*

42 *The New Spaghetti Western.*

43 *The New Spaghetti Western.*

44 *The New Spaghetti Western.*

45 Moon Charania, "Django Unchained, Voyeurism Unleashed." *Contexts*,12(3) (2013), 58–60.

46 Frantz Fanon, *Black Skin, White Masks* (Syracuse, NY: Grove Press, 2008).

47 See Hill Collins, *Black Sexual Politics.*

48 Ishmael Reed, "Black Audiences, White Stars, and Django Unchained," *Wall Street Journal*, December 28, 2012, http://blogs.wsj.com/speakeasy/2012/12/28/black-audiences-white-stars-and-django-unchained/

12

Guess Who's Coming to Get Her: Stereotypes, Mythification, and White Redemption

Ryan J. Weaver and Nichole K. Kathol

In recent memory, few films have polarized audiences like Quentin Tarantino's *Django Unchained* (2012). While the film received an abundance of mostly positive reviews from critics, Django aroused a sizable group of objectors to voice outrage at the film's portrayal of American slavery. The question remains: how should we view the significance of this film? Is *Django Unchained* an important contribution to the historical record, is it the product of a racist, rabid director as some have claimed, or is it an attempt to start a "race war" as Nation of Islam Minister Louis Farrakhan argues?[1]

Upon its release, a sizable group of film critics focused on ethical questions regarding the way *Django Unchained* (2012) represented American slavery and the accuracy of the history shown in the film. This was just one of a handful of controversies surrounding the film which also included debates about gratuitous violence and offensive language. Several commentators were offended by Tarantino's purposeful historical revisionism. Many voiced concerns that the filmmaker played fast and loose with history in *Django* and they recognized the risks implicit in doing this with a film about slavery.[2] Yet, a more favorable outlook was offered by critics who dismissed the importance of dogmatic cinematic accuracy and saw the film's historical elasticity as an advantage in critiquing the sins of American slavery.[3]

The extent to which Hollywood filmmakers may take license in representing real historical events has been a long-standing point of contention among historians of cinema. Vast disagreement exists as to the inherent value of historical accuracy in Hollywood film. Academic writing recognizes both the possibilities for new exploration and discussion.[4] It also has the potential for spreading misinformation and offending audiences through Hollywood's representations of history.[5] The consensus stemming from this debate is that Hollywood films can have a significant impact on the ways in which an audience thinks about the past.

This chapter uses this debate as a starting point for our examination of *Django Unchained*. Critical response to the film was polarizing, and this reaction is due in large part to a filmmaker who told a story loosely constrained by historical boundaries of accuracy and truth. While we have familiarized ourselves with the debate outlined earlier, we argue that ultimately it presents limitations for the critical exploration of film. Questions as to the worthiness of Hollywood film for teaching audiences about the past (given their vast popularity and influence) seem less interesting than questions about roles films play in teaching us about ourselves. The questions driving our exploration of *Django Unchained* focus on uncovering the function that a revisionist history of American slavery serves for present-day audiences.

We argue that Tarantino's *Django Unchained* attempts to rectify the mythic potential of American slavery by offering mainstream, white audiences a redemptive exit from the lingering sins of this history. *Django's* two protagonists occupy long-standing cinematic stereotypes: the cowboy and the Magical Negro. Over the course of the film, the stereotypes are inverted between the protagonists (a slave and his white owner). As stereotypes are laid upon nontraditional, new characters their cooperation in the film may be read in alternative ways. We extend James Snead's concept of "mythification" in order to demonstrate that the semiotic valuation of characters is jarred loose from the bodies that ordinarily occupy traditional representations.[6] The symbolic meaning of stereotypes is transferred among the protagonists in *Django Unchained*. While this juxtaposition of inverted stereotypical characters is license for many to see the film's narrative techniques as progressive, we argue that this is a veneer of progressivism, and that ultimately the film offers representations of the protagonists, American slavery and its legacy which are deeply conservative. *Django* provides an attractive view of history for white, mainstream audiences in which both renegade slaves and heroic whites battled wicked slavers for life and liberty. The heroism of the two main characters in *Django Unchained* not only offers redemption from the lingering sins of slavery, but the film also works to protect white supremacy and further post-racial discourses in American culture.

The following section reviews the literature which provides a methodological entry point for analyzing *Django Unchained*. We review foundational literature on the form and function of stereotypes. As rhetorical forms, stereotypes perform important cultural work in that they function as narratives with coded meanings and valuations that largely remain consistent over time. There is a direct relationship between the rhetorical forms that stereotypes embody and the cultural ideologies that they produce. Stereotypes teach us about ourselves. We illustrate the way in which stereotypes as rhetoric fit within a broader set of symbols that influence the way audiences view themselves and their collective past. In this case, *Django Unchained* projects and plays with a powerful set of historical stereotypes—the American cowboy and the Magical Negro. The film, when set within a broader rhetorical framework of post-racial discourse, allows white audiences to purge lingering historical guilt and make it so that they are less likely to interrogate white supremacy and contemporary forms of racism.

Stereotypes and ideology

Stereotypes commonly are thought of as pejorative—as devices which essentialize large groups of minorities. However, when Walter Lippmann introduced the term he did not completely see the function of stereotypes as one of abuse.[7] In fact, Lippmann lays out a definition of stereotypes which frames purpose as one of necessity and utility in addition to their limitations and problematic implications.[8] Lippmann argues,

> A pattern of stereotypes is nor neutral. It is not merely a way of substituting order for the great blooming, buzzing confusion of reality. It is not merely a short cut. It is all these things and something more. It is the guarantee of our self-respect; it is the projection upon the world of our own sense of our own value, our own position and our own rights. The stereotypes are, therefore, highly charged with the feelings that are attached to them. They are the fortress of our tradition, and behind its defenses we can continue to feel ourselves safe in the position we occupy.[9]

There is a broad sense of collectivity from the passage quoted above. Lippmann's use of "our" and "we" reflects a view of stereotypes which shows them to possess a significant role in identity formation and maintenance. His use of these pluralistic pronouns suggests that one of the most powerful (and problematic) functions of stereotypes is to generate consensus among members of a society. Stereotypes tell us what to think about others as well as what to think about ourselves. Stereotypes are "charged with feeling," which is another way of saying that they are reflective of our collective attitudes of other groups as well as the inherent value we see in ourselves and the groups to which we belong. Lippmann goes on to say that the consensus generated from stereotypes is more apparent than real.[10] Lippmann shows stereotypes to be rhetorical—they express particular versions of reality. Further, the "tradition" alluded to by Lippmann is central to the power wielded by stereotypes.[11] Those with control over the dominant projections of cultural stereotypes almost always use them to show themselves as more traditional and "belonging" than groups without the power to influence stereotypes. Stereotypes are central to the ways we think about ourselves and others. In this way, stereotypes—a rhetorical form—serve an ideological function.

When stereotypes are represented visually, they contain an implicit narrative. Unlike social types (hero, villain, helper, etc.) which appear in almost every plot and will serve a wide range of functions in different stories, stereotypes carry with them a history of the character which is consistent across narratives. Stereotypes are characters that appear in many cultural texts. They are used by storytellers to tap into historical symbols which drive plot development, create drama and conflict, and convey meaning to an audience. As symbolic forms they are developed by filmmakers in the mise-en-scène (casting, dialogue, dress, etc.) constructed by elements of the narrative (characters, plot, setting, themes) and performed by actors (dialect, body language).

Importantly, stereotypes exist independently of any particular film character. In some instances, stereotypes dislocate from the characters that ordinarily inhabit the symbolic form. They become mobile, and in many cases are transferred to other adjacent characters in a film. James Snead identifies this device as mythification in his analysis of Merriam C. Cooper's 1933 *King Kong*.[12] The author argues that

> [m]ythification involves realization that filmic codes describe an interrelationship between images. American films do not merely feature this or that debased black image or this or that glorified white hero in isolation, but rather they correlate these images in a larger scheme of semiotic valuation.[13]

The juxtaposition and relationship between characters is central to the symbolic meaning that those characters create. Furthermore, Snead suggests that the symbolic meaning is transferrable, arguing that "*King Kong* is a noteworthy example of 'the coded black'— in this case the carrier of blackness is not a human being, but an ape, but we shall see that the difference can easily be bridged."[14] The critic identifies a noteworthy example of this filmic device from a famous sequence at the beginning of *King Kong*. As the crew of the Venture encounters the inhabitants of Skull Island for the first time, we see them in a ritual ceremony preparing to sacrifice a young woman to Kong. In addition to face paint, spears, and headdresses, one of the first things the viewer sees is that several islanders are dressed as apes. Snead argues that this "cinematic marking" drives the primary narrative force of the film: the terror embodied by Kong (who audiences will meet a few minutes later) is transferred to the islanders from the very first moments that we meet them.[15] Thus, the terror of the film—black male sexual predation—is embodied not only by Kong but more importantly by the human black bodies in close proximity to white women.

Toplin provides similar analysis of the 1988 film *Mississippi Burning*.[16] As the author explores questions about historical authenticity in film and the ways in which a film aids public thinking about the past, stereotypes are shown to play a significant role in contributing to what an audience remembers about media representations. While stereotypes may be manipulative and essentializing, they are the cinematic devices which are most likely to leave an impression in an audience's collective memory about the veracity of the past. Toplin argues that the terror of a film like *Mississippi Burning* for white audiences is the transference of negative stereotypes of poor, uneducated blacks to proximate white populations.[17] The terror of seeing whites contracting negative black stereotypes in Mississippi in 1964 is the takeaway for white audiences in 1988, and the film may have had political and ideological implications which retrenched anti-black attitudes at the time of its release.

Stereotypes shift in *Django Unchained*. The protagonists in the film—a German bounty hunter and an American slave—occupy stereotypes that have a long-standing history in American cinema. The cowboy and the Magical Negro are familiar symbolic forms to American film going audiences. Because each stereotype has appeared in many films over time, each possesses an implicit narrative that creates expectations for audiences. There would be nothing unusual about the German bounty hunter playing the stereotypical cowboy role and the American slave as the Magical Negro. However, it is significant when those stereotypes are jarred loose from the bodies by which they are traditionally occupied. Audiences are invited not only to think differently about the history represented on film, but about the vestiges of that history as it pertains to their lives today. The shifting stereotypes in *Django Unchained* have ideological implications as audiences may think differently about the present-day implications of American slavery and their relationship to that history.

The following section briefly reviews the lineage of the cowboy and the Magical Negro in American cinema. Each of these symbolic forms is shown to be popular recurring characters in film and each possesses characteristics which are important to our analysis of *Django Unchained*.

The cowboy

Most cultures have developed some variation of a macho, heroic semi-barbarian mythic character, yet none have the international popularity and publicity of the North American cowboy. The most likely point of origin of the myth of the cowboy is the American frontier—the Wild West. Eric Hobsbawm argues that the original image of the Wild West contains two elements: "the confrontation of nature and civilization, and of freedom with social constraint."[18] American settlers who move from bondage to independence (which characterizes American independence from Europe and the idea of manifest destiny in the eighteenth and nineteenth centuries) bring civilization to the Wild West and tame it. It is the cowboy who is the first citizen of the settled West—a guardian—who simultaneously represents a rugged individualist spirit but who functions to kowtow the Wild West so that it is habitable for American settlers.

In one of the more comprehensive sociohistorical excavations of the iconography of the American cowboy, William Savage recognizes that "the cowboy in various guises is popularly accepted by Americans as a symbol, indicative of his stature as myth."[19] The author recognizes that cowboys did not leave behind a wealth of documents that historians find useful, and therefore researchers have had difficulty writing this history. Thus, the collective memory of the American cowboy is a composite that remains obscure. It is a synthesis of images that include Buffalo Bill Cody, the Marlboro Man, the masterpieces of Charles M. Russell and Frederic Remington, screen icons like the Lone Ranger, John Wayne, and Clint Eastwood, as well as the presidency of Ronald Reagan.

Because the cowboy is a composite of a wide variety of real people as well as fictitious characters a typology of the American cowboy hero has been difficult to formulate with precision. Yet, there is a consensus about three formal characteristics that are common of the mythic character throughout most textual representations. First, the cowboy possesses a commonsense faculty of mind which explains much of his popularity in American history and culture. The cowboy's pragmatism reflects what Americans see as virtuous in themselves— the middle-class virtue of common sense has much to do with how America came to be in the first place.[20] The cowboy's common sense is paired together with the second formal characteristic of the mythic character—his sense of justice as a righter of wrongs. Described as a philosophical observer of the human condition, the wisdom of the cowboy is arguably the best weapon in his arsenal.[21] In his discussion of the evolution of the cowboy hero in American literature and film, Savage sees the cowboy's analytical skill set as a consistent marker of his prowess as a hero:

> They knew exactly what to do and when to do it, whether the task was to win the lady or save the day. And they could overthrow evil by any of several techniques drawn from their arsenal of cowboy skills. Deprive them of sidearms, but no matter. They would first outwit then outpunch any enemy. It occurred to Americans between boxes of popcorn, that brains were the cowboy's most potent weapon. Against cowboy intellect even the worst villain, the most outrageous despoiler of human rights, bank vaults, or local sovereignty, was only a hopeless dunce who could not postpone his fate and came inevitably to the bar of justice, usually a little worse for the wear.[22]

The cowboy's intellect appeared God-given as he received no formal education. He was schooled and skilled in the ways of nature. He survived in the wilderness among wild animals and wild men. Thus, he represented the promise of America in a cowboy suit: individualist spirit, strong work-ethic, and a commonsense morality.

The final characteristic common to almost all cowboy representations is a capacity for violence. Paired with his commonsense wisdom, the cowboy knows when and against whom to display violence. While violence has been bemoaned by critics of the Western film genre, it is almost always central to the rising action, climax, and resolution of most cowboy films.[23] A cowboy's use of violence is engrained in the character because he suffers, and his heroism is a result of his ability to overcome (his as well as others') suffering. The cowboy is always provoked, and whether he must come to the defense of a helpless woman or protect homesteaders from a ruthless cattle baron, he is ready to die when the chips are down.

Americans have been remarkably loyal to the cowboy for what we see of ourselves in the character and for what we do not. We want to imagine ourselves as pragmatic, wise people driven by a sense of individualist spirit just like the cowboy. However, the cowboy attains his mythic status because of his superhuman drive toward virtue and his willingness to die for it.

The Magical Negro

Mainstream American audiences likely identify less with the second stereotypical cinematic character at the center of our investigation. The Magical Negro character has its origins in mid–twentieth century American film when a demand emerged out of the Civil Rights Movement for more positive black characters.[24] The actor who is remembered most for his roles cast as the "ebony saint" is Sidney Poitier "who championed the cause of assimilation through the repeated portrayal of a friendly, desexualized black man" in films like *Lilies of the Field* (1963) and *Guess Who's Coming to Dinner* (1967).[25] The character has evolved into the twenty-first century with some of the more notable examples being Morgan Freeman as God in *Bruce Almighty* (2003) and *Evan Almighty* (2007), Will Smith in *The Legend of Bagger Vance* (2000), and Gloria Foster and Mary Alice who play "the Oracle" in *The Matrix* films.

The central purpose of the Magical Negro character is to assist and serve whites who are broken and down on their luck. This character is unpacked extensively by Matthew Hughey who argues that

> [t]he Magical Negro has become a stock character that often appears as a lower class, uneducated black person who possesses supernatural or magical powers. The powers are used to save and transform disheveled, uncultured, lost, or broken whites (almost exclusively white men) into competent, successful, and content people within the context of the American myth of redemption and salvation.[26]

The author goes on to argue that these characters resonate powerfully for audiences and collectively they function to preserve and protect attitudes of white supremacy. The Magical Negro's powers exist to serve damaged white characters, and this cinematic relationship reinforces a "normative climate of white supremacy within the context of the American myth of redemption and salvation whereby whiteness is always worthy of being saved and strong depictions of blackness are acceptable as long as they serve white identities."[27] This relationship between broken white characters and blacks with magical powers is reflective of the way that racism evolves and changes its form. Identifying what he calls "cinethetic racism," Hughey argues that while there is a public, overt celebration of racial harmony and equality, there remains an ongoing, covert discomfort and distrust of nonwhite people.[28]

Hughey's thorough investigation of the Magical Negro outlines the four most common thematic elements that embody the character: (1) economic extremity and (2) cultural deficiency while he or she possesses (3) folk wisdom and (4) primordial magic.[29] Further, the Magical Negro is present in film to serve the white protagonist, and in so doing redeems broken white characters by assisting with their socioeconomic mobility, moral salvation, and romantic relationships. The recurring narrative theme throughout films in which the Magical Negro stereotype appears is that he or she is almost always positioned as financially and materially inferior to white, but morally superior. The Magical Negro is almost always too eager and willing to help broken, down-on-their-luck white characters and seems almost wholly uninterested in improving his own financial and material lot in life.

While the Magical Negro has largely been ignored by academic scholarship, popular audiences are well familiar with this character as the stereotype has appeared in some of the highest grossing films in the last two decades: *The Matrix* films (1999, 2003, 2003), the *Blade* trilogy (1998, 2002, 2004), *The Green Mile* (1999), *What Dreams May Come* (1998), *Unbreakable* (2000), *The Legend of Bagger Vance* (2000), *City of Angels* (1998), *O Brother, Where Art Thou?* (2000), *Pirates of the Caribbean: Dead Man's Chest* (2006), *Pirates of the Caribbean: At World's End* (2007), *Happy Gilmore* (1996), *Bruce Almighty* (2003), *Evan Almighty* (2007). The prevalence of the character in the last fifteen years in major motion pictures suggests that the character has attained a level of popularity among mainstream audiences. There is an audience for films which feature interracial cooperation and seemingly reflect progressive racial attitudes—even if those films deploy covert representations of debasing, racist black characters and normative, heroic white representations.

An interesting offshoot of this phenomenon—of "cinethetic racism"—is instances when stereotypes become movable and transferrable among film characters. What does it mean to see a white protagonist adopt the characteristics of the Magical Negro stereotype? Similarly, what is the narrative and historical implications of a black protagonist acquiring the power of his white counterpart? Initially, one may see the nontraditional, cinematic stereotype swap as a slick narrative maneuver to disrupt the racist representations that accompany many of the Magical Negro films. However, in our analysis to follow, we argue that as stereotypical roles are switched between the protagonists in *Django Unchained* the film protects attitudes of white supremacy and offers mainstream, white audiences freedom from the historical sins of slavery.

Inverted stereotypes in *Django Unchained*

Set in the American South "three years before the start of the Civil War," *Django Unchained* stars Jamie Foxx as Django Freeman, an ex-slave who is bought by Dr. "King" Schultz, a German bounty hunter played by Christoph Waltz. After Django assists Schultz with executing a warrant, both men set off on a quest to free Django's wife, Broomhilda, a slave owned by the brutal Calvin Candie played by Leonardo DiCaprio. Over the course of the film, Schultz trains Django as a fellow bounty hunter and the two characters develop a close partnership. In the process of freeing Broomhilda, Schultz sacrifices his own life to kill her captor. Django is captured following a gun fight after the death of Candie and Schultz. Threatened with a return to slavery en route to a mine, Django is able to escape and return to the Candie plantation to free Broomhilda a second time. He guns down Candie's remaining henchmen, plants dynamite throughout the mansion, and watches it explode before riding off into the sunset with his wife.

Over the course of the film, both Dr. "King" Schultz and Django Freeman experience a transformation of character types when the two men meet and form a partnership. Schultz purchases Freeman from the Speck Brothers, and offers Django his freedom in exchange for his assistance in identifying the Brittle Brothers for whom Schultz possesses a warrant. From the initial moments of their first meeting, we see Schultz begin to enact and embody the characteristics of the Magical Negro. From his sudden, unlikely appearance out of the mist to his principled decision to pay for Django even after killing one of the Speck Brothers and leaving the other to die at the hands of vengeful slaves. We argue in our analysis that Schultz's becoming the Magical Negro presents him as compassionate ally of Django. At one point, Schultz identifies himself as a conscientious objector to slavery—even as a slave owner himself. The function of Shultz as the Magical Negro is to present a historical vision of the antebellum South where even white slave owners could object to the institution of slavery and be seen as the heroic saviors of American slaves. The offering to white audiences of *Django Unchained* is of redemption—freedom from the historical sins and lingering guilt whites may feel from being implicated and benefitting from slavery. Further, Schultz's transformation to the Magical Negro invests the white protagonist with special power projects attitudes of white supremacy and heroism.

Dr. "King" Schultz as the Magical Negro

It seems unlikely that the name bestowed upon Dr. "King" Schultz by Tarantino is a coincidence. Just as the name "Django" evokes the popular cowboy character from Sergio Corbucci's 1966 Italian Western, *Django*, Schultz's name serves as an allusion to the Civil Rights leader. Dr. Martin Luther King Jr. who arguably played a role in the development of the Magical Negro stereotype's rise in popularity during the middle of the twentieth century. Juxtaposed with the far more militant and radical Malcolm X, King's policy of nonviolent protest during the Civil Rights Movement was much more tolerable for anxious whites.[30] Filmmakers during this time included the "black saint" character in a wide array of films in order to attract white audiences, and the Magical Negro is an outgrowth of that initial stereotype.[31] The association between Dr. "King" Schultz and Dr. Martin Luther King Jr. indicates to the audience that Schultz likely possesses compassion for blacks/slaves/Django and may work to liberate those characters later in the film.

The very first time we meet Dr. "King" Schultz it is as he emerges mysteriously from the forest in the middle of the night. He appears unexpectedly which gives the impression that he is out of place. The sudden and unexpected appearance of Schultz is interesting given that this is a common occurrence with Magical Negro characters. Hughey argues that sudden dis/appearing acts are typical of the Magical Negro to suggest that he does not ordinarily belong in the world of the white characters, that he is present for only a limited amount of time, and that he departs when his work of assisting whites has finished.[32] It is not that these characters are not interesting or integral to the development of the narrative; it is that they exist without lives of their own.[33]

Schultz's exit from the film is far more sudden and dramatic than his entrance. At the end of the film, Django and Schultz locate Broomhilda at Candyland, Candie's plantation, and devise a plan to free her. Candie becomes suspicious of the bounty hunters and attempts to extort a high price from the two men in retaliation for the plot. Schultz submits to Candie's demands and agrees to pay the full amount to Candie. After the paperwork is signed, Candie demands that Schultz shake his hand to finalize the deal. Revolted by Candie's demanding behavior, Schultz refuses the handshake and shoots Candie in the heart with a gun he had concealed in his sleeve. Schultz turns to Django to apologize before being shot by one of Candie's henchmen.

The death of Dr. "King" Schultz is the emotional climax of the film. It is the culmination of the character's evolution throughout the film from being a passive observer to the institution of slavery to being willing to sacrifice his own life to save two slaves who he has befriended. Hughey identifies many examples of the Magical Negro character sacrificing his or her life at the end of a film.[34] There is no greater honor for the Magical Negro than the opportunity to give one's life to assist and save white people. Sometimes this sacrifice happens metaphorically as in *Bruce Almighty* (2003) when at the end of the film after saving the white protagonist, God, played by Morgan Freeman is returned to life as a servant/janitor "leaving audiences with the suggestion that this placement is his 'authentic' earthly form."[35] The Magical Negro is required to "walk off into the sunset" because an ongoing friendship between black and white characters would disrupt the racial status quo. Once he has fulfilled his purpose by redeeming white lives (sometimes by giving his own) he is no longer welcome in the proximity of whites. His continued presence would raise a host of difficult questions which the film likely cannot resolve (Figure 12.1).

In addition to Dr. King Schultz's dramatic dis/appearing acts, he possesses and displays folk wisdom constantly throughout the film. The Magical Negro's folk wisdom is characterized as "unexplainable knowledge" separate from intelligence which is aimed at freeing a white person's better character to help him or her resolve dilemmas.[36] As a doctor, Schultz's folk wisdom is more informed than the typical Magical Negro character. For example, after freeing a chain gang of slaves he encourages them to head North "to a more enlightened area of the country" but before riding away on his horse adds, "Oh, and on the off chance that there's any astronomy aficionados amongst you, the North Star is THAT ONE." Schultz and Django form a partnership and Schultz agrees to mentor Django as a bounty hunter in order to increase his profits. Around the campfire one night, Schultz learns that Django is a married man and hopes to one day be reunited with this wife, Broomhilda. Surprised that Django has a

FIGURE 12.1 *A final disappearance*

wife with a German name (who also speaks German), and in a clear case of foreshadowing, Schultz tells Django of the German legend of Broomhilda:

> Dr. "King" Schultz: Well, Broomhilda was a princess. She was a daughter of Wotan, god of all gods. Anyways, her father is really mad at her.
>
> Django: What she do?
>
> Dr. "King" Schultz: I can't exactly remember. She disobeys him in some way. So he puts her on top of the mountain.
>
> Django: Broomhilda's on a mountain?
>
> Dr. "King" Schultz: It's a German legend, there's always going to be a mountain in there somewhere. And he puts a fire-breathing dragon there to guard the mountain. And he surrounds her in a circle of hellfire. And there, Broomhilda shall remain. Unless a hero arises brave enough to save her.
>
> Django: Does a fella arise?
>
> Dr. "King" Schultz: Yes, Django, as a matter of fact, he does. A fella named Siegfried.
>
> Django: Does Siegfried save her?
>
> Dr. "King" Schultz: [Nods] Quiet spectacularly so. He scales the mountain, because he's not afraid of it. He slays the dragon, because he's not afraid of him. And he walks through hellfire ... because Broomhilda's worth it.
>
> Django: I know how he feel.[37]

Recalling the legend of Broomhilda causes Schultz to reflect on his partnership with Django. It is just after this exchange that Schultz reveals that his attitudes toward slavery and Django specifically have started to change. Schultz proposes that the two men partner together through the winter and once the snow melts he will travel with Django to Mississippi to search for Broomhilda. Django, expectedly skeptical of Schultz as no white man has ever offered him assistance, asks his partner why he cares about what happens to him. Schultz's reply reveals an evolution in his thinking:

> Dr. "King" Schultz: Well frankly, I've never given anybody their freedom before. And now that I have I feel vaguely responsible

for you. You're just not ready to go off on your own, it's that simple. You're too green, you'll get hurt. Plus when a German meets a real life Siegfried, it's kind of a big deal. As a German, I'm obliged to help you on your quest to rescue your beloved Broomhilda.[38]

Schultz slowly comes to the realization that his purpose (in much of the remainder of the film) will be to assist Django as he seeks to find and rescue his wife. Schultz gradually slips into the role typical of the Magical Negro—his purpose will mirror that of his partner's. Schultz will put himself in tremendous danger in order to help Django rescue Broomhilda, and in the end, he will die for this cause.

The Magical Negro is often in possession of magical powers which is what gives him the ability to perform his duties in the white world. Magic makes it possible for the Magical Negro "to teach, guide and instruct the white man on how to reclaim his social positioning, mental keenness and material success."[39] This quality of the Magical Negro serves the fetishistic needs of the filmmakers to transform the black–white partnership into a good/service which is used to redeem whites.

Schultz, who plays a trickster figure, and has a taste for theater and masquerade, is in possession of magic which is deployed to free Django and Broomhilda. In fact, to free Django from the Speck Brothers and Broomhilda from Calvin Candie, Schultz ejects a concealed Derringer hidden up his sleeve to kill each of the slavers. Beyond that, Schultz uses disguise and trickery multiple times during the film. Before Schultz and Django set out to locate the Brittle Brothers and secure their first bounty together, he dresses Django in a powder blue satin Little Lord Fauntleroy outfit—a costume that would not be out of place in the court of Marie Antoinette. He tells Django:

Dr. "King" Schultz: It's part of "The Act." You're playing a character. Your character is The Valet. This is what The Valet wears. Remember what I told you. During the act, you can never break character. [40]

At the end of the film as the two men set out to locate and free Broomhilda, Schultz concocts a scenario in which he is looking to purchase Mandingo fighters and Django is his assistant with an eye for evaluating talent. It is a ruse used to penetrate Candyland which ultimately works. Schultz and Django are able to purchase Broomhilda. The "act" allows Schultz to complete the narrative arc of his character as he martyrs himself by shooting the evil slaver Calvin Candie through the heart.

Dr. "King" Schultz possesses many of the hallmarks of the Magical Negro character. His sudden appearance at the beginning of the film as well as his sacrificial death at the end convey the sense that he existed to free Django, train him as a bounty hunter, and reunite him with his wife. Once his work is completed and after an evolution is his moral objections toward slavery, Schultz makes the most dramatic exit possible by ridding the world of the most evil slave owner in the South. Along the way, Schultz dispenses wisdom and employs magic and theatrics to train and assist Django as he struggles to get back to his wife.

Audiences see the Magical Negro stereotype embodied by a white character toiling for the salvation of black slaves in *Django Unchained*. The film offers an ideological view of American slavery that likely will comfort white audiences in the present day. With a white Magical Negro protagonist, *Django Unchained* depicts white people—even those who owned slaves—as heroes willing to give their lives as a symbolic moral objection to slavery.

Django as cowboy

The first indication that Django is playing the role of the cowboy is his name. Just as Dr. King Schultz's name is an allusion to the Civil Rights leader, the name "Django" unmistakably refers to the 1966 Spaghetti Western starring Franco Nero in the eponymous role. *Django* (1966), directed by Sergio Corbucci, shares similar aspects of plot with Tarantino's film. Django is a drifter who rescues a woman from a gang of murderous thieves whose leader is responsible for the death of his wife. In both films, the motivation for each of the Django characters is revenge for the enslavement or murder of their wives. Each character is extraordinarily proficient with a gun, each man suffers in pursuit of revenge, and each man pursues his revenge with a pragmatic sense of justice. That there is some mirroring of characters and plot is confirmed in *Django Unchained* as Franco Nero makes a cameo appearance as an Italian Mandingo fighter manager. Nero questions Foxx about his character's name and asks him to spell it—a direct reference to Nero's role as Django in the 1966 film.

While shown to be a brutal vigilante, Jaime Foxx's Django dispenses justice with an exactitude that typifies the pragmatism of the American cowboy. Violence is dispensed only toward those most deserving of his wrath—evil slavers, the Ku Klux Klan, and criminals who have murdered innocent people. Tarantino is careful to show the audience that Django is not carelessly bloodthirsty in his pursuit of vengeance and that he is guided by a sense of morality not possessed by the villains he kills. As Django prepares to kill and collect his first bounty, the conversation with his mentor reveals his internal struggle with having to kill a man with which he has no grievance.

> Django: Smitty Bacall is a farmer?
> Dr. "King" Schultz: No. Smitty Bacall is a stagecoach robber who's hiding out as a farmer, because there's a seven thousand dollar bounty on his head. And he's all yours.
> Django: [aims the rifle with his finger on the trigger . . . but he hesitates]
> Dr. "King" Schultz: Ooh, what happened to Mr. I-Wanna-Kill-White-Folks-For-Money?
> Django: His son's with him.
> Dr. "King" Schultz: Good. He'll have a loved one with him. Maybe even share a last word. That's better than most get, and a damn sight better then he deserves.
> Django: [still hesitates]
> Dr. "King" Schultz: Put down the rifle. Don't worry, I'm not mad at you. Take out Smitty Bacall's handbill. Read it aloud. Consider it today's lesson.
> Django: "Wanted, dead or alive. Smitty Bacall and The Smitty Bacall Gang. For murder and stagecoach robbery. Seven thousand dollars for Smitty Bacall. One thousand and five hundred dollars for each of his gang members. Known members of The Smitty Bacall Gang are as follows, DANDY MICHAELS, GERALD NASH, and CRAZY CRAIG KOONS."

Dr. "King" Schultz: Well done. Bravo. THAT is who Smitty Bacall is. If Smitty Bacall wanted to start a farm at twenty-two, they would never of printed that. But Smitty Bacall wanted to rob stagecoaches, and he didn't mind killing people to do it. You want to save your wife by doing what I do? This is what I do. I kill people, and sell their corpses for cash. His corpse is worth seven thousand dollars. Now quit your pussyfootin' and shoot him.[41]

It is crucial for this moment of dialogue to appear at the outset of Django's training as a bounty hunter, and it is significant that this scene occurs in the West (mountains appear in the background). The audience is shown his hesitation to kill—even those people wanted for murder and robbery. As he is developing his marksmanship, Django is also finding his moral center—a code of ethics that does not seem comfortable for him initially as he sets his sights on Smitty Bacall. His acquiescence of the demands of being a bounty hunter forces a confrontation with a moral dilemma early in the film. That Django struggles with killing another man reveal early signs of heroism and the struggle that a hero will face in a corrupt world. The hesitation that grips Django before shooting and killing Smitty Bacall is noteworthy for what it reveals about his character, but it is the only time in the film he will show indecision in his action. As he and Schultz make their way to Mississippi to locate and free Broomhilda, Django is exact in seeking vengeance and it is clear that his victims are all deserving of their fate.

Django Unchained ends with a flashback scene in which Schultz is shown in awe of Django's quick draw and marksmanship with a gun. In the final line of dialogue in the film Schultz bestows upon Django the moniker which confirms his placement in the pantheon of classic cinematic cowboys.

Dr. "King" Schultz: "You know what they're going to call you?" "The fastest gun in the South." [42]

Django is a deadly shot from any distance on any occasion. Even though Django receives training from Schultz, his mentor is bewildered at the proficiency of his partner with a gun. In fact, there is no explanation provided within the film's narrative to account for the reason of Django's natural skill. His natural born talent as a marksman suggests that he possesses some of the magic of the Magical Negro stereotype that is shifting to his partner throughout the film. Both Schultz and Django have traits of both stereotypes—the cowboy and the Magical Negro. Schultz is a bounty hunter/cowboy and Django is a Magical Negro, and it is because of each man's proximity to the other that makes a transfer of stereotypical attributes possible. This is the crux of mythification.

Implications

There are three important implications of this study—each of which show *Django Unchained* as a film which reinforces the ideology of white supremacy and frees mainstream, white audiences from the lingering historical guilt felt as a result of their collusion with the institution of slavery.

First, the inversion of stereotypes is critical to the ideological work performed by the film. Dr. "King" Schultz possesses the character traits and performs the duties of the Magical Negro. Throughout the film, we see him appear suddenly and mysteriously, dispense folk wisdom, and engage in trickery. Schultz even performs a bit of magic in the form of a hidden Derringer up his sleeve. In the end, he dies the death of a martyr in order to rid the world of the evil Calvin Candie and guarantee the freedom of Django and Broomhilda. All of this is in addition to his name which alludes to the Civil Rights pioneer, Dr. Martin Luther King, Jr.

Dr. "King" Schultz is a complex character to read rhetorically because over the course of the film he purchases slaves, frees slaves, murders evil slave owners, and plays the part of the Magical Negro stereotype. However, it is this character more than any other that embodies the redemptive spirit of the film. Author Roxane Gay challenged the premise of *Django Unchained* as an unconventional revenge fantasy from the vantage point of a slave, arguing instead that the film is "a white man's slavery revenge fantasy" where black people are largely incidental.[43] Gay (2013) insists that *Django Unchained* isn't about a black man reclaiming his freedom, but about "a white man working through his own racial demons and white guilt."[44]

It is Dr. "King" Schultz's character with whom which mainstream white audiences are asked to identify. The other white characters in the film—Calvin Candie, Candie's henchmen, the Brittle Brothers, the Speck Brothers—are portrayed as caricatures. Each of these characters is "either hilariously stupid or sadistically depraved" and the audience has no choice but to "hate the brutal, Erskine Caldwell-like inbreeding-type cretins; because they are obviously cruel and depraved beyond redemption, it is okay to kill them all."[45] The audience has no incentive to identify with these characters—in fact the filmmaker leaves the audience with no choice but to identify with Schultz. It is the evolution of his character that is most attractive to contemporary white audiences who are less likely to see themselves as one-dimensional evil slavers and more likely to imagine themselves as morally conflicted and ultimately liberators.

His attitudinal evolution toward slavery—from slave owner to passive objector, finally to an expression of moral outrage in the form of murdering Candie resulting in his own death—is an invitation for present-day audiences to imagine themselves in his position. While he evolves to reject the institution of slavery, his character begins by being complicit with it. Schultz finds slavery repulsive after using it for his own objectives—a problem many white people likely faced during the era of slavery. It is a dilemma many mainstream, white audience members imagine themselves having to negotiate. That Schultz devotes the last six months of his life to mentoring, serving, and dying for Django and his wife is a less common experience white people undertook in the antebellum South. However, it is possible that contemporary audiences will see Schultz's sacrifice as indicative of the actions of many progressive whites of the era—even reformed slave owners. It is Schultz's sacrifice to Django and Broomhilda that offers redemption to contemporary white audiences.

The second major finding of this study is that Jamie Foxx's portrayal of Django offers redemption from white guilt like his film counterpart, and more importantly, the character reinforces attitudes of white supremacy. Django—part Magic Negro and part cowboy—embodies a mixture of freedom and individualism typical of almost all iconic American cowboys. Pragmatic, judicious, and a righter of wrongs,

Django fits squarely within the pantheon of American cowboy iconography which includes the likes of John Wayne, Clint Eastwood, and Buffalo Bill Cody. The major difference between those men and Django is that the latter is black. Yet, he is no less stoic and larger-than-life than his cinematic predecessors. Schultz may be the hero of the film, but Django is the historical hero. It is the cold and calculated freed slave who makes revenge his mission to free his wife (and the other slaves of Candyland). The instance of the freed-slave-turned-cowboy-vigilante likely was a rare occurrence in the antebellum South. Yet, if audiences extrapolate from the history of this film, the renegade former slave was a deadly threat to malicious slave owners. Contemporary audiences may take solace in the realization that cruel slavers received their comeuppance from gallant freed slaves seeking justice—however distorted this history actually may be.

This is not to say that slaves and freed former slaves did not play a significant role in achieving ending American slavery and achieving their freedom. In fact, just the opposite is true. Everyday acts of struggle and resistance coupled with the constant feeling of desperation by millions of American slaves characterize more fully their lived experience in the antebellum South. There are many historical examples of freed slaves who, once sold from their spouses, went to great lengths and risked their lives to find and rescue them.[46] We know of the historical examples of Denmark Vesey, Nat Turner, and others who risked death and torture to organize with other slaves and free them.

Yet, this history is not represented in *Django Unchained*. Once freed by Schultz, Django assists with his capitalist enterprise initially by searching for, killing and collecting bounties. Django does not organize with the other slaves of Candyland in order to free them. In fact, one of the last people Django kills in the film is Stephen—Calvin Candie's loyal house slave played by Samuel L. Jackson. Django is not as interested in freeing slaves as he is (to paraphrase him) in killing white people and getting paid for it. He has freed his wife—the only slave worth saving. Now that he is reunited with Broomhilda he is restored and repaired as a man. Initially freed to serve a white, capitalist entrepreneur, as Django rides off into the sunset at the end of the film the audience imagines him continuing the work of his martyred mentor.

As we have shown in this chapter, the stereotypes portrayed by Django and Schultz are inverted—the white guy is helping the black guy find his black wife. Ordinarily it is the individual being helped by the Magical Negro character that is damaged or deficient. However, in this film, the Magical Negro character played by Schultz is morally deficient—he is a slave owner. It is in the presence and ownership of Django that Schultz is able to evolve and change his attitudes. Again, while Django as the renegade cowboy is the historical hero, his attitudinal evolution makes Schultz the hero of the film. The purpose of the partnership between the two protagonists in the film (in addition to rescuing Broomhilda) is to rid the South of evil, malicious whites (the cartoonish villains of the film). Evil whites are eradicated from the South in order to purify and protect and salvage the good whites worth saving. In this way, *Django Unchained* reifies attitudes of white supremacy.

Finally, *Django Unchained* reflects a broader cultural consensus of the onset of a post-racial America. This film is Tarantino's most popular and highest grossing project to date. We have argued earlier that one of the reasons for the film's overwhelming popularity among mainstream, white audiences is that it offers transcendence from the lingering guilt of slavery and institutional forms of racism. Additionally, the film's seemingly progressive narrative is consistent with recent celebrations of America's post-racial landscape. Almost entirely due to the election of Barack Obama as the nation's forty-fourth president, some analysts suggest that distinctions of race would no longer be important and race would no longer stand as a barrier to anyone working to attain even the highest political office in the country. For many, Obama's assent to the presidency symbolized the end of an era in which African Americans and other minorities could make reasonable arguments about the barriers racism presented in the United States. These arguments were not offered solely by the political right. The actor and energetic Obama supporter Will Smith essentially agreed with the previous sentiment by saying the following: "I love that all of our excuses have been removed. African American excuses have been removed. There's no white man trying to keep you down, because if he were [sic] really trying to keep you down, he would have done everything he could to keep Obama down."[47]

The inversion of the Magical Negro and cowboy stereotypes played by nontraditional character actors confirms attitudes of a post-racist society. White slave owners realized the errors of their ways, reformed, and were willing to die for the freedom of slaves. Black heroic cowboys easily acquired the skill and courage to seek revenge for the evils of slavery. The historical revisionism of the film projects a vision of the antebellum South in which the institutional racism of the era was resolved long ago by reformed whites and vigilante blacks. In that case, there is little reason to be concerned about the derivative effects of slavery as they have been resolved. In this way, *Django Unchained* reinforces deeply conservative ideological thinking which says that there is little need for social welfare programs, that discussions of race and racism are in the past, and that the victims of oppression will find their inner hero who shall overcome on his or her own.

Notes

1   Omali Yeshitela, "Django Unchained or Killing Whitey to Protect White Power," *UhuruNews.Com*, http://uhurunews.com/story?resource_name=killing-whitey-while-protecting-white-power-a-review-of-django-unchained (accessed January 20, 2013).

2   Roxane Gay, "Surviving Django," *Buzzfeed Community*, http://www.buzzfeed.com/roxanegay/surviving-django-8opx (accessed January 5, 2013); Aisha Harris, "Conservatives Freak Out About Django Unchained," *Slate*, December 19, 2012, http://www.slate.com/blogs/browbeat/2012/12/19/django_unchained_and_racism_drudge_report_rehashes_tarantino_n_word_flap.html; Erin A. Kaplan, "'Django' an Unsettling Experience for Many Blacks," *Los Angeles Times*, December 28, 2012; Adelle Platon, "Spike Lee Slams Django Unchained: 'I'm Not Gonna See it,'" *VIBE*, December 21, 2012, http://www.vibe.com/article/spike-lee-slams-django-unchained-im-not-gonna-see-it.

3   Jelani Cobb, "Tarantino Unchained," *New Yorker*, January 2, 2013, http://www.newyorker.com/online/blogs/culture/2013/01/how-accurate-is-quentin-tarantinos-portrayal-of-slavery-in-django-unchained.html.

4   Simon Schama, "Clio Has a Problem," *The New York Times Magazine*, September 29, 1991, 32–34; Robert B. Toplin, *History*

by Hollywood: The Use and Abuse of the American Past (Urbana: University of Illinois Press, 1996), 7–8.

5 Daniel Leab, "The Moving Image as Interpreter of History—Telling the Dancer from the Dance," in *Image as Artifact: The Historical Analysis of Film and Television*, ed. John E. O'Connor (New York: Robert E. Krieger Publishing Company, 1990), 69–95; Michael Parenti, *Make-Believe Media: The Politics of Entertainment* (New York: Cengage Learning, 1991), 30–32; Pierre Sorlin, *The Film in History: Restaging the Past* (New York: Barnes and Noble Imports, 1980), 39–66.

6 James Snead, *White Screens/Black Images: Hollywood from the Dark Side* (New York: Routledge, 1994), 4.

7 Walter Lippmann, *Public Opinion* (New York: Macmillan, 1956), 96.

8 Lippmann, *Public Opinion*, 85–91.

9 Lippmann, *Public Opinion*, 96.

10 Lippmann, *Public Opinion*, 92–93.

11 Lippmann, *Public Opinion*, 95–96.

12 Snead, *White Screens/Black Images*.

13 Snead, *White Screens/Black Images*, 4.

14 Snead, *White Screens/Black Images*, 8.

15 Snead, *White Screens/Black Images*, 23–27.

16 Toplin, *History by Hollywood*, 26–44.

17 Toplin, *History by Hollywood*, 34–36.

18 Eric Hobsbawm, *Fractured Times: Culture and Society in the 20th Century* (London: Little, Brown Book Group, 2013), 302.

19 William W. Savage, *The Cowboy Hero: His Image in American History and Culture* (Norman, OK: University of Oklahoma Press, 1979), 3.

20 Savage, *The Cowboy Hero*, 20–21.

21 Joe B. Frantz and Julian E. Choate, *The American Cowboy: The Myth and the Reality* (Norman: University of Oklahoma Press, 1955), 6.

22 Savage, *The Cowboy Hero*, 23.

23 James Horowitz, *They Went Thataway* (New York: E.P. Dutton & Co, 1976), 7–9.

24 David Draigh and Gail Sussman Marcus, "In the Heat of the Night," *American Museum of the Moving Image*, http://www.movingimage. us/site/education/content/guides/Heat%20of%20the%20Night%20 SM.pdf, 3 (accessed 2001).

25 Matthew Hughey, "Cinethetic Racism: White Redemption and Black Stereotypes in 'Magical Negro' Films," *Social Problems* 56,3 (2009), 545.

26 Hughey, "Cinethetic Racism," 544.

27 Hughey, "Cinethetic Racism," 548.

28 Hughey, "Cinethetic Racism," 551.

29 Hughey, "Cinethetic Racism," 556–566.

30 Herbert Shapiro, *White Violence and Black Response: From Reconstruction to Montgomer* (Amherst: University of Massachusetts Press, 1988), 428–454.

31 Draigh and Marqus, "In the Heat of the Night."

32 Hughey, "Cinethetic Racism," 559–560.

33 Rita Kempley, "Too Too Divine. Movies' 'Magic Negro' Saves the Day—But At The Cost Of His Soul," *The Black Commentator*, 49 (2003), 1, http://blackcommentator.com/49/49_ magic.html (accessed November 1, 2013).

34 Hughey, "Cinethetic Racism," 556.

35 Hughey, "Cinethetic Racism," 556.

36 Robert M. Entman and Andrew Rojecki, *The Black Image in the White Mind: Media and Race in America* (Chicago: University of Chicago Press, 2001), xvir.

37 Quentin Tarantino, "Django Unchained," *The Internet Movie Script Database*, www.imsdb.com/scripts/Django-Unchained.html (accessed November 26, 2013).

38 Tarantino, "Django Unchained."

39 Hughey, "Cinethetic Racism," 561.

40 Tarantino, "Django Unchained."

41 Tarantino, "Django Unchained."

42 Tarantino, "Django Unchained."

43 Gay, "Surviving Django."

44 Gay, "Surviving Django."

45 Yeshitela, "Django Unchained or Killing Whitey to Protect White Power."

46 Yeshitela, "Django Unchained or Killing Whitey to Protect White Power."

47 "Reflections on Living History," *USA Today*, January 21, 2009, 14A.

13

Django Blues: Whiteness and Hollywood's Continued Failures

David J. Leonard

Quentin Tarantino is a good *white* filmmaker. Irrespective of his talents and his ability to remix stories, traditions, and aesthetics, his opportunities, his platform, his opportunities and his voice are aided and abetted by the privileges of whiteness; he is a product of the symbolic and material value bestowed upon of white masculinity inside and outside of Hollywood. If Tarantino is the main force behind each and every one of his films, from *Pulp Fiction* to *Django*, his whiteness is both his co-producer and his agent. Embodied in a myriad of ways, the fact that Tarantino is consistently imagined as an innovator, as an auteur, as transformative, and as a new type of filmmaker is a testament to the power of whiteness. In fact, at his best he is someone who recycles, samples, and remixes; at his worst he is a biter who is cashing in on his whiteness. His films, especially evident with *Django*, are vehicles for the accepted tropes, aesthetics, and ideological meanings of Hollywood. Tarantino is indicative of the hegemonic representations of blackness within Hollywood.

This chapter contains and builds upon a previous essay "Django Blues," which appeared in *The Crisis* (April 2013, 26–29). http://www.academia.edu/3249551/Django_Blues.

As with so many films about African American history and life, *Django* is ultimately a story of whiteness. Akin to *Glory, Mississippi Burning, Amistad*, and countless other films, *Django* is a story of white redemption. As with many Hollywood films dealing with slavery, race, and the South, the focus of the film was ultimately on reconciling "a divided white self."[1] *Django* works to reunify a divided white self; by killing and destroying the white supremacist self, unification of the fragmented white body and nation is possible. In other words, as whiteness is redeemed and the nation purges the corrupting white racist from its mix, the nation (and whiteness) can rightfully coalesce around goodness and civilization. Whereas other films position the good white person as the savior and source of redemption., *Django* privileges Tarantino as the white savior and desired white subject. As filmmaker, as a white person who doesn't see race, who can use the n-word without it meaning anything, who isn't a racist because he tells people so, Tarantino is the only good white American associated with the film. With this in mind, this chapter, thus, accepts the task of analyzing *Django* and its deployed compass in whiteness. Focusing particularly on the themes of white redemption and its deployment of a white-centered narrative, it argues that *Django* is a story of whiteness (and white masculinity). In the end, it is a movie that stars Tarantino as himself and as the great white savior. In seeking to center Tarantino and his revolutionary narrative about slavery, *Django* renders the story of African American slavery, and particularly resistance, as peripheral. As with other films on African American history, whiteness exists in a spotlight with blackness serving and existing as a backdrop for white greatness. Similarly, *Django* imagines whiteness as both good and evil; those bad whites, those who embody slavery and white supremacy, are pathologized and mocked, as to make clear that whiteness is not the problem. In the end, *Django* serves Tarantino and his narrative about himself, failing to get beyond the dominant tropes, narratives, and representations central to the history of Hollywood.

Blackness displaced

Django unchained is not a film about blackness, black humanity, black people, the black community, or black history; as a film about whiteness, blackness is displaced, erased, and ignored, continuing a tradition of films set in history that use blackness as a vehicle for the celebration and redemption of whiteness. From *Gone with the Wind* to *Glory*, from *Mississippi Burning* to *The Help*, Hollywood representations of slavery, Jim Crow, and American racism has centered white bodies. In these films, white saviors (and their exceptional nature) are front and center, whereupon liberation and freedom results from the assistance, kindness, and brilliance of whites. *Django* follows suit, rendering Schultz, whose liminal whiteness is complicated by his German background, as a co-star to *Django*. Like *Django* himself, he is different and exceptional; he's not like other whites and therefore is able to repel the hegemonic trappings of white masculinity during slavery. Shultz's outsider status, alongside of Django's exceptionality, is ideal in the struggle for redemption and reunification.

Schultz not only frees Django, and provides weaponry for other slaves, but sets in motion the revenge and redemption that guides the film. Without Schultz, there is no freedom, there is no redemption, and there is no black life; without Schultz, Black Death remains a fixture of democracy. Scott Schomburg reflects on the significance of whiteness within *Django*:

> In the official screenplay, Django is identified as "our hero," not Schultz. Yet, while Tarantino's script builds intentionally toward Django's bloody revenge, it remains inside Schultz's narrative. That is, *Django Unchained* is not merely a slave revenge tale; it is an exploration of the limits and possibilities of the white ally: the white progressive who stands *within* the dominant group and imagines it possible to stand *against* the dominant group's injustices. And while Django struggles against white masters in truly original cinematic moments, the terror undergirding the narrative is this: Django is no longer in chains, but he is *not yet free*. He never escapes the world of Dr. Schultz, the enlightened white liberal. Approaching Tarantino's narrative universe through this lens illuminates the instability of white progressives in a world of white masters and black slaves, a world into which we continue to live. Schultz's one-handed hatred of slavery cannot evade the crisis of whiteness: the totalizing temptation for Schultz to remain the master even in his efforts to help vindicate Django.[2]

Django, however, remixes the classic white savior narrative, thus representing another cinematic deployment of what Thomas Bogle describes as a "Huckfinn fixation," in which "the white hero grows in stature from his association with the dusty black."[3] Embodying a liberal humanist perspective on race, such narratives emphasize interracial friendships and breaking down social distance as an important step toward not only racial reconciliation but also personal growth, particularly for whites. In *Django*, Dr. Schultz and Django follow suit, forming a biracial buddy insurrection, which doesn't challenge slavery but instead the violent and horrifying consequences experienced by one family. However, more than the cinematic inscription of the biracial buddy film, its narrative operates through a vision of America as a nation of biracial buddies; the film not only bridges the gap and the tension between "the races" but provides a vehicle for redemption and a loving relationship in the future.

Because of the centering of Tarantino and the grandiose vision of national redemption and reconciliation, his film could not overly use the white savior trope because the true white savior is not visible on screen. Ultimately the film could not give viewers too much to celebrate as it relates to Schultz since the ultimate star of the film is Tarantino, the filmmaker, the writer, and the auteur. In some sense, Tarantino rather than Schultz is Huck to Django's Jim. And the centering of Schultz, the focus on Tarantino, and the narrative focus on a divided white self, relegates African American characters to the periphery.

One of the most troubling aspects of *Django* is its representation of African Americans. In an effort to legitimize the exceptional nature of Django, the film plays up the complicity, passivity, and acceptance of enslavement. From Stephen (Samuel L. Jackson) to those who sat idly by swinging in the face of white supremacist terror, *Django* offers a myriad of representations that imagine blacks as ineffective and incapable of resistance. Even Broomhilda (Kerry Washington) is a flat character who lacks much development. All of film's black characters are background, giving meaning to the film's true stars: Jamie Foxx, Christoph Waltz, and Quentin Tarantino. Mirroring other interracial buddy films, *Django* refuses to take the spotlight off of them, transforming the buddy pic into a ménage à trois of racial redemption and reunification. The seeming erasure of enslaved and free blacks, who challenged white supremacy, who defied enslavement and dehumanization, and who otherwise survived a society built around "Black Social Death,"[4] is important both cinematically and historically. Salamishah Tillet makes this clear arguing that Tarantino deploys the exceptional narrative at the expense of others:

> As we cheer Django on in his revenge, we ought to ask ourselves: What happened to all the other slaves in America? Those who had neither Django's guile nor guns? If we are serious about avenging the past, we must deal with the legacy of their lives in our present.

The emphasis on Django's exceptionalism results in the erasure of widespread resistance from slaves. From breaking tools to sabotaging crops, from runaways to slave insurrections, the history of slavery is one of both resistance and retribution. Harriet Tubman, Henry Box Brown, Denmark Vessey, Nat Turner, the Haitian Revolution, and the German Coast Uprising are but a few examples. In 1855, Celia, a nineteen-year old slave, who had been raped for five years on a Missouri plantation, beat Robert Newsome, her enslaver and rapist, to death.[5] With a club hand, she put an end this terror and terror; she exacted justice. *Django* doesn't simply erase this history, but in imagining it in fantastical terms, in centering multiple white saviors, it yet again replicates the long-standing narrative about the lack of resistance all while imaging Django as exceptional, as special, as unique to the larger history of slavery. Worse yet, as the film is constructed through Tarantino's imagination, he too becomes exceptional since he "discovers" and "creates a world" that purportedly did not exist. He brings a narrative that he claims has been unavailable within Hollywood. He is Django's creator despite the fact that history is filled with enslaved Africans who resisted white supremacy, who exacted revenge not only on slave masters but on Hollywood with its perpetuation of racist stereotypes.

Whiteness and Django

The privilege and freedom endowed by whiteness is evident in the inclusion of a scene mocking the Klan. The attempt here is to lampoon their inability to see through their hoods, thereby showing their ridiculousness. While there can be power in mocking and belittling one of America's great perpetrators of violence and terror, not all filmmakers are able to use these representational devices in every instance. Would a black filmmaker be able to write and direct a revenge film against Al Qaeda whereupon members of the terrorist group were imagined as bumbling fools for the sake of comedy? Would we see the power in satire in this context? What about a film by an Arab filmmaker about the Holocaust; would purportedly satirical representations of Nazis get a green light from Hollywood and ample praise from mainstream media?[6] Would such a film ever be made?

There is also a lot of danger in the scene. To imagine white supremacy as unique to the stupid and ignorant, to reduce the history of violence and terror to backwards morons, is to erase the centrality of white supremacy within the levers and instruments of power. The Klan was a mainstream terrorist organization. At one point, for example, the Klan had 250,000 members in Indiana alone (which constituted 30 percent of Indiana's white males) and was bringing in 2,000 new members each week. The governor and half (!) of the elected members of the Indiana General Assembly were members of the Klan. While comforting to imagine the Klan and white supremacist terrorists as bumbling fools, it is also dangerous in that the entrenched nature of white supremacy becomes lost. Akin to the Jerry Springerization of racism within talk shows, which embody a long-standing tradition of imagining white supremacy as Southern, as a pathology of "poor white trash," and as a result of ignorance and stupidity as opposed to power and ideology, the scene confines racism to the narrow corridors of the backwards and stupid. Yes, it ethers those confined to the corridor, leaving untouched the institutions and individuals who have been central to a white supremacist project. This scene (and the use of comedy throughout the film) mediates the tension resulting from representations of slavery.

While using humor as a source of resistance was central to the history of enslaved communities, its inclusion in *Django* betrays that tradition, offering relief rather than power and transcendence. Often following a scene of violence, one that embodied the trauma and pain of American slavery, the insertion of comedic relief felt like a mechanism to assuage white viewer discomfort. The efforts to comfort white viewers, to privilege their feelings and desires, is evident throughout the film, and throughout Hollywood's treatment of the black experience.

Recognizing that meaning is not fixed and that viewers bring their own oppositional gaze into the theater,[7] it is important to also consider these comedic moments that flatten, individualize, and pathologize white supremacy within the film's larger narrative.

Refashioning of Tarantino as savior, as the true star of the film, is part of *Django's* redemption of whiteness. The film's pathologizing and mocking of white supremacy ("look it's over there" as opposed to recognizing racism as core to the American project), and its representation of violence, furthers its efforts to elevate, celebrate, and redeem whiteness. Throughout the film, Tarantino imagined violence through spectacle, through caricature, and through an almost cartoonish representation. He seemingly distances the violence of slavery from whiteness, from hegemonic institutions, and the nation as a whole. As such, its inclusion was often more gratuitous and spectacular as opposed to evidence of the horrors of slavery and the trauma resulting from white supremacy. It fails to offer a sustained critique of white supremacy and its mechanisms of violence. There were moments where the cinematic gaze was infused with a pleasure in the violence, and that troubled me. Those scenes were early in the film—the scene involving the dogs and slave fights—and I had to look away because the purpose seemed to be about eliciting pleasure from its (white) viewers. The camera's gaze conveys pleasure and joy in these spectacular images. Tamura Lomax concurs, arguing

> He doesn't take the time to deal with or allow us to sit with the trauma. He doesn't allow us to feel the pain of the characters; he doesn't encourage viewers to reflect on the psychic pain of Black Death or the countless victimizations of white supremacy. We should problematize all of this, but perhaps QT's offering us a mockery on life. Sometimes we take pleasure in hideous violence (isn't this why it's videotaped so rampant and callously?). Sometimes we find alibis for engaging the taboo. Sometimes violence is selfish. Sometimes it's unprovoked. And sometimes it's illiberal. However, sometimes violence may be just, cathartic, or imagined as some sort of source of power. What happens

when, for a great many of us, our origins as subjects are entangled with what we refer to as violence? This is a winding conundrum.[8]

The film fails to convey the outrage; it neglects the importance of spotlighting trauma through bringing the cruelty and violence of anti-black racism and slavery into visibility amid constant chatter of a post-racial America. Rather there seems to be an effort to transport viewers into this extreme spectacle of violence. A cinematic gaze that finds power and pleasure in violence seemingly erases the history of white supremacy, from slavery to lynching, from Emmett Till to the Birmingham church bombing. The pleasure and power exhibited in the film's gaze cannot be read outside of Tarantino's own whiteness. He rarely accounts for the trauma and terror that is at the core of America's history, doing little to create a world that accounts for the pain on screen and in theaters across the nation. Instead, he flaunts his privilege, turning slavery into a playground for his fantasies about masculinity, violence, and redemption.

The leading man: Quentin Tarantino

The production and widespread distribution of *Django* is the embodiment of the power of whiteness. The operationalizing of white privilege does not end with production and distribution—the ability to make and have the movie seen—but is also evident in the types of representations and narratives provided in *Django*. "As a black filmmaker, I find that I wrestle with thoughts of 'responsibility'; 'who will see it,' 'what impact will it have on the discourse in America,' 'what images will I be projecting to our youth/to the world,'" writes Tanya Steele. "I've often noted, even in film school, white filmmakers don't have that burden. They were free to write, to be, to create without thinking about this stuff. I'm certain they thought about other things but, the burden of race was not in their baggage."[9] This is evidenced in Tarantino's privilege and his re-appropriation of violence and slavery as a cinematic playground. Whiteness immunizes Tarantino and the other white viewers from the direct impact of slavery's history. He is not the descendant of slaves; none of his family was likely mauled to death by dogs, whipped into submission, or sexually violated during this time. Honorée Fanonne Jeffers, who writes about Tarantino's detached relationship to the history of slavery and a life not defined by "shed[ing] tears because of something you lost that you can't even name that lost." An associate professor of English at the University of Oklahoma, she concludes that "no parasitic White man who likes to poke fun at the misery suffered by long dead, displaced Africans can do justice to the history of the Transatlantic slave trade."[10] The detached relationship from the history, and the violence, impacts the narrative and the camera's gaze. "He simply uses slavery as a way to create 'new' kill/torture scenes. And those scenes are simply par for the course in this gory movie," notes Tanisha Ford, an assistant professor of Women, Gender, Sexuality Studies at the University of Massachusetts-Amherst.[11] His whiteness, his detached relationship to the history of slavery and lynchings, is on full display.

As with so many films about African American history and life, *Django* is ultimately a story of whiteness. *Django* is a story of white redemption. Ishmael Reed, who argues that *Django* is a film that is ultimately a story about Dr. "King" Schultz (Christoph Waltz) and Leonardo DiCaprio (Calvin Candie), concludes,

> The real stars of "Django Unchained," however, are Waltz and Leonardo DiCaprio. DiCaprio is master of a plantation where Django's wife Broomhilda (seriously), is being held, and has apparently been passed around among the "Mandingos" who are trained to participate in slave fights for the entertainment of DiCaprio and his friends. The movie's "star," Foxx, is there for the audience that used to sit in the balcony at southern movie houses. He performs in a movie within a movie. A sort of "Harlem On The Prairie." This was an ingenuous bit of marketing.[12]

As with many Hollywood films dealing with slavery, race, and the South, the focus of the film was ultimately on reconciling a divided white self. According to Hernan Vera and Andrew Gordon, "the white self is an invention, a fiction that we take for real and rarely question."[13] These "sincere fictions" necessitate work, reunification, and efforts to explain and mend any ruptures to a unified whiteness.[14] Slavery or white supremacy puts into question the unified white body given the visibility of evil. Films are crucial in uniting and refiguring a normalized whiteness.

As such, *Django* works to reunify a divided white self; by killing and destroying the white supremacist self, that unification is possible. Whereas other films position the good white person within the film, *Django* privileges Tarantino as the white savior and desired white subject.

At the same time, Tarantino imagines Django as himself; in fact, he longs to be *Django*, who he imbues with raw sexuality, coolness, and a level of courage that leads him to "whip ass." He destroys evil and wins the affection of the leading lady, all while rocking shades, using the n-word over and over again, and swaggering around on a house wearing "electric blue dandy outfit complete with ruffle kerchief."[15] Tarantino, like so many white youth, fetishize blackness, imagining "everything but the burden." This isn't surprising given that in 2007, Tarantino told *British GQ*, "I do believe in past lives and stuff like that…I know I was a black slave in America. I think maybe even like three lives" (In Quintero 2013; Wenn 2007). Citing his "feeling" and just "knowing," Tarantino makes clear that this is sufficient evidence of his possession of a "ghetto pass."

Even in his current life, Tarantino imagines himself as not just deeply influenced and connected to the black community, but as ostensibly black.

> I kind of grew up surrounded by black culture. I went to an all black school. It is the culture that I identify with. I can identify with other cultures too; we all have a lot of people inside of us, and one of the ones inside of me is black. Don't let the pigmentation fool you; it is a state of mind. It has affected me a lot in my work.[16]

Reflective of a history of minstrelsy and bell hooks' idea of "eating the other," a tendency to imagine blackness as monolithic and cultural, Tarantino's history as a filmmaker is one where he, as Lawrence Ross reminds us, sees "Blackness as some cultural accessory that can be worn without the real implication of being black." His ability to try on the Other, to claim Otherness, even as to cashes in on his whiteness checks, is emblematic of privilege. Jamilah Lemieux, editor at Ebony.com notes, "I think he's an entitled White dude who is super high on his privilege and success."[17] Not surprisingly, his inner blackness or his "state of mind" has surely not led to many obstacles throughout his career.

The sense of entitlement and the efforts to reimagine himself as a white filmmaker, with a "black inner essence," who is able to bring representations otherwise impossible into the American landscape, are clear when Tarantino laments the failures of *Roots* or celebrates the film for its ability to construct a narrative around black revenge. Yet, his sense of entitlement and self-importance is equally evident with his repeated us of the n-word within *Django, Pulp Fiction*, and his larger cinematic biography. Able to use the word because of his "inner blackness" and his experience, albeit in new ways given his whiteness, Tarantino positions himself as exceptional in both his imagination and his execution of language and image. Unlike his black counterparts, whose usage of the "n-word" has become mundane and scrutinized, as part of the everyday vernacular, and his white counterparts, whose usage fits within a larger history of white supremacy, Tarantino stands apart. In fact, he defends his use of the "n-word," arguing that its inclusion reflects his desire to be historically accurate. Unlike others, who have sanitized history, he is brave to include because it reflects the racial im(morality) and violence of Texas, Tennessee, and Mississippi in the 1850s. He shrugs off criticism (dismissing it in fact):

> Personally, I find [the criticism] ridiculous. Because it would be one thing if people are out there saying, "You use it much more excessively in this movie than it was used in 1858 in Mississippi." Well, nobody's saying that. And if you're not saying that, you're simply saying I should be lying. I should be watering it down. I should be making it more easy to digest. No, I don't want it to be easy to digest.[18]

The "historic accuracy" piece is hard to swallow—given the film's erasure of the Black Codes, given its Spaghetti Western aesthetics, and the inclusion of "B-word" and "MF," both which were not widely used until after the 1920s. The fact that Tarantino uses the word in virtually every movie should at least give pause that its deployment in *Django* cannot be chalked up to historic accuracy or the time/space that the film takes place. Joel Randall makes this clear, identifying the pattern of usage (200 times in six films) in his entire body of work:

> You've obviously been suffering withdrawal from your beloved n-word, because you've returned to overusing the word seemingly on steroids. You volley the n-word around in *Django Unchained* over 110 times, all under the guise of "historical accuracy." But that's

bullshit. You're not concerned about being historical *or* accurate. You just have some sick obsession with the n-word, and it's way more racist than historic. Here, let me show you, as we take a walk down memory lane through your employment of the n-word like it was the most privileged extra in Hollywood.[19]

Rather than debate why/appropriateness of its use, I am more invested in the Tarantino's dismissal of any criticism. The sense of entitlement and the realized/cashed in on privilege are visible with the constant iteration of this word. It embodies the "inner black essence," a source of authentication—only black people can say the word yet Tarantino can; since Tarantino uses the word inside and outside of films, and since only black people are allowed to use the word Tarantino must indeed have a special "inner blackness."

In the end, Tarantino's use of the n-word in this film, and in others where his argument about historical necessity is less cogent, reflects a larger pattern of fetishizing blackness. The ability to say the word, to do what other whites are purportedly not able to participate in, becomes an instance where he becomes the embodiment of the exceptional white body. He becomes cool, he becomes racially progressive, and he becomes the hipster white dude that can say the n-word and get away with it. At the same time, it, like *Django*, becomes part of a narrative that positions Tarantino as a source of cohesion and unification of a divided white self (between racist and nonracist, between those who use the word and those who don't) and a divided nation. His ability to transform the meaning/reaction to this word, his ability to bring a new story into the collective imagination, and his elevation of a narrative that both black and white can embrace symbolize the investment in white savior and bridging the gap of a divided white self.

In other words, Tarantino's use of the n-word reflects his "black inner essence" and his exceptionalism. Irrespective of his "black inner essence," Tarantino also positions his whiteness as worthy of celebration. He routinely celebrates himself as providing a story that is otherwise unavailable and that will ultimately empower black America. Although others heap praise for his going where no other filmmaker will go, and offer accolades for being a white guy telling these stories, Quentin is his own greatest cheerleader.

In an interview with *The Los Angeles Times*, Tarantino made this clear: "Even for the movie's biggest black detractors, I think their children will grow up and love this movie. I think it could become a rite of passage for young black males."[20] Purportedly providing black youth with a narrative and understanding of slavery, much of Tarantino's promotion of the film centers around its supposed impact and importance to black America. "I would be surprised if, in five years, that every Black person in America hasn't seen my film," Tarantino told *Ebony*. "I don't know if they are all going to see it on opening weekend, but within five years, everyone will have seen this movie. Why wouldn't you?" (Keith 2012).

In this context, Tarantino defines his importance against the failures of Hollywood and black artists to deliver authentic representation. Imagining himself as an outsider, he often criticizes the same industry that provides opportunities otherwise not available to artists of color. He cites the importance of his film in his ability to make a cinematic masterpiece otherwise not available, to tell a story, that others in Hollywood have yet to tell. Describing *Roots* as "inauthentic" and "corny," Tarantino imagines *Django* as a corrective to this important film. "When you look at Roots, nothing about it rings true in the storytelling, and none of the performances ring true for me either," he states. "I couldn't get over how oversimplified they made everything about that time. It didn't move me because it claimed to be something it wasn't."[21] Reflective of a level of arrogance and entitlement, Tarantino positions *Django* as a source of redemption and transformation.

Similar to *The Help, Red Tails, The Blindside*, and countless other films that turn African American history into a place for white heroes (in the film, its marketing, or its production narrative), *Django* is ultimately a story of whiteness; it embodies and celebrates the power and privilege resulting from whiteness. Films about black people, or films dealing with race, are increasingly reserved for white filmmakers. According to Sarah J. Jackson, Assistant Professor in Communication Studies at Northeastern University, "Having a well-respected white filmmaker on a film about race makes that film less threatening and more appealing to the people making decisions behind the scenes AND arguably also makes 'mainstream' (again read as white) audiences more likely to see that film because they see it as 'safe.'"[22] Jelani Cobb makes a similar point about *Django* when he writes, "I's not likely that a black director would've gotten a budget to even attempt such a thing."[23] Films about white America and American history (read white history) are also reserved for white artists. The diversity on screen has not translated into a range of stories and narratives and most certainly behind the camera.

Read against Tarantino's claims of blackness, his usage of the n-word, and his ability to get Hollywood support, even for a film that has a black hero kill countless white characters, the power of whiteness is on full display here: Tarantino has the freedom to claim the Other, yet he also gets to cash in on his whiteness. "Some people have the freedom to insult others, who do not have the social power to curtail, prevent, or disallow it. Not can those insulted disseminate a response, insulting or not, as loudly and widely as their insulter can," writes Sean Tierney in "Quentin Tarantino in Black and White." "When we factor race into that construct, 'freedom' can suddenly appear much the same as privilege, grounded as it is in social power."[24] Tarantino's career is emblematic of this racially produced freedom not only to insult and mock, but to ... the freedom to borrow and sample, to turn histories of violence into a cinematic playground, and to claim fantasy and history in the same sentence. He, as Eric Deggans notes, "gets to do what black artists should also get to do";[25] he reaps the benefits of racism while denying not only his position within this larger American racial matrix, but claiming blackness. It is not simply that he gets to make a film like *Django* with a huge budget and massive distribution deal; it is not simply that he has a huge media platform to promote the film, reviews in virtually every media outlet, and showings in city after city, town after town, and suburb after suburb; it is also that he gets to tell stories, imagine alternative realities, play with aesthetics and techniques (black filmmakers are asked to "keep it real"), and in the end tell different types of stories from the Holocaust to slavery, from urban America and gangster picks to Kung Fu.

Tarantino even has the privilege to reconstitute racism and whiteness. It is not surprising that the representations of whiteness in *Django* are simplistic and flat at times, particularly in the case of those secondary roles. Just as *Pulp Fiction* had the requisite ignorant racists who raped Marcellous Wallace, *Django* redeems whiteness by constructing racism, ignorance, and pathology in the Southern, white-trashed body. Whiteness, his own whiteness, is redeemed through the Othering of the undesired white body as Southern, as trash, as uneducated, as stupid, as lazy and uncivilized. The imagining of white racism as Southern, as poor, as uneducated, and pathological is a long-standing practice, which is comforting because it once again locates racism as not central to the American project; it locates racism elsewhere, all while reifying a central message to every Tarantino film: his exceptionalism.

Conclusion

Almost a year later, I am still wrestling with my thoughts, criticisms, and frustration with *Django*. These reactions, and my immediate ambivalence after watching the film, are conditioned by my own whiteness; that white privilege infects my gaze so much so that the emotionality, the appeal, and the power of a black hero, a hero like Django whose swagger, aesthetic, and refusal to take any shit from white America means something different to me. In a society, in a cinematic landscape, where white masculinity is validated, celebrated, and elevated, I recognize that my reaction to the film is clouded by the privileges of whiteness.

Evident in my own internal questions and at times contradictory feelings about the film, it is clear *Django* has been successful in prompting discussion and debate, which of course is a good thing. But why is this film, and not the brilliant work of Ava DuVernay, whose *Middle of No Where* is one of the best films of 2012, the center of media debates? Is it because it doesn't privilege white feelings, narratives of whiteness, or white artists? Is it because they don't tell stories that empower white America or have enough white actors participating in them? It is because it doesn't imagine blackness as spectacle, as flat and one-dimensional. DuVernay beautifully describes her film in the following way:

> … So often when I see African-American performances on screen, it is in the voice of spectacle. I don't feel like race is spectacle. Race is me. I'm a black woman. We are black people. And as we move

around our daily lives, it is not a spectacle; it is the norm.... We just live, we exist. I can see those kinds of very nuanced character studies 100 times a day if I wanted to with white characters, yet it would be a struggle to find it with people of color—black brown or otherwise.... So those were the attempts that I made with the script, a simple story told with, hopefully, some depth in terms of the character development, (and) deviating from what we usually see from African-American archetypes within those situations.[26]

It's safe to say that whereas *Middle of Nowhere* chronicles the everyday experiences of African Americans, thereby avoiding the spectacle, the fantastic, and the sensational, *Django* imagines blackness and African American histories through the spectacularized, and sensationalized white fantasy. Is that what sells? Why didn't *Pariah* or *Beasts of a Southern Wild* compel the same national media interest and commercial support as *Django* and *The Help*? One can only hope that the future will bring equal attention and visibility to films like *Middle of Nowhere* and *12 Years a Slave*, and shared opportunity and freedom for all filmmakers.

Notes

1 Vera Hernan and Andrew M. Gordon, *Screen Saviors: Hollywood Fictions of Whiteness* (New York: Rowman & Littlefield Publishers, 2003).

2 Scott Schomburg, "The Enduring World of Dr. Schultz: James Baldwin, Django Unchained, and the Crisis of Whiteness," September 6, 2013, http://theotherjournal.com/2013/09/12/the-enduring-world-of-dr-schultz-james-baldwin-django-unchained-and-the-crisis-of-whiteness/#disqus_thread (accessed November 10, 2013).

3 Thomas Bogle, *Toms, Coons, Mulattoes, Mammies and Bucks: An Interpretive History of Blacks in American Films* (New York: Continuum Publishers, 2001). 140).

4 See: Lisa Marie Cacho, *Social Death: Racialized Rightlessness and the Criminalization of the Unprotected* (New York: New York University Press, 2012).

5 Douglas Linder, "Celia, A Slave, Trial (1855): An Account," (2011) http://law2.umkc.edu/faculty/projects/ftrials/celia/celiaaccount.html (accessed November 10, 2013).

6 See here David Denby, *"Django Unchained*: Put-On, Revenge, and the Aesthetics of Trash" (January 22, 2013), http://www.newyorker.com/online/blogs/culture/2013/01/django-unchained-reviewed-tarantinos-crap-masterpiece.html (accessed November 11, 2013); Nicole Sperling and Ben Fritz, "'Django,' Unchained, Looks at U.S. Past" (December 15, 2012), http://articles.latimes.com/2012/dec/15/entertainment/la-et-mn-quentin-tarantino-django-unchained-20121215 (accessed November 10, 2013); Peter Travers, "Django Unchained" (December 13, 2012), http://www.rollingstone.com/movies/reviews/django-unchained-20121213#ixzz2kTJYjoW4 (accessed November 11, 2013).

7 Tamura Lomax pushed my thinking here:

> Regardless of what we may think of QT's racial politics, his parodies of whiteness, the Klan, master-class incest, white brilliance, etc., are disruptive. They provide a different kind of narrative, further revealing the human-made character of racism, thus allowing us to find humor in the demonic. The presence of the comedic in no way diminishes the cruelty of history. We're too clever for that. Black folks have long used jokes to lessen the racial yoke. We don't always have to (or want to) relive the tragic. Sometimes comedic rage works just fine. And rest assured, meaning is never limited to the producer. We're always rearranging signs and symbols in order to make the most sense out of them.

Tamura Lomax and David Leonard, "Django Unchained: A Critical Conversation Between Two Friends" (December 31, 2012), http://thefeministwire.com/2012/12/django-unchained-a-critical-conversation-between-two-friends/ (accessed November 10, 2013).

8 Lomax and Leonard 2013.

9 Tanya Steele, "Tarantino's Candy (Slavery in the White Male Imagination)," December 27, 2012. http://blogs.indiewire.com/shadowandact/tarantinos-candy-slavery-in-the-white-male-imagination (accessed November 10, 2013).

10 Facebook post.

11 Facebook post.

12 Ishmael Reed, "Black Audiences, White Stars and 'Django Unchained'" (December 28, 2012), http://blogs.wsj.com/speakeasy/2012/12/28/black-audiences-white-stars-and-django-unchained/ (accessed November 10, 2013).

13 Vera and Gordon 2003, 1.

14 Vera and Gordon 2003, 17.

15   Richard Lawson, "'Django Unchained': Trouble in the South" (December 13, 2012), http://www.theatlanticwire.com/ entertainment/2012/12/django-unchained-review/59970/ (accessed November 10, 2013).

16   Adrian Wootton, "Quentin Tarantino interview (I) with Pam Grier, Robert Forster and Lawrence Bender," January 5, 1998, http://www.theguardian.com/film/1998/jan/05/quentintarantino. guardianinterviewsatbfisouthbank1 (retrieved November 10, 2013).

17   Email to the author.

18   Abdul Siddiqui, "Quentin Tarantino N-Word Video: Django Director Uses Racial Epithet at the Golden Globes" (January 14, 2013), http://www.policymic.com/articles/23194/quentin-tarantino-n-word-video-django-director-uses-racial-epithet-at-the-golden-globes/344575 (accessed November 10, 2013).

19   Joel Randall, "An Open Letter to Quentin Tarantino" (December 24, 2012), http://razorhorizon.tumblr.com/post/38730290043/an-open-letter-to-quentin-tarantino (accessed November 10, 2013).

20   Sperling and Fritz 2012.

21   In Karu Daniels, "Django Unchained: Selling Slaves as Action Figures" (January 6, 2013), http://www.thedailybeast.com/ articles/2013/01/06/django-unchained-selling-slaves-as-action–figures.html#url=/articles/2013/01/06/django-unchained-selling-slaves-as-action–figures.html (accessed November 10, 2013).

22   Email to the author.

23   William Jelani Cobb, "Tarantino Unchained" (January 2013), http:// www.newyorker.com/online/blogs/culture/2013/01/how-accurate-is-quentin-tarantinos-portrayal-of-slavery-in-django-unchained.html (accessed November 10, 2013).

24   Sean Tierney, "Quentin Tarantino in Black and White," in *Critical Rhetorics of Race*, ed. Michael G. Lacy and Kent A. Ono (New York: New York University Press, 2011), 93.

25   Eric Deggans, "Tarantino is the Baddest Black Filmmaker Working Today" (December 27, 2012), http://www.salon.com/2012/12/27/ tarantino_is_the_baddest_black_filmmaker_working_today/ (accessed November 10, 2013).

26   Ava DuVernay in Christy Grosz, "OSCARS Q&A: Ava DuVernay" (January 3, 2013), http://www.deadline.com/2013/01/ava-duvernay-middle-of-nowhere-oscars/ (accessed November 10, 2013).

Works Cited

ABC News. "'Django Unchained': Tarantino, DiCaprio, Foxx Answer Critics" (2013) http://youtube/JMUhaCXPyg8 (accessed September 6, 2013).

Agamben, G. *Homo Sacer. Sovereign Power and Bare Life*. Stanford, CA: Stanford University Press, 1998.

Ahmed, O. "*Django Unchained*—Re-imagining Slavery," *Ellipsis: The Accents of Cinema*, http://omarsfilmblog.blogspot.com/2013/01/django-unchained-dir-quentin-tarantino.html (accessed November 27, 2013).

Alvarez, L. and Buckley, C. "Zimmerman Is Acquitted in Killing of Trayvon Martin." *The New York Times*, July 14, 2013, http://www.nytimes.com/2013/07/15/us/george-zimmerman-verdict-trayvon-martin.html.

Anderson, M.J. "New Film: *Django Unchained* (2012)," *Tativille: A Place for Cinema & the Visual Arts*, http://tativille.blogspot.com/2013/01/new-film-django-unchained-2012_25.html (accessed November 29, 2013).

Andrews, W.L. *To Tell a Free Story: The First Century of Afro-American Autobiography, 1760–1865*. Urbana: University of Illinois Press, 1986.

———— "The Representation of Slavery and the Rise of Afro-American Literary Realism, 1865–1920." In *Slavery and the Literary Imagination*, ed. D.E. McDowell and A. Rampersad, 62–80. Baltimore: Johns Hopkins University Press, 1989.

Anon. "Reflections on Living History." *USA Today*, January 21, 2009: 14A.

————. *The Nibelungenlied. The Lay of the Nibelungs*. Translated with an Introduction and Notes by Cyril Edwards. Oxford: Oxford University Press, 2010.

————. *Django Unchained*, Review, December 30, 2012, "*The Cinephiliac*," http://thecinephiliac.wordpress.com/2012/12/30/django-unchained/ (accessed November 1, 2013).

————. "Tarantino ließ sich von Wagner Inspirieren." *Deutsche Welle*, n.d. http://www.dw.de/tarantino-ließ-sich-von-wagner-inspirieren/a-16524893 (accessed January 17, 2013).

Apter, D.E. *Ideology and Discontent*. Glencoe: The Free Press of Glencoe, 1964.

Arendt, H. *Eichmann in Jerusalem*. New York: Penguin Books, 2006.

Arron, S. "'What's Next, What's West," *OAH Magazine of History* (November 2005): 22–25.

Awkward, M. *Burying Don Imus*. Minneapolis: University of Minnesota Press, 2009.

Bantum, B. "We Should All Be Terrified," *Brian Bantum*, http://brianbantum.wordpress.com/2013/07/14/we-should-all-be-terrified/ (accessed August 7, 2013).

Baudrillard, J. *The Transparency of Evil: Essays on Extreme Phenomenon*, translated by James Benedict. New York, NY: Verso Publishing, 1993.

———— *Simulation and Simulacrum*, translated by Sheila Faria Glaser. Ann Arbor, MI: University of Michigan Press, 1994.

Beecher Stowe, H. "Uncle Tom's Cabin; Or, Life Among the Lowly" *In The Oxford Harriet Beecher Stowe Reader*, ed.J.D. Hedrick, New York: Oxford University Press, 1999.

Beethoven, Ludwig van, *Fidelio*. http://classical-music-opera.com/ludwig-van-beethoven/fidelio-summary-synopsis.html (accessed November 27, 2013).

bell hooks. *Black Looks: Race and Representation*. Cambridge, MA: South End Press, 1992.

————. *Where We Stand: Class Matters*. New York: Routledge, 2000.

Benjamin, W. *The Origin of German Tragic Drama*. translated by John Osborne, Introduction by George Steiner. London and New York: Verso, 2009.

Benson Jr, Al. and Kennedy, W.D. *Lincoln's Marxists*. Greetna. LA: Pelican, 2011.

Berger Peter, L. and Luckmann, T. *The Social Construction of Reality: A Treatise in the Sociology of Knowledge*. Garden City, NY: Doubleday, 1967.

Berlant, L. "The Face of America and the State of Emergency." In *Disciplinarity and Dissent in Cultural Studies*, ed. C. Nelson and D.P. Gaonkar, 397–439. New York: Routledge, 1996.

Blair, J. *First Steps Toward Globalization: Nineteenth Century Exports of American Entertainment Forms*. Quoted in R. Wagnleitner and E. May. *Here, There and Everywhere: The Foreign Politics of American Popular Culture*. Hanover, NH: University Press of New England, 2000.

Blight, D.W. *Frederick Douglass' Civil War: Keeping Faith in Jubilee*. Baton Rouge: Louisiana State University Press, 1989.

———— ed. *Narrative of the Life of Frederick Douglass, an American Slave, Written by Himself: With Related Documents*. 2nd ed. Boston: Bedford/St. Martin's, 2003.

Bluhm, W.T. *Ideologies and Attitudes: Modern Political Culture*. Englewood Cliffs: Prentice Hall, 1974.

Blum, S. "Mississippi Ratifies 13th Amendment Abolishing Slavery ... 147 Years Late," http://www. theguardian.com/world/2013/feb/18/mississippi-us-constitution-and-civil-liberties (accessed November 11, 2013).

Bogle, D. *Toms, Coons, Mulattoes, Mammies, and Bucks: An Interpretive History of Blacks in American Films*. New York, NY: Continuum Publishing Company, 1999.

Bolter, J.D. and Grusin, R. "Remediation" *Configurations*, 4, 3 (1996): 311–358.

Boxofficemojo. "Django Unchained" http://www.boxofficemojo.com/movies/?id=djangounchained.htm (accessed November 26, 2013).

Boyd, T. *The New H.N.I.C.: The Death of Civil Rights and the Reign of Hip Hop*. New York: New York University Press, 2003.

Brown, P. *The Body and Society: Men, Women, and Sexual Renunciation in Early Christianity*, 2nd ed. New York: Columbia University Press, 2008.

Brown, W., Iordanova, D. and Torchin, L. *Moving People, Moving Images: Cinema and Trafficking in the New Europe*. St Andrews: St Andrews Film Studies, 2010.

Burghardt Du Bois, W.E. *John Brown*. Philadelphia: G. W. Jacobs, 1909, 340.

Burke, K. *A Grammar of Motives*. Berkeley, CA: University of California Press, 1969.

Burnard, T.G. *Mastery, Tyranny, and Desire: Thomas Thistlewood and His Slaves in the Anglo-Jamaican World*. Chapel Hill: University of North Carolina Press, 2004.

Cacho, L.M. *Social Death: Racialized Rightlessness and the Criminalization of the Unprotected*. New York: New York University Press, 2012.

Campbell, K.K. "The Ontological Foundations of Rhetorical Theory." *Philosophy and Rhetoric*, 3 (1970): 97–108.

Campbell, J. and Moyers, B. *The Power of Myth*. Harpswell: Anchor Publishing, 1988.

Carpenter, R. "Revisiting Janice Rushing about 'The Western Myth' (More Important Now than Ever Before)," *Southern Journal of Communication*, 71, no.2 (2006): 179–182.

Chabon, M. *The Amazing Adventures of Kavalier & Clay*. London: 4th Estate, 2010.

Charania, M. "Django Unchained, Voyeurism Unleashed." *Contexts*, 12, no. 3 (August 12, 2013): 58–60.

Clark, E.B. "'The Sacred Rights of the Weak': Pain, Sympathy, and the Culture of Individual Rights in Antebellum America." *Journal of American History*, 82 (September 1995): 463, 466–467.

Cobb, J. "How Accurate Is Quentin Tarantino's Portrayal of Slavery in Django Unchained?" *The New Yorker*, January 2, 2013, http://www.newyorker.com/online/blogs/culture/2013/01/how-accurate-is-quentin-tarantinos-portrayal-of-slavery-in-django-unchained.html.

Coleman, R.M. *Say It Loud! African-American Audiences, Media, and Identity*. New York, NY: Routledge, 2002.

Conrad, J. "'Henry James: An Appreciation' from *Notes on Life and Letters* in 'The Author on Art and Literature.'" In *Heart of Darkness: A Norton Critical Edition*, 4th ed, ed. P.B. Armstrong, 286–288. New York and London: W.W. Norton & Company, 2006.

———— "Heart of Darkness." In *Heart of Darkness: A Norton Critical Edition*, 4th ed, ed. P.B. Armstrong, 3–77. New York and London: W.W. Norton & Company, 2006.

Cooper, J.F. "The Last of the Mohicans. A Narrative of 1757." In *The Leatherstocking Tales*, ed. Blake Nevius. New York: The Library of America, 1985.

Copjec, J. *Imagine There's No Woman: Ethics and Sublimation.* Cambridge: MIT, 2002.

Corcoran, F. "Cultural Studies: From Old World to New World." *Communication Yearbook* (1989): 602.

Cornish, A. "Tarantino On 'Django,' Violence and Catharsis." National Public Radio December 28, 2012. http://www.npr.org/templates/transcript/transcript.php?storyId= 168193823 (accessed July 9, 2013).

Crain, C. *American Sympathy. Men, Friendship, and Literature in the New Nation.* New Haven/London: Yale University Press, 2001.

Dahlhaus, C. *Ludwig van Beethoven, Approaches to His Music.* Oxford: Oxford University Press, 1991.

Daniels, K. "Django Unchained: Selling Slaves as Action Figures," January 6, 2013. http://www.thedailybeast.com/articles/2013/01/06/django-unchained-selling-slaves-as-action-figures.html (accessed November 10, 2013).

Dassanowsky, R. von. "Introduction: Locating Mr. Tarantino or, Who's Afraid of Metacinema?" In *Quentin Tarantino's Inglourious Basterds: A Manipulation of Metacinema*, ed. R. von Dassanowsky, ix–xi. New York and London: Continuum, 2012.

Davis, C. "Mindhole Blowers: 20 Facts about *Blazing Saddles* that Might Leave Your Mind Aglow with Whirling, Transient Nodes of Thought Careening Through a Cosmic Vapor of Invention." *Pajiba* (2012), http://www.pajiba.com/seriously_random_lists/mindhole-blowers-20-facts-about-blazing-saddles-that-might-leave-your-mind-aglow-with-whirling-transient-nodes-of-thought-careening-through-a-cosmic-vapor-of-invention-.php (accessed September 2, 2013).

DeMott, B. *The Trouble with Friendship. Why Americans Can't Think Straight About Race.* New York: The Atlantic Monthly Press, 1995.

Deggans, E. "Tarantino is the Baddest Black Filmmaker Working Today," December 27, 2012. http://www.salon.com/2012/12/27/tarantino_is_the_baddest_black_filmmaker_working_today/ (accessed November 10, 2013).

Denby, D. "'Django Unchained': Put-On, Revenge, and the Aesthetics of Trash," *New Yorker*, January 22, 2013, http://www.newyorker.com/

online/blogs/culture/2013/01/ django-unchained-reviewed-tarantinos-
crap-masterpiece.html. (accessed November 11, 2013).

Derrida, J. *The Politics of Friendship*, translated by George Collins.
London/New York: Verso, 2005.

Dimock, W.C. "Crowdsourcing History: Ishmael Reed, Tony Kushner,
and Steven Spielberg Update the Civil War." *American Literary
History*, no. 4 (2013): 896–914.

Döring, M. "Die narratologische Küste. Küstenbilder in zwei Romanen
und Kurzgeschichten Guy de Maupassants." In *Küstenbilder—Bilder
der Küste. Interdisziplinäre Ansichten, Ansätze und Konzepte*, ed.
M. Döring, W. Settekorn, and Hvon Storch, Hamburg: Hamburg
University Press, 2006.

Draigh, D. and Marcus, G.S. "In the Heat of the Night," *American
Museum of the Moving Image*. http://www.movingimage.us/site/
education/content/ guides/Heat%20of%20the%20Night%20SM.pdf.

Dudziak, M. *Cold War Civil Rights: Race and the Image of American
Democracy*. Princeton NJ: Univeristy Press, 2000.

Dyson, M.E. *Reflecting Black: African-American Cultural Criticism*.
Minneapolis: University of Minnesota Press, 1993.

Ebert, R. "Faster Quentin! Thrill! Thrill!" *Roger Ebert's Journal*, January
7, 2013. http://www.rogerebert.com/rogers-journal/faster-quentin-
thrill-thrill (accessed July 13, 2013).

Eisner, L.H. *The Haunted Screen. Expressionism in the German Cinema
and the Influence of Max Reinhardt*, translated by Roger Greaves.
Berkeley/Los Angeles: University of California Press, 1969.

Eliade, M. *The Myth of the Eternal Return or, Cosmos and History*.
Princeton: Princeton University Press, 1954.

——— *Myth and Reality*. New York: Harper, 1963.

Entman, R.M. and Rojecki, A. *The Black Image in the White Mind:
Media and Race in America*. Chicago: University of Chicago Press,
2001.

Fanon, F. *The Wretched of the Earth*. Boston: Grove Press, 2005.

——— *Black Skin, White Masks*. Grove press: Syracuse, NY, 2008.

Fiske, J. *British Cultural Studies and Television*. New York, NY: St.
Martin's Press Inc, 1996, Quoted in J. Storey *What is Cultural
Studies? A Reader*. New York, NY: St. Martin's Press Inc., 1996,
115–147.

Foner, E. *The Fiery Trial: Abraham Lincoln and American Slavery*.
New York: W. W. Norton, 2010, 313–314, *Globe* quotes on 314.

Fortson, R. "Correcting the Harms of Slavery: Collective Liability, the
Limited Prospects of Success for a Class Action Suit for Slavery
Reparations, and the Reconceptualization of White Racial Identity."
African American Law & Policy Report, 6, no. 71 (2004): 71–127.

Frantz, J.B. and Choate, J.E. *The American Cowboy: The Myth and the Reality*. Norman: University of Oklahoma Press, 1955.

Gabriel, D. "Hollywood's Slavery Films Tell Us More about the Present than the Past." *Colorlines* (2013), http://colorlines.com/archives/2013/01/slavery_in_film.html (accessed August 29, 2013).

Garrigus, J. "Free Coloureds." In *The Routledge History of Slavery*, ed. G. Heuman and T. Burnard, 237–243. London: Routledge, 2011.

Gates, H.L. Jr. *Thirteen Ways of Looking at a Black Man*. New York: Vintage, 1997.

———. "Were There Slaves Like Stephen in 'Django'?" *The Root* (2013). http://www.theroot.com/views/were-there-slaves-stephen-django (accessed August 30, 2013).

———. "Tarantino 'Unchained,' Part 1: 'Django' Trilogy? In the First of a Q&A Series, the Director Tells Our Editor-in-Chief about His Next Black Film." *The Root*, December 23, 2012. http://www.theroot.com/views/tarantino-unchained-part-1-django-trilogy?page=0,4 (accessed July 9, 2013).

——— "Tarantino 'Unchained,' Part 2: On the N-Word—In the Second of a Q&A Series, He Talks Critics and Django's Depiction of Slavery with Henry Louis Gates Jr." *The Root*, December 25, 2012. http://www.theroot.com/views/tarantino-unchained-part-2-n-word?page=0,1&wpisrc=obinsite (accessed July 9, 2013).

——— "Tarantino 'Unchained,' Part 3: White Saviors," *The Root*, December 24, 2012. http://www.theroot.com/views/tarantino-unchained-part-3-white-saviors?page=0,4&wpisrc=obinsite (accessed July 9, 2013).

——— "Did Dogs Really Eat Slaves, Like in 'Django'? 100 Amazing Facts About the Negro: Plus, whether Slaves Rode Horses or Had Mandingo Death Matches" *The Root*, January 14, 2013. http://www.theroot.com/views/did-dogs-really-eat-slaves-django?page=0,0 (accessed July 9, 2013).

Gauntlett, D. *Media, Gender, Identity*. London: Routledge, 2002.

Gay, R. "Surviving Django." *Buzzfeed Community*. http://www.buzzfeed.com/roxanegay/surviving-django-8opx (accessed January 5, 2013).

Gehrts, H. "Der Sinn der Blutsbrüderschaft." *Märchenspiegel*, Braunschweig: Märchenstiftung Walter Kahn, 1993, n.p.

Geller, T.L. "Queerying Hollywood's Tough Chick: The Subversions of Sex, Race, and Nation in The Long Kiss Goodnight and The Matrix." *Frontiers: A Journal of Women Studies*, 25, no. 3 (2004–2005): 8–34.

Gibson, K.L. and Heyse, A.L. "Depoliticizing Feminism: Frontier Mythology and Sarah Palin's "The Rise of the Mama Grizzlies," *Western Journal of Communication*, 78, no. 1 (2014): 97–117.

Gillens, M. *Why America Hates Welfare: Race, Media and the Politics of Anti-Poverty Policy*. Chicago, IL: University of Chicago Press, 1999.

Glover, J. *Humanity: A Moral History of the Twentieth Century*. New Haven, CT: Yale University Press, 1999.

Gobin, A. "Technologies of Control: Visual Arts and the African Slave Body from the 18th Century to the Present." *Research and Practice in Social Sciences*, 2, no. 2 (2007): 126.

Godbeer, R. *The Overflowing of Friendship. Love Between Men and the Creation of the American Republic*. Baltimore: The Johns Hopkins University Press, 2009.

Gormley, P. *New Brutality Film: Race and Affect in Contemporary Hollywood Cinema*. Bristol: Intellect Ltd, 2005.

Gould, S.J. *The Mismeasure of Man*. New York: W.W. Norton, 1981.

Gray, H. *Watching Race: Television and the Struggle for "Blackness."* Minneapolis: University of Minnesota Press, 1995.

Gregg, R. *Symbolic Inducement and Knowing: A Study in the Foundation of Rhetoric*. Columbia: University of South Carolina Press, 1984.

Grønstad, A. *Transfigurations: Violence, Death and Masculinity in American Cinema*. Amsterdam: Amsterdam University Press, 2008.

Gross, T. "Quentin Tarantino, 'Unchained' and 'Unruly,'" interview with National Public Radio's Terry Gross, January 2, 2013, http://www.npr. org/2013/01/02/168200139/quentin-tarantino-unchained-and-unruly (accessed November 11, 2013).

Grossberg, L. "Strategies of Marxist Cultural Interpretation." *Critical Studies in Mass Communication*, 1 (1984): 392–421.

——— *We Gotta Get Out of this Place: Popular Conservatism and Postmodern Culture*. New York: Routledge, 1992.

Grosz, C. "OSCARS Q&A: Ava DuVernay," January 3, 2013. http://www. deadline.com/2013/01/ava-duvernay-middle-of-nowhere-oscars/ (accessed November 10, 2013).

Gunning, T. *The Films of Fitz Lang: Allegories of Vision and Modernity*. London: BFI Press, 2001.

Haas, T. *The Pursuit of Public Journalism: Theory, Practice, and Criticism*. New York: Routledge, 2007.

Hahn, S. "Forging Freedom." In *The Routledge History of Slavery*, ed. G. Heuman and T. Burnard, London: Routledge, 2011.

Hale, G.E. *Making Whiteness: The Culture of Segregation in the South, 1890–1940*. New York: Vintage Books, 1999.

Hall, S. "Notes on Deconstructing 'The Popular.'" In *People's History and Socialist Theory*, ed. R. Samuel, 227–240. London: Routledge and Kegan Paul, 1981.

——— "On Postmodernism and Articulation: An Interview with Stuart Hall." *Journal of Communication Inquiry*, 10, 2 (1986): 45–60.

——— "Old and New Identities, Old and New Ethnicities." In *Culture, Globalization, and the World-system*, ed. A. King, 41–68. London: Macmillan, 1991.

———— "Cultural Studies and Its Theoretical Legacies." In *Cultural Studies*, ed. L. Grossberg, C. Nelson, P.A. Treichler, L. Baughman, and J. Macgregor Wise, 277–294. New York: Routledge, 1992.

————. "New Ethnicities." In *Stuart Hall: Critical Dialogues in Cultural Studies*, ed. D. Morley and K.-H. Chen, 441–449. New York: Routledge, 1996.

———— *Representation: Cultural Representation and Signifying Practices*. London: Sage, 1997.

Halttunen, K. "Humanitarianism and the Pornography of Pain in Anglo-American Culture." *American Historical Review*, 100 (April 1995): 303–334.

Hamilton, D. "Representing Slavery in British Museums: The Challenges of 2007." In *Imagining Transatlantic Slavery*, ed. C. Kaplan and J. Oldfield, New York: Palgrave, 2010.

Hamilton, E. and Cairns, H. *The Collected Dialogues of Plato*. Princeton, NJ: Princeton University Press, 1962.

Haraway, D. *A Cyborg Manifesto: Science, Technology and Socialist— Feminism in the Late Twentieth Century. The Cybercultures Reader*. London: Routledge, 2000.

Harris, A. "Was There Really 'Mandingo Fighting,' Like in *Django Unchained?*" *Slate*, December 24, 2012. http://www.slate.com/blogs/browbeat/2012/12/24/django_unchained_ mandingo_fighting_were_any_slaves_really_forced_to_fight.html (accessed November 11, 2013).

———— "Conservatives Freak Out About Django Unchained." *Slate*, December 19, 2012. http://www.slate.com/blogs/browbeat/2012/12/19/django_unchained_and_racism_drudge_report_rehashes_tarantino_n_word_flap.html.

———— "When Blaxploitation Went West: Django Unchained Seems Tame by Comparison." *Slate*, December 25, 2012. http://www.slate.com/articles/arts/culturebox/2012/12/django_unchained_tarantino_s_movie_seems_tame_compared_with_the_blaxploitation.html (accessed November 20, 2013).

Harris-Perry, M. *Sister Citizen: Shame, Stereotypes, and Black Women in America*. New Haven, CT: Yale University Press, 2011.

Hasse, J. "Küste als Raum der Erholung und der Freizeit." In *Küstenbilder—Bilder der Küste. Interdisziplinäre Ansichten, Ansätze und Konzepte*, ed. M. Döring, S. Wolfgang, and Hvon Storch, Hamburg: Hamburg University Press, 2006.

Hathaway, J. "*Django Unchained* Stereoscopic Photo," *What the…*, January 14, 2013, http://jahathaway.wordpress.com/2013/01/14/django-unchained-stereoscopic-photo/ (accessed July 8, 2013).

Hellmuth, L. *Die germanische Blutsbrüderschaft. Ein typologischer und volkskundlicher Vergleich*. Rudolstadt: Edition Roter Drache, 2010.

Henretta, J.A., R. Edwards, and R.O. Self, eds. *America: A Concise History 5th, vol. 1, To 1877*. Boston: Bedford/St. Martin's, 2012.

Hertzberg, H. "Djangled Nerves," *The New Yorker*, March 7, 2013. http://www.newyorker.com/online/blogs/hendrikhertzberg/2013/03/djangled-nerves.html.

Heuman, G. "Slave Rebellions." In *The Routledge History of Slavery*, ed. G. Heuman and T. Burnard, London: Routledge, 2011.

Hewitt, A. "The Bad Seed: 'Auschwitz and the Physiology of Evil.'" In *Radical Evil*, ed. J. Copjec, 74–105. New York: Verso, 1996.

Hill Collins, P. *Black Sexual Politics: African Americans, Gender, and the New Racism*. New York: Routledge, 2005.

Hillier, J. *Cahiers du cinéma: The 1950s: Neo-realism, Hollywood, New Wave*. Cambridge, Mass: Harvard University Press, 1985.

Hobsbawm, E. *Fractured Times: Culture and Society in the 20th Century*. London: Little, Brown Book Group, 2013.

Hoeveller, D.L. and Cass, J. "Mapping Orientalism: Representations and Pedagogies." In *Interrogating Orientalism: Contextual Approaches and Pedagogical Practices*, ed. D. Hoeveller and J. Cass, Columbus, OH: Ohio State University Press, 2006.

Hollywood Reporter, December 2012. http://www.hollywoodreporter.com/news/spike-lee-django-unchained-is-406313 (accessed July 13, 2013).

Honoré, A. "The Nature of Slavery." In *The Legal Understanding of Slavery. From the Historical to the Contemporary*, ed. J. Allain, Oxford: Oxford University Press, 2012.

Horowitz, J. *They Went Thataway*. New York: E.P. Dutton & Co, 1976.

Hudlin, R. "Django Unchained Producer's Diary" http://www.hudlinentertainment.com/pages/goodies/hudlins-huddle.php?p=10&g=7.

Hughey, M. "Cinethetic Racism: White Redemption and Black Stereotypes in 'Magical Negro' Films." *Social Problems*, 56, no.3 (2009): 543–577.

Ignatiev, N., and John G., eds. *Race Traitor*. New York: Routledge, 1996.

IMDB. "Django Unchained: Awards" http://www.imdb.com/title/tt1853728/awards?ref_=tt_awd (accessed November 26, 2013).

Indiana, G. *Salò or the 120 Days of Sodom*. London: BFI, 2000.

Jacobs, H. *Incidents in the Life of a Slave Girl, Written by Herself*. ed. L. Maria Child. Boston: Published for the Author, 1861.

Jansson, D.R. "'A Geography of Racism': Internal Orientalism and the Construction of American National Identity in the Film Mississippi Burning." *National Identities*, 7, no. 3 (2005): 265–285.

Jenkins, H. "'Quentin Tarantino's Star Wars?' Digital Cinema, Media Convergence, and Participatory Culture." In *Rethinking Media Change: The Aesthetics of Transition*, ed.D. Thorburn, Cambridge, MA: MIT Press, 2003.

Jhally, S. *The Codes of Advertising: Fetishism and the Political Economy of Meaning in Consumer Society.* New York, NY: Routledge, 1990.

——— and Lewis, J. *Enlightened Racism: The Cosby Show, Audiences, and the Myth of the American Dream.* Boulder, CO: Westview, 1992.

Kaes, A. *Shell Shock Cinema. Weimar Culture and the Wounds of War.* Princeton/Oxford: Princeton University Press, 2009.

Kant, I. *Religion Within the Limits of Reason Alone.* New York: Harper Torchbooks, 1960.

———, "What is Englightenment? (1784)" *Modern History Sourcebook,* Fordham University, http://www.fordham.edu/halsall/mod/kant-whatis.asp (accessed August 1, 2013).

Kantrowitz, S. "'Django Unchained's' White Abolitionist Vision." *HNN: History News Network,* January 28, 2013, http://hnn.us/article/150272 (accessed November 11, 2013).

Kaplan, E.A. "'Django' an Unsettling Experience for Many Blacks," *Los Angeles Times,* 2012, http://articles.latimes.com/2012/dec/28/entertainment/la-et-django-reax-2-20121228 (accessed September 2, 2013).

Kaufmann, J.-C. *Frauenkörper—Männerblicke: Soziologie des Oben-ohne.* Konstanz: UVK Verl.-Ges, 2006.

Keeling, K. *The Witch's Flight: The Cinematic, the Black Femme, and the Image of Common Sense.* Durham, NC: Duke University Press, 2007.

Keith, A.E. "[INTERVIEW]: Quentin Tarantino, Untamed," December 12, 2012. http://www.ebony.com/entertainment-culture/interview-quentin-tarantino-untamed-999#axzz2kIfBa2ZA. (accessed November 10, 2013).

Kempley, R. "Too Too Divine. 'Movies' 'Magic Negro' Saves the Day— But at the Cost of His Soul." *The Black Commentator,* 49 (2003): 1. http://blackcommentator.com/49/49_ magic.html. (accessed November 1, 2013.)

Ken, P. "An Interview with Danny Strong." *IGN,* May 19, 2003. http://www.ign.com/articles/2003/05/19/an-interview-with-danny-strong (accessed February 28, 2013).

Kerrigan, J. *Revenge Tragedy: Aeschylus to Armageddon.* Oxford: Clarendon, 1996.

Kipnis, L. "(Male) Desire and (Female) Disgust: Reading *Hustler.*" In *Cultural Studies,* ed. L. Grossberg, C. Nelson, P.A. Treichler, L. Baughman, and J. Macgregor Wise, 373–391. New York: Routledge, 1992.

Kracauer, S. *From Caligari to Hitler. A Psychological History of the German Film.* Edited by Leonardo Quaresima, revised and expanded edition. Princeton: Princeton University Press, 2004.

Krauskopf, P. "Deutsche Zeichen, deutsche Helden." In *Jahrbuch der Karl-May-Gesellschaft 1996,* ed. C. Roxin and H. Schmiedt, 365–393.

Hans Wollschläger. Hamburg: Karl-May-Gesellschft, 1996. http://www.karl-may-gesellschaft.de/kmg/seklit/JbKMG/1996/365.htm (accessed December 26, 2012).

Lacan, J. "Seminar V: The Formation of the Unconscious: Seminar of 21-5-58." Unpublished Manuscript http://www.lacanonline.com/index/quotes/ (accessed June 14, 2013).

Larson, S. *Media and Minorities: The Politics of Race in News and Entertainment*. Lanham, MD: Rowman & Littlefield, 2006.

Lawrence, K. "Karl Marx on American Slavery," *Freedom Information Service* 1976, http://www.sojournertruth.net/marxslavery.pdf. (accessed July 8, 2013).

Lawson, R. "'Django Unchained': Trouble in the South," December 13, 2012. http://www.theatlanticwire.com/entertainment/2012/12/django-unchained-review/59970/ (accessed November 10, 2013).

Leab, D. "The Moving Image as Interpreter of History—Telling the Dancer from the Dance." In *Image as Artifact: The Historical Analysis of Film and Television*, ed. J.E. O'Connor, New York: Robert E. Krieger Publishing Company, 1990.

Lee, S. (with Ralph Wiley). *By Any Means Necessary: The Trials and Tribulations of the Making of "'Malcolm X'" ... Including the Screenplay*. London: Vintage, 1993.

——— "The Newest Hottest Spike Lee Joint" (2013), http://www.kickstarter.com/projects/spikelee/the-newest-hottest-spike-lee-joint (accessed September 6, 2013).

Lessig, L. *Remix: Making Art and Commerce Thrive in the Hybrid Economy*. New York: Penguin, 2008.

Lessing, G.E. *Nathan the Wise, Minna von Barnhelm, and Other Plays and Writings*. Edited by Peter Demetz, foreword by Hannah Arendt. New York: Continuum, 2004.

Levi-Strauss, C. *The Savage Mind*. Chicago: University of Chicago Press, 1966.

Levin, D. *Richard Wagner, Fritz Lang, and the Nibelungen. The Dramaturgy of Disavowal*. Princeton: Princeton University Press, 1998.

Lincoln, A. "The Gettysburg Address." http://www.abrahamlincolnonline.org/lincoln/speeches/gettysburg.htm (accessed November 11, 2013).

Linder, D. "Celia, A Slave, Trial (1855): An Account," 2011. http://law2.umkc.edu/faculty/projects/ftrials/celia/celiaaccount.html (retrieved November 10, 2013).

Lippmann, W. *Public Opinion*. New York: Macmillan, 1956.

Lockley, T.J. "Race Relations in Slave Societies," in *The Routledge History of Slavery*. ed. Gad Heuman and Trevor Burnard. London: Routledge, 2011.

Lomax, T. and Leonard, D. "Django Unchained: A Critical Conversation between Two Friends," December 31, 2012, http://thefeministwire.

com/2012/12/django-unchained-a-critical-conversation-between-two-friends/ (accessed November 10, 2013).

Lotringer, S. "'Domination and Servitude': Introduction to Jean Baudrillard" In *The Agony of Power*, ed.Jean Baudrillard, translated by Ames Hodges, Los Angeles, CA: Semiotext(e), 2010.

Lott, E. *Love and Theft: Blackface Minstrelsy and the American Working Class*. New York: Oxford University Press, 1993.

Lovejoy, P.E. "'Freedom Narratives' of Transatlantic Slavery." *Slavery & Abolition*, 32, no. 1 (March 2011): 95.

Low, S.M. "Anthropological Theories of Body, Space, and Culture." *Space and Culture*, 6, no. 1 (2003): 9–18.

Löw, M. "The Social Construction of Space and Gender," *European Journal of Women's Studies*, 13, no. 2 (May 1, 2006): 119–133.

Macnab, G. "Quentin Tarantino—The Good, the Bad and the Movie Geek," http://www.independent.co.uk/arts-entertainment/films/features/quentin-tarantino--the-good-the-bad-and-the-movie-geek-2283148.html, Friday May 13, 2011.

Mailloux, S. "Re-Marking Slave Bodies: Rhetoric as Production and Reception," *Philosophy and Rhetoric*, 35, no. 2 (2002): 96–119.

Malinowski, B. *Magic, Science and Religion and Other Essays*. Garden City: Doubleday, 1948.

Mamdani, M. *When Victims Become Killers: Colonialism, Nativism, and the Genocide in Rwanda*. Princeton, NJ: Princeton University Press, 2001.

Mancini, A. "The New Spaghetti Western: The Southern." Iperstoria. Testi letterature linguaggi (www.iperstoria.it). Rivista semestrale. Numero 2, ottobre 2013. http://www.iperstoria.it/joomla/numeri/15-saggi/80-mancini-prova-2 (accessed November 28, 2013).

Manovich, L. *The Language of New Media*. Cambridge: MIT Press, 2001.

Marche, S. "*Django Unchained* Is a Better Movie about Slavery than *Lincoln*," *Esquire*, December 24, 2012, http://www.esquire.com/blogs/culture/django-unchained-lincoln-slavery-14895534 (accessed November 11, 2013).

Marcotte, A. "*Django Unchained*: A Movie about Other Movies about the 19th Century." *Raw Story* (2013). http://www.rawstory.com/rs/2013/01/03/django-unchained-a-movie-about-other-movies-about-the-19th-century/ (accessed September 2, 2013).

Marcus, R. "A Cliffhanger in the White House." *The Washington Post* (2012), http://articles.washingtonpost.com/2012-11-20/opinions/35510873_1_fiscal-cliff-mary-lincoln-13th-amendment (accessed September 2, 2013).

Marlowe, W. Gertrude. "Keckley." In *American National Biography Online*, http://www.anb.org/articles/20/20-00530.html (accessed November 11, 2013).

Martin-Jones, D. "Schizoanalysis, Cinema and the Spaghetti Western." In *Deleuze and the Schizoanalysis of Cinema*, ed. I. Buchanan and P. MacCormack, 75–88. London: Continuum, 2008.

Marx, K. *The Poverty of Philosophy: A Reply to M Proudhon's Philosophy of Poverty*. New York: International Publishers, n.d.

May, K. *Winnetou III*. Freiburg: Fehsenfeld (1909). http://www.karl-may-gesellschaft.de/kmg/primlit/reise/gr09/kptl_7.htm (accessed July 20, 2013).

Mazierska, E. (ed.) *Work in Cinema: Labour and the Human Condition*. London: Palgrave Macmillan, 2013.

——— *From Self-Fulfilment to Survival of the Fittest: The Representation of Work in European Cinema from the 1960s to the Present Day*. New York, Oxford: Berghahn (Forthcoming).

McGee, P. *Bad History and the Logics of Blockbuster Cinema: Titanic, Gangs of New York, Australia, Inglourious Basterds*. New York: Palgrave Macmillan, 2012.

McKeown, N. "Seeing Things: Examining the Body of the Slave in Greek Medicine," *Slavery & Abolition*, 23, no. 2 (August 2002): 29.

McPherson, J.M. "The Second American Revolution," in *Abraham Lincoln and the Second American Revolution*, 3–22. New York: Oxford University Press, 1991.

Medhurst, M.J. "George W. Bush at Goree Island: American Slavery and the Rhetoric of Redemption." *The Quarterly Journal of Speech*, 96, no.3 (2010): 257–277.

Miller, D.A. *The Epic Hero*. Baltimore/London: The Johns Hopkins University Press, 2000.

Molloy, S. "The Instruction of Suffering: Kant's Theological Anthropology for a Prodigal Species." Unpublished Manuscript, University of Edinburgh, 2013, 16.

Morgan, J.L. "Gender and Family Life." In *The Routledge History of Slavery*, ed. G. Heuman and T. Burnard, London: Routledge, 2011.

Morris, S.M. "Django Unchained and Why Context Matters," January 6, 2013, http://www.crunkfeministcollective.com/2013/01/06/django-unchained-and-why-context-matters/.

Moser, K. and Ravasani, D. "Amerika's dreckige Geschichte." *3sat*, January 8, 2013. http://www.3sat.de/page/?source=/kulturzeit/tips/166980/index.html (accessed January 10, 2013).

Moviemaniacs. "Django Unchained: Meet the Press" (2013), http://youtu.be/-1QpScB-HJg (accessed September 6, 2013).

Mstrmnd. "The Last Auteur: *Django Unchained*," *Mstrmnd*, http://www.mstrmnd.com/log/2390 (n.d.) (accessed July 8, 2013).

Mullins, W.A. *The Concept of Ideology: An Analysis and Evaluation*. Seattle: University of Washington Press, 1969.

Oprah Winfrey Network. "Oprah, Spielberg, Daniel Day-Lewis talk about 'Lincoln.'" *The Huffington Post* (2012), http://www.huffingtonpost.

com/2012/11/29/oprah-spielberg-daniel-day-lewis-lincoln_n_2207277.
html (accessed September 6, 2013).

———. "Exclusive: Jamie Foxx Addresses Critics of *Django Unchained*"
(2013), http://youtu.be/xrolCfnrkG8 (accessed September 6, 2013).

Oschema, K. "Das Motiv der Blutsbrüderschaft." In *Riten, Gesten,
Zeremonien. Gesellschaftliche Symbolik in Mittelalter und Früher
Neuzeit*, ed. E. Bierende, S. Bretfeld, K. Oschema, 47–51. Berlin/
New York: Walter de Gruyter, 2008.

Osterweil, W. "Hollywoodin Revolt?" *Dissent* (October 1, 2013).

O'Hehir, A. "Is Tarantino Good for the Jews?' *Salon* (August 13, 2009).
http://www.salon.com/2009/08/13/basterds/

Palmer, L. "Why 'Django Unchained' Is Subversively Complex and
Disappointingly Simple," *FilmSchoolRejects*, December 29, 2012.
http://www.filmschoolrejects.com/features/why-django-unchained-is-
subversively-complex-and-disappointingly-simple-lpalm.php.

Parenti, M. *Make-Believe Media: The Politics of Entertainment.*
New York: Cengage Learning, 1991.

Parker, E. "Chain Gang." *Vibe* (December 2012/January 2013).

Patterson, R.J. "'Woman Thou Art Bound': Critical Spectatorship, Black
Masculine Gazes, and Gender Problems in Tyler Perry's Movies."
Black Camera. 3, no, 1 (2011): 9–30.

Penley, C. *NASA/TREK: Popular Science and Sex in America.* New York:
Verso, 1997.

Perry, S.P. "Douglas MacArthur as Frontier Hero: Converting Frontiers
in MacArthur's Farewell to Congress," *Southern Communication
Journal*, 77, no. 4 (2012): 263–286.

——— "Django Unchained and Undisturbed Frontier Hero Archetype,"
18th Biennial NCA/AFA Conference on Argumentation, 2013
(forthcoming).

Platon, A. "Spike Lee Slams Django Unchained: 'I'm Not Gonna See it.'"
VIBE, December 21, 2012. http://www.vibe.com/article/spike-lee-
slams-django-unchained-im-not-gonna-see-it.

Prince, R. *Sam Peckinpah and the Rise of Ultraviolent Movies.* London:
The Athlone Press,1998.

Quintero, S. "I Should've Been Motherfuckin' Black Mamba': What
the Poetic License of Quentin Tarantino Reveals about His Racial
Politics," February 2, 2013. http://blackartemis.blogspot.com/2013/02/
i-shouldve-been-motherfuckin-black.html (accessed November
10, 2013).

Quintin, "*Django Unchained* (Quentin Tarantino, US)," *Cinemascope*
54, http://cinema-scope.com/currency/django-unchained-quentin-
tarantino-us/ (accessed November 1, 2013)

Radway, J.A. *A Feeling for Books: The Book-of-the-Month Club, Literary
Taste, and Middle-class Desire.* Chapel Hill: University of North
Carolina Press, 1997.

Randall, J. "An Open Letter to Quentin Tarantino," December 24, 2012. http://razorhorizon.tumblr.com/post/38730290043/an-open-letter-to-quentin-tarantino (accessed November 10, 2013).

Reece, C. "Snowball's Chance in Hell: *Django Unchained*" *The Hooded Utilitarian* (2013). http://www.hoodedutilitarian.com/2013/01/snowballs-chance-in-hell-django-unchained/ (accessed August 30, 2013).

Reed, I. "Black Audiences, White Stars and 'Django Unchained,'" December 28, 2012. http://blogs.wsj.com/speakeasy/2012/12/28/black-audiences-white-stars-and-django-unchained/ (accessed November 10, 2013).

Rhines, J. *Black Film, White Money*. New Brunswick, NJ: Rutgers University Press, 1996.

Rich, F. "The *Lincoln* Consensus: A Bipartisan Coalition Praises Stephen Spielberg's Latest Film." *New York*, 2013. http://nymag.com/news/frank-rich/spielbergs-lincoln-politics-2013–2/ (accessed September 6, 2013).

Richardson, M.D. "Vengeful Violence: Inglourious Basterds, Allohistory, and the Inversion of Victims and Perpetrators." In *Quentin Tarantino's Inglourious Basterds: A Manipulation of Metacinema*, ed. R. von Dassanowsky, 93–112. New York and London: Continuum, 2012.

Rodman, G.B. *Elvis After Elvis: The Posthumous Career of a Living Legend*. New York: Routledge, 1996.

——— "Race … and Other Four Letter Words: Eminem and the Cultural Politics of Authenticity." *Popular Communication*, 4, 2 (2006): 95–121.

Rowland, R.C. "On Mythic Criticism." *Communication Studies*, 41 (1990): 101–116.

——— and Frank, D.A. *Shared Land/Conflicting Identity: Trajectories of Israeli & Palestinian Symbol Use*. East Lansing: Michigan State University Press, 2002, 1990.

Rushing, J.H. "The Rhetoric of the American Western Myth." *Communication Monographs*, 50, no. 1 (1983): 14–32.

——— "Mythic Evolution of the 'New Frontier' in Mass Mediated Rhetoric." *Critical Studies in Mass Communication*, 3, no. 3 (1986): 265–296.

——— "Evolution of 'The New Frontier' in *Alien* and *Aliens*: Patriarchal Co-optation of the Feminine Archetype." *Quarterly Journal of Speech*, 75, no. 1 (1989): 1–24.

Salwen, M. "Cultural Imperialism: A Media Effects Approach." *Critical Studies in Mass Communication*, 8, no. 1 (1991): 29–38, Special Issue: Cultural Diversity.

Savage, W.W. *The Cowboy Hero: His Image in American History and Culture*. Norman, OK: University of Oklahoma Press, 1979.

Schama, S. "Clio Has a Problem." *The New York Times Magazine* (September 29, 1991): 32–34.

Schiller, H. "Not Yet the Post-Imperialist Era." *Critical Studies in Mass Communication* 8, no.1 (1991): 13–28.

Schlipphacke, H. "*Inglourious Basterds* and the Gender of Revenge." In *Quentin Tarantino's Inglourious Basterds: A Manipulation of Metacinema*, ed. R. von Dassanowsky, 113–133. New York/London: Continuum, 2012.

Schomburg, S. "The Enduring World of Dr. Schultz: James Baldwin, Django Unchained, and the Crisis of Whiteness," September 6, 2013. http://theotherjournal.com/2013/09/12/the-enduring-world-of-dr-schultz-james-baldwin-django-unchained-and-the-crisis-of-whiteness/#disqus_thread (accessed November 10, 2013).

Schweitzer, I. *Perfecting Friendship. Politics and Affiliation in Early American Literature*. Chapel Hill: The University of North Carolina Press, 2006.

Scott, F. "*Django Unchained* Upends the Western: A History of Violence." *Village Voice*, Wednesday, December 19, 2012. http://www.villagevoice.com/2012-12-19/film/django-unchained-upends-the-western/ (accessed July 9, 2013).

Scott, A.O. "The Black, the White and the Angry: Quentin Tarantino's 'Django Unchained' Stars Jamie Foxx." *New York Times*, December 24, 2012. http://movies.nytimes.com/2012/12/25/movies/quentin-tarantinos-django-unchained-stars-jamie-foxx.html?pagewanted=all&_r=0 (accessed July 13, 2013).

Shapiro, H. *White Violence and Black Response: From Reconstruction to Montgomery*. Amherst: University of Massachusetts Press, 1988.

Shils, E. "The Concept and Function of Ideology," In *International Encyclopedia of the Social Sciences*, ed. D.L. Sills, New York: Macmillan, 1968.

Shugart, H.A. "Counterhegemonic Acts: Appropriation as a Feminist Rhetorical Strategy," *Quarterly Journal of Speech*, 83, no 2 (1997): 210–229.

Sidbury, J. "Resistance to Slavery." In *The Routledge History of Slavery*, ed. G. Heuman and T. Burnard, London: Routledge, 2011.

Siddiqui, A. "Quentin Tarantino N-Word Video: Django Director Uses Racial Epithet at the Golden Globes," January 14, 2013. http://www.policymic.com/articles/23194/quentin-tarantino-n-word-video-django-director-uses-racial-epithet-at-the-golden-globes/344575 (accessed November 10, 2013).

Silver, D. "Collective Responsibility and the Ownership of Actions." *Public Affairs Quarterly*, 16, no. 3 (2002): 287–304.

Slatta, R. "Making and Unmaking the Frontier Myth." *European Journal of American Culture*, 29, no. 2 (2010): 81–92.

Slotkin. *Regeneration Through Violence: The Mythology of the American Frontier*. Norman, OK: University of Oklahoma Press, 1973.

Snead, J. *White Screens/Black Images: Hollywood from the Dark Side.* New York: Routledge, 1994.

Snowden, F.M. *Before Color Prejudice: The Ancient View of Blacks.* Cambridge, Mass: Harvard University Press, 1983.

Sontag, S. "Notes on Camp." In *Against Interpretation and Other Essays*, ed. Sontag, 275–293. London: Penguin, 2009.

Sorlin, P. *The Film in History: Restaging the Past.* New York: Barnes and Noble Imports, 1980.

Sperling, N. "'Django Unchained': Quentin Tarantino on His Funniest Scene Yet." December 26, 2012. http://articles.latimes.com/2012/dec/26/entertainment/la-et-mn-django-unchained-quentin-tarantino-funniest-scene-20121226 (accessed November 11, 2013).

———— and Fritz, B. "'Django,' Unchained, Looks at U.S.' Past," December 15, 2012. http://articles.latimes.com/2012/dec/15/entertainment/la-et-mn-quentin-tarantino-django-unchained-20121215 (accessed November 10, 2013).

Srinivasan, S. "The Grand Illousion." In *Quentin Tarantino's Inglourious Basterds: A Manipulation of Metacinema*, ed. R. von Dassanowsky, 1–14. New York and London: Continuum, 2012.

Stead, N. "The Value of Ruins: Allegories of Destruction in Benjamin and Speer," *Form/Work: An Interdisciplinary Journal of the Built Environment*, No. 6 (October 2003), 51–64. http://naomistead.files.wordpress.com/2008/09/stead_value_of_ruins_2003.pdf (accessed November 27, 2013).

Steele, T. "Tarantino's Candy (Slavery in the White Male Imagination)." December 27, 2012. http://blogs.indiewire.com/shadowandact/tarantinos-candy-slavery-in-the-white-male-imagination (accessed November 10, 2013).

Stewart, J. "Message in the Music: Political Commentary in Black Popular Music from Rhythm and Blues to Early Hip Hop." *The Journal of African American History*, 90, no. 3 (2005): 196–225.

Stone, R. "Spike Lee Calls 'Django Unchained' 'Disrespectful.'" *Rolling Stone* (December 27, 2012). http://www.rollingstone.com/music/news/spike-lee-calls-django-unchained-disrespectful-20121227.

Storey, J. *An Introductory Guide to Cultural Theory and Popular Culture.* Athens, GA: University of Georgia Press, 1993.

Streeter, C. "Was Your Mama Mulatto? Notes toward a Theory of Racialized Sexuality in Gayl Jones's Corregidora and Julie Dash's Daughters of the Dust." *Callaloo*, 27, no. 3 (2004): 768–787.

Susan, O.A., Stein, S.R. and Vande Berg, L.R. *Bad Girls: Cultural Politics and Media Representations of Transgressive Women.* New York, NY: Peter Lang Publishing, 2007.

Suskind, A. *The Wall Street Journal* quoted in *Moviefone* http://news.moviefone.com/2012/12/16/christoph-waltz-django-unchained-interview/ (accessed November 27, 2013).

Tarantino, Q. "*DJANGO UNCHAINED* Script." *The Internet Movie Script Database.* http://www.imsdb.com/scripts/Django-Unchained.html. (accessed November 30, 2013).

———— and Guru-Murthy, K. "Tarantino Uncut: When Quentin met Krishnan." http://www.channel4.com/news/tarantino-uncut-when-quentin-met-krishnan-transcript. (January 10, 2013.)

Tascon, S. "Considering Human Rights Films, Representation, and Ethics: Whose Face?" *Human Rights Quarterly,*34, no., 3 (2012): 864–883.

Tierney, S. "Quentin Tarantino in Black and White." In *A Critical Rhetorics of Race,* ed.M.G.L. Lacy, and K. Ono, 81–97. New York: New York University Press, 2011.

Tillet, S. "Quentin Tarantino Creates an Exceptional Slave." December 25, 2012. http://inamerica.blogs.cnn.com/2012/12/25/opinion-quentin-tarantino-creates-an-exceptional-slave/ (accessed November 10, 2013).

Toplin, R.B. *History by Hollywood: The Use and Abuse of the American Past.* Urbana: University of Illinois Press, 1996.

Townes, E.M. *Womanist Ethics and the Cultural Production of Evil.* New York: Palgrave Macmillan, 2006.

Travers, P. "Django Unchained," December 13, 2012. http://www.rollingstone.com/movies/reviews/django-unchained-20121213#ixzz2kTJYjoW4 (accessed November 11, 2013).

Trefousse, H.L. *Carl Schurz: A Biography.* New York: Fordham University Press, 1998.

Urbain, J.-D. *At the Beach.* Minneapolis: University of Minnesota Press, 2003.

Vahabzadeh, S." Warum Tarantino Sklaverei und Holocaust vergleicht." *Süddeutsche.de,* January 10, 2013. http://www.sueddeutsche.de/kultur/roter-teppich-fuer-neuen-tarantino-film-1.1568666 (accessed January 12, 2013).

van Whye, J. *The History of Phrenology on the Web.* http://www.historyofphrenology.org.uk/texts/2002van_wyhe.htm (accessed November 1, 2013).

Vera, H. and Gordon, A.M. *Screen Saviors: Hollywood Fictions of Whiteness.* New York: Rowman & Littlefield Publishers, 2003.

Von Eschen, P. *Satchmo Blows Up the World: Jazz Race and Empire During the Cold War.* Cambridge, MA: Harvard Press, 2004, Quoted in R. Wagnleitner and E. May. *Here, There and Everywhere: The Foreign Politics of American Popular Culture.* Hanover, NH: University Press of New England, 2000.

Von Wilpert, G. "Sekundenstil." In *Sachwörterbuch der Literatur,* ed. G. von Wilpert, Fifth edition. Stuttgart: Alfred Kröner Verlag, 1969.

Wagner, R. "Der Nibelungen-Mythus. Als Entwurf zu einem Drama." In *Gesammelte Schriften und Dichtungen von Richard Wagner,* 3rd edition, volume 2. 156–166. Leipzig: Verlag von E. W. Fritzsch, 1897.

———— *Der Ring des Nibelungen. Ein Bühnenfestspiel für drei Tage und einen Vorabend. Dritter Tag: Siegfried.* Stuttgart: Philipp Reclam, 1997.

———— *Der Ring des Nibelungen. Ein Bühnenfestspiel für drei Tage und einen Vorabend. Zweiter Tag: Siegfried.* Stuttgart: Philipp Reclam, 1997.

Waldstreicher, D. *Slavery's Constitution: From Revolution to Ratification.* New York: Hill and Wang, 2009, 3, See also George William Van Cleve, *A Slaveholder's Union: Slavery, Politics, and the Constitution in the Early American Republic* (Chicago: University of Chicago Press, 2010).

Walker, A. *"Faces of the Week*—Quentin Tarantino Interview." BBC. May 14, 2004. http://news.bbc.co.uk/2/hi/uk_news/magazine/3712013.stm (accessed February 28, 2013).

Wander, B. "Black Dreams: The Fantasy and Ritual of Black Films." Film Quarterly, 29, No. 1 (Autumn, 1975): 2–11.

Weimer, W.B. "Why All Knowledge Is Rhetorical." *Journal of the American Forensic Association,* 20 (1983): 63–71.

Weld, T.D. *American Slavery As It Is: Testimony of a Thousand Witnesses. 1839; repr.* New York: Arno Press, 1968.

Wenn. "Tarantino Embraces Past Lives," May 2, 2007. http://www.contactmusic.com/news/tarantino-embraces-past-lives_1029799 (accessed November 10, 2013).

White, A. "Still Not a Brother." *CityArts: New York's Review of Culture* (2012). http://cityarts.info/2012/12/28/still-not-a-brother/ (accessed August 30, 2013).

Wiggins, D. "Great Speed but Little Stamina: The Historical Debate of Black Athletic Superiority." *Journal of Sports History,* no. 2 (1989). ibrary.la84.org/SportsLibrary/JSH/JSH1989/JSH1602/jsh1602d.pdf (accessed November 29, 2013).

Wilentz, S. "Lincoln in Hollywood, from Griffith to Spielberg," *New Republic,* December 21, 2012, http://www.newrepublic.com/article/books-and-arts/magazine/111242/the-lost-cause-and-the-won-cause (accessed November 11, 2013).

Williams, R. *Culture and Society 1780–1950.* London: Chatto and Windus: Penguin Books: Harmondsworth, 1958.

Wood, J. "Niggers, Negroes, Blacks, Niggaz, and Africans." *Village Voice* (September 17, 1991): 38–39.

Wootton, A. "Quentin Tarantino Interview (I) with Pam Grier, Robert Forster and Lawrence Bender," January 5, 1998, http://www.theguardian.com/film/1998/jan/05/quentintarantino.guardianinterviewsatbfisouthbank1 (accessed November 10, 2013).

Wyatt-Brown, B. *Honor and Violence in the Old South.* New York/Oxford: Oxford University Press, 1986.

Yeshitela, O. "Django Unchained or Killing Whitey to Protect White Power," *UhuruNews.Com*. http://uhurunews.com/story?resource_ name=killing-whitey-while-protecting-white-power-a-review-of-django-unchained (accessed January 20, 2013).

Zakarin, J. "Spike Lee: 'Django Unchained' is 'Disrespectful,' I Will Not See It." The Hollywood Reporter. http://www.hollywoodreporter.com/ news/spike-lee-django-unchained-is-406313 (accessed January 20, 2013).

Zimbardo, P. *The Lucifer Effect: Understanding How Good People Turn Evil*. New York: Random House Trade Paperback Edition, 2008.

Žižek, S. "Death's Merciless Love." http://www.lacan.com/zizek-love. htm.

Notes on Contributors

Chante Anderson is a graduate student of speech communication at the Texas Southern University's School of Communication. He also serves as the department's graduate assistant. Chante received his BA in speech communication from Morgan State University in Baltimore, Maryland. His professional background is in broadcast journalism (WCBS-TV, KTVO-TV) and marketing communications.

Reynaldo Anderson is Assistant Professor of Teacher Education and Humanities at Harris-Stowe State University, Saint Louis, MO, and currently serves as a member of the Executive Board for the Missouri Arts Council. He was recognized by Gov. Jay Nixon of Missouri in 2010 for his leadership in Humanities in the Saint Louis community. Reynaldo publishes research in regard to several dimensions of the African American experience, social media, and the African Diaspora and recently participated as a visiting lecturer at the Ghana Institute of Management and Public Administration (G.I.M.P.A.) in Accra, Ghana.

William Brown is Senior Lecturer in Film at the University of Roehampton, London, He is the author of *Supercinema: Film-Philosophy for the Digital Age* (Berghahn, 2013), as well as of numerous other texts. He has also directed four zero-budget feature films, including *En Attendant Godard* (2009), *Afterimages* (2010), *Common Ground* (2012), and *China: A User's Manual (Films)* (2012).

Robert von Dassanowsky is Professor of German and Film Studies at the University of Colorado, Colorado Springs, and also works as an independent film producer. A member of the European Academy of Sciences and Arts, the European Film Academy, and a Fellow of the Royal Historical Society, his books include *Austrian Cinema: A History* (2005), *New Austrian Cinema*, co-edited with

Oliver C. Speck (2011), *The Nameable and the Unnameable: Hugo von Hofmannsthal's "Der Schwierige" Revisited*, co-edited with Martin Liebscher (2011), *Quentin Tarantino's Inglourious Basterds: A Manipulation of Metafilm*, ed. (2012), and *World Film Locations: Vienna*, ed. (2012). His study, *Screening Transcendence: Film under Austrofascism and the Hollywood Hope 1933–1938*, is forthcoming.

Heather Ashley Hayes is Assistant Professor of Rhetoric Studies at Whitman College. She specializes in teaching on rhetorics of social justice, civic engagement, and activism. Her scholarly work explores the relationship between violence, race, power, and discourse. She is currently working on a book project centered around the technology of drones as part of the global war on terror, specifically dealing with the implications drone use in the Middle East and North Africa by the United States has for understanding the relationship between rhetoric and racialized violence.

Gregory L. Kaster teaches at the Department of History, Gustavus Adolphus College, where he is responsible for teaching undergraduate courses in U.S. history, including the first half of the American survey. His current research is centered on American Manhood and Masculinity.

Nichole K. Kathol is Assistant Professor of Communication and Women's Studies at the University of Wisconsin-Barron County. She received her PhD from the University of Kansas and her master's degree from Miami University of Ohio. Her areas of expertise include intersectional rhetorics of gender, race, sexuality, and violence. Nichole is the president of the Barron County Domestic Abuse Project, a nonprofit organization which provides community education, victim advocacy, financial support, and transitional housing for victims of domestic abuse in Barron County, WI.

David J. Leonard is Associate Professor in the Department of Critical Culture, Gender and Race Studies at Washington State University, Pullman, and the author of *Screens Fade to Black: Contemporary African American Cinema*. He is also the coeditor (with C. Richard King) of *Commodified and Criminalized: New Racism and African Americans in Contemporary Sports* and of *Visual Economies of/in Motion: Sport and Film*. David is the author of the just released *After Artest: The NBA and the Assault on Blackness* (SUNY Press, 2012).

Alexander Darius Ornella is Lecturer in Religion at the University of Hull. He is interested in the intersection between religion and popular culture, in particular how people "do" and practice religion today. He has published widely on today's visual culture, such as film, and the ideas of the human transmitted in and through images.

Margaret Ozierski has recently finished her PhD at the Department of Romance Studies at Duke University. She currently teaches courses on French and Film Studies at Virginia Commonwealth University.

Samuel P. Perry is Assistant Professor in the Baylor Interdisciplinary Core at Baylor University. He received his PhD in Communication from Georgia State University. He is the author of "'Strange Fruit,' Ekphrasis, and the Lynching Scene" in *Rhetoric Society Quarterly* and "Douglas MacArthur as Frontier Hero: Converting Frontiers in MacArthur's Farewell Address" in the *Southern Communication Journal*. Sam is currently working on a book project concerning the use and appropriation of lynching images in the antilynching movement.

Gilbert B. Rodman is Associate Professor of Communication Studies at the University of Minnesota, where his research and teaching focus on cultural studies, media studies, popular culture, media technologies, intellectual property, and the politics of race and ethnicity. He is the author of *Elvis After Elvis: The Posthumous Career of a Living Legend* (Routledge 1996), *Why Cultural Studies?* (Blackwell, forthcoming), one of the co-editors of *Race in Cyberspace* (Routledge, 2000), and the editor of *The Race and Media Reader* (Routledge, 2014).

Oliver C. Speck currently teaches Film Studies at Virginia Commonwealth University, School of World Studies. Oliver Speck's scholarly writing focuses on narrative strategies and the representation of memory and history in French, German, and other European cinema. His book *Funny Frames: The Filmic Concepts of Michael Haneke* (Continuum, NY: 2010) explores how a political thinking manifests itself in the oeuvre of the Austrian director, suggesting that the constant shifting of frames of reference in his films is needed to open up ethical perspectives. Oliver has also co-edited a volume on *New Austrian Film* (with Robert von Dassanowsky, Berghahn, NY: 2011).

D.L. Stephenson is Associate Professor in the Department of Communication and Media Arts at Western Connecticut State University, where she teaches courses in communication ethics, critical studies in rhetoric, communication theory, persuasion and propaganda in media, and critical studies in media. She currently serves as program planner for the Eastern Communication Association's Law and Ethics Division. She spent fourteen years working as a newspaper journalist in Western Massachusetts, where she began her study and critique of hegemonic media practices. She has been teaching at the college level since 1992, after earning a Master of Science degree in Rhetoric and Technical Communication at Michigan Technological University. She earned a doctorate in Communication in 2006 from the University of Massachusetts, Amherst.

Kate E. Temoney is a PhD candidate in the Department of Religion at Florida State University and former Auzenne Fellow and Editorial Assistant for the *Journal of Religious Ethics* (Wiley-Blackwell). Her research interests include Buddhist ethics, human rights, the problem of evil, and the just war tradition. Her dissertation treats the role of religious rhetoric and institutionalized religion in the former Yugoslavia and Rwanda genocides.

Dara Waldron is Lecturer in Critical and Contextual Studies in the School of Art and Design, Limerick Institute of Technology. Dara is the author of *Cinema and Evil: Moral Complexities and the Dangerous Film* (Cambridge Scholars Publishing, 2013).

Ryan J. Weaver is Senior Lecturer of Communication at the University of Wisconsin-Barron County and Lecturer of Communication and Women's Studies at the University of Wisconsin-Eau Claire. He earned his doctorate from the University of Kansas in Communication Studies with an emphasis in rhetorical theory and criticism. His research interests lie at the intersections of gender and sexuality, race, and public address.

Alina Dana Weber is Assistant Professor of German in the Department of Modern Languages and Linguistics at Florida State University. Her published articles explore legends in media, cultural transfers in German festivals and performances, Native American theatrical representations, and the touching points between Freud's notion of the uncanny and performance concepts. Dana is currently completing a monograph on the intersections of literature, folklore, and performance in German festivals entitled *Blood-Brothers and Peace-Pipes. Transcultural Negotiation of Difference in German Wild West Festivals*.

Index